THE
ASEAN
REGIONAL
FORUM

The **Institute of Southeast Asian Studies (ISEAS)** was established as an autonomous organization in 1968. It is a regional centre dedicated to the study of socio-political, security and economic trends and dev elopments in S outheast Asia and its wider geostrategic and economic environment. The Institute's research programmes are the Regional Economic Studies (RES, including ASEAN and APEC), Regional Strategic and Political Studies (RSPS), and R egional Social and Cultural Studies (RSCS).

ISEAS Publishing, an established academic press, has issued almost 2,000 books and journals. I t is the largest scholarly publisher of r esearch about S outheast Asia from within the r egion. ISEAS P ublishing wor ks with many other academic and trade publishers and distributors to disseminate impor tant r esearch and analyses from and about S outheast Asia to the r est of the world.

THE
ASEAN
REGIONAL
FORUM

RODOLFO C. SEVERINO

ISEAS

INSTITUTE OF SOUTHEAST ASIAN STUDIES

Singapore

First published in Singapore in 2009 by
Institute of Southeast Asian Studies
30 Heng Mui Keng Terrace
Pasir Panjang
Singapore 119614

E-mail: publish@iseas.edu.sg
Website: <http://bookshop.iseas.edu.sg>

The responsibility for facts and opinions in this publication rests exclusively with the author and his interpretations do not necessarily reflect the views or the policy of the publisher or its supporters.

ISEAS Library Cataloguing-in-Publication Data

Severino, Rudolfo C.
   The ASEAN Regional Forum
   1. ASEAN Regional Forum.
   2. National security—Southeast Asia.
   3. National security—Pacific Area.
   I. ASEAN.
   II. ASEAN Regional Forum.
   III. Title.
UA830 S49   2009

ISBN 978-981-4279-25-3 (hard cover)
ISBN 978-981-4279-38-3 (PDF)

Photo Credit: Cover image©iStockphoto.com
Typeset by Superskill Graphics Pte Ltd
Printed in Singapore by Utopia Press Pte Ltd

CONTENTS

ABOUT THE AUTHOR

Rodolfo C. Severino is the head of the ASEAN Studies Centre at the Institute of Southeast Asian Studies in Singapore and a frequent speaker at international conferences in Asia and E urope. H aving been S ecretary-General of the Association of Southeast Asian Nations from 1998 to 2002, he completed a book, entitled *Southeast Asia in Search of an ASEAN Community* (published by ISEAS in 2006), on issues facing ASEAN, including the security, economic, and other challenges confronting the region. He has also produced a book on ASEAN in ISEAS' S outheast Asia B ackground S eries. S everino co-edited *Whither the Philippines in the 21st Century?*, a collection of papers on many aspects of Philippine life by eminent scholars and observers of the Philippine scene, in which he wrote the concluding chapter. He is currently working on a book on the Philippine national territor y. H is views on ASEAN and Southeast Asia have been published in *ASEAN Today and Tomorrow*, a compilation of his speeches and other statements. H e writes articles for journals and for the press.

As ASEAN Senior Official for the Philippines, Severino was involved in the establishment of the ASEAN R egional Forum in 1994. He is one of the Experts and E minent P ersons r egistered b y the P hilippines for the ARF . Before assuming the position of ASEAN S ecretary-General, S everino was Undersecretary of Foreign Affairs of the Philippines. In the Philippine Foreign Service, Severino served in Malaysia, China and the U nited States. He has a Bachelor of Ar ts degr ee in the humanities from the A teneo de M anila University and a M aster of Ar ts degr ee in international r elations from the Johns Hopkins University School of A dvanced International Studies.

PREFACE

Ambassador K. Kesavapany, Director of the forty-year-old Institute of Southeast Asian Studies in Singapore, where I am a Visiting Senior Research Fellow and now head of the ASEAN Studies Centre, suggested that I write a book on the ASEAN Regional Forum.

The ARF is the only region-wide forum that deals with political and security issues in the Asia-Pacific. Inaugurated in mid-1994, the ARF initially encompassed Southeast Asia, Northeast Asia, Oceania, Papua New Guinea, the United States, Canada, the European Union, and Russia. Since then, it has expanded to include four countries in South Asia as well. Yet, no book devoted exclusively to it had been published, although an enormous number of book chapters, monographs, papers and articles had been written on it or on certain aspects of it. The one exception I know of is the book by Takeshi Yuzawa, *Japan's Security Policy and the ASEAN Regional Forum* (London and New York: Routledge, 2007), but, as the title suggests, it is specifically from the viewpoint of Japan's role in the ARF and in the context of its broad security policy.

Many of these works offer penetrating insights into the nature, potential, shortfalls and direction of the ARF. I do not intend to repeat or add to their analyses, many of which are excellent and to which this book owes much. What the book seeks to do is to establish certain facts about the ARF in some detail, so as to help illuminate its true character and what it can and cannot do, its potential and its limitations, as an institution and process *sui generis* in the unique circumstances of the Asia-Pacific in the current phase of its history. It does so on the ARF's own terms and not in terms of the experience of other regional institutions and processes and without wishing that it were something else. At the same time, it ackno wledges that the ARF can ev olve and, to a cer tain extent and at a cer tain pace, has ev olved and does evolv e.

In the book, I review the environment in which the ARF was conceiv ed and initiated and the for ces that led to it and shaped it.   The original participation in the ARF explains much of its natur e and reflects and shapes its purposes and limitations. Each step in the expansion of the forum is examined for its implications and motivations. A   ccording to its original Concept P aper, annex ed her e, the first stage in the ARF'   s evolution is confidence-building. The book takes a look at the ways that the forum seeks to carry this out and whether they hae succeeded. The next stage is "preventive diplomacy". The book discusses the questions of why the ARF is not able to deal with inter-state disputes in pæventive terms, much less with those within nations, and why its future in "preventive diplomacy" may lie in cooperation on non-traditional, non-militar y thr eats to the security of all.   The book details the increasing number of activities that take place between ministerial meetings, activities that the media and the public generally ignore, and seeks to evaluate their worth. O ne of the for um's limitations in terms of activism and implementation is its lack of adequate egion-wide operative institutions. The book examines why this is so, despite the pgress that has been made in setting up cer tain rudimentary ARF institutions. F inally, I attempt my o wn assessment of the ARF , its achievements and shortfalls, in the light of the limitations imposed b y its composition and objectiv es, liberally citing the evaluation of r esponsible bodies and thoughtful scholars.

I do not bring theor etical constructs to this book. What I do bring to it are the experiences and insights that I gained as ARF SOM leader for the Philippines from the forum's beginnings to the end of 1997 and as ASEAN Secretary-General from the first day of 1998 to the last day of 2002, and fm research and inter views thereafter.

In the writing of this book, I had much help fom many people. Without them, the book could not have been done. I thank them all. Ambassador Kesavapany urged me to write the book and gae me frequent encouragement to see it through. Many others gave generously of their time, their knowledge and their insights in my inter views with them. I cite sev eral of them in the text or in the endnotes or in both. U   nfortunately, space limitations hav e prevented me fr om mentioning the others. The same holds tr ue for those whose wor ks I have consulted. I thank them all. S   pecial thanks go to the anonymous refer ees for their ver y useful suggestions, most of which found their way into the manuscript. Needless to say, I alone am responsible for the contents of the work, including its many shortcomings. I thank Triena Ong and her crew at the Publications Unit of ISEAS for shepherding the book through to the light of day. Finally, and not least, I thank my wife, Weng, for the support, patience and tolerance that she offered during the many hours, days, weeks and months that I devoted to working on this book.

1

THE BEGINNINGS

On 28 January 1992, almost a quarter of a century after the founding of the Association of Southeast Asian Nations, the leaders of the then-six members of ASEAN — S ultan H assanal Bolkiah of B runei D arussalam, P resident Soeharto of I ndonesia, P rime M inister M ahathir M ohamad of M alaysia, President Coraz on Aquino of the P hilippines, P rime M inister Goh Chok Tong of Singapore, and Prime Minister Anand Panyarachun of Thailand — met in S ingapore.

It was only the four th meeting of ASEAN' s leaders in the association 's almost twenty-five years of existence. Several important decisions were made at that summit. [1]

One of those decisions was to create the ASEAN Free Trade Area. AFTA was to be achiev ed primarily through the Common E ffective P referential Tariff scheme, which would entail dropping, in agreed tranches and according to a common timetable, tariffs on intra-ASEAN trade to 0–5 per cent b y a definite date. To "supervise, coordinate and review" this process, they set up the ministerial-level AFT A Council. H owever, the leaders also r ecognized that integrating the r egional economy, which was AFT A's ultimate purpose, required more than the reduction and removal of tariffs. Thus, they committed their countries to the elimination of quantitativ e restrictions and other non-tariff barriers to intra-ASEAN trade within specified time frames. They called on ASEAN to "encourage and facilitate fr ee movement of capital and other financial resources". They committed ASEAN to the dev elopment of "safe, efficient and inno vative transportation and communications infrastr ucture networks". They str essed the impor tance of str engthening postal and telecommunications ser vices.

The Singapore Summit reiterated ASEAN's perennial concern over energy security, emphasizing in its declaration " cooperation in energy security , conservation and the search for alternative fuels. Recognizing the importance of ASEAN awar eness among the people of S outheast Asia, the ASEAN leaders directed "the expansion of ASEAN Studies as part of Southeast Asian Studies in the school and univ ersity curricula".

With respect to ASEAN' s management, the leaders decided to meet formally every three years, with an "informal" summit in each of the years in-between. Since then, the distinction betw een formal and informal summits has been r emoved, with ASEAN S ummits now held annually and the new ASEAN Char ter pr escribing at least twice-y early S ummit meetings. The Secretary-General was to be designated as the ASEAN S ecretary-General (as against the previous designation of S ecretary-General of the ASEAN Secretariat), appointed on merit and accorded ministerial status. The Secretariat was to r ecruit its professional staff openly but " ensure representation of all ASEAN countries in the Secr etariat". Until then, the pr ofessional staff had been seconded to the S ecretariat by their r espective governments.

Before the 1992 ASEAN S ummit, ASEAN had been at the for efront of the political and diplomatic r esistance to Vietnam's incursion into and subsequent occupation of Cambodia, an occupation — and an ASEAN effort — that lasted from 1979 to 1989, when Vietnamese troops withdrew from Cambodian soil. ASEAN had also played a pr ominent role in the sear ch for a diplomatic resolution to the Cambodian problem. The search included the Jakarta I nformal M eetings of 1988 and 1989, sponsor ed by ASEAN and convened by Indonesia, and the P aris Conference that began in 1989. The weight of the five permanent members of the U nited N ations S ecurity Council, plus J apan, and consultations and compromises among them contributed significantly to the diplomatic endeavour That endeavour ended with the conclusion of the P aris Peace Agreements in 1991.

At their S ingapore S ummit the ASEAN leaders pledged to help "in ensuring the full implementation " of the P aris Agr eements and in the "reconstruction" of Vietnam, Laos and Cambodia. They reiterated ASEAN's commitment to "forge a closer relationship based on friendship and cooperation with the Indochinese countries". These were the highest-level expressions of ASEAN's effort, begun after the reunification of Vietnam and resumed after the withdrawal of Vietnamese for ces from Cambodia, to r each out to the Indochinese states across the Southeast Asian divide.

From a strategic viewpoint, all these measur es would help str engthen Southeast Asian and As ia-P acific stability in an uncer tain time. R egional economic integration, including transportation and communication networks,

Demonstration by the Special Unit of the Beijing Military Command during the ARF Security Policy Conference, Beijing, China, 4–6 November 2004. *Source: Reproduced with the kind permission of the ASEAN Secretariat.*

"Operational demonstration viewed on board the RSS Endurance Landing Ship Tank during the ARF CBM "Regional Cooperation in Maritime Security", Singapore, 2–4 March 2005. *Source: Reproduced with the kind permission of Ministry of Defence, Singapore.*

Field demonstration at the Qingdao Fire-fighting Brigade during the 6th ARF Inter-Sessional Meeting on Disaster Relief (ISM on DR), Qingdao, China, 18–20 September 2006. *Source: Reproduced with the kind permission of the ASEAN Secretariat.*

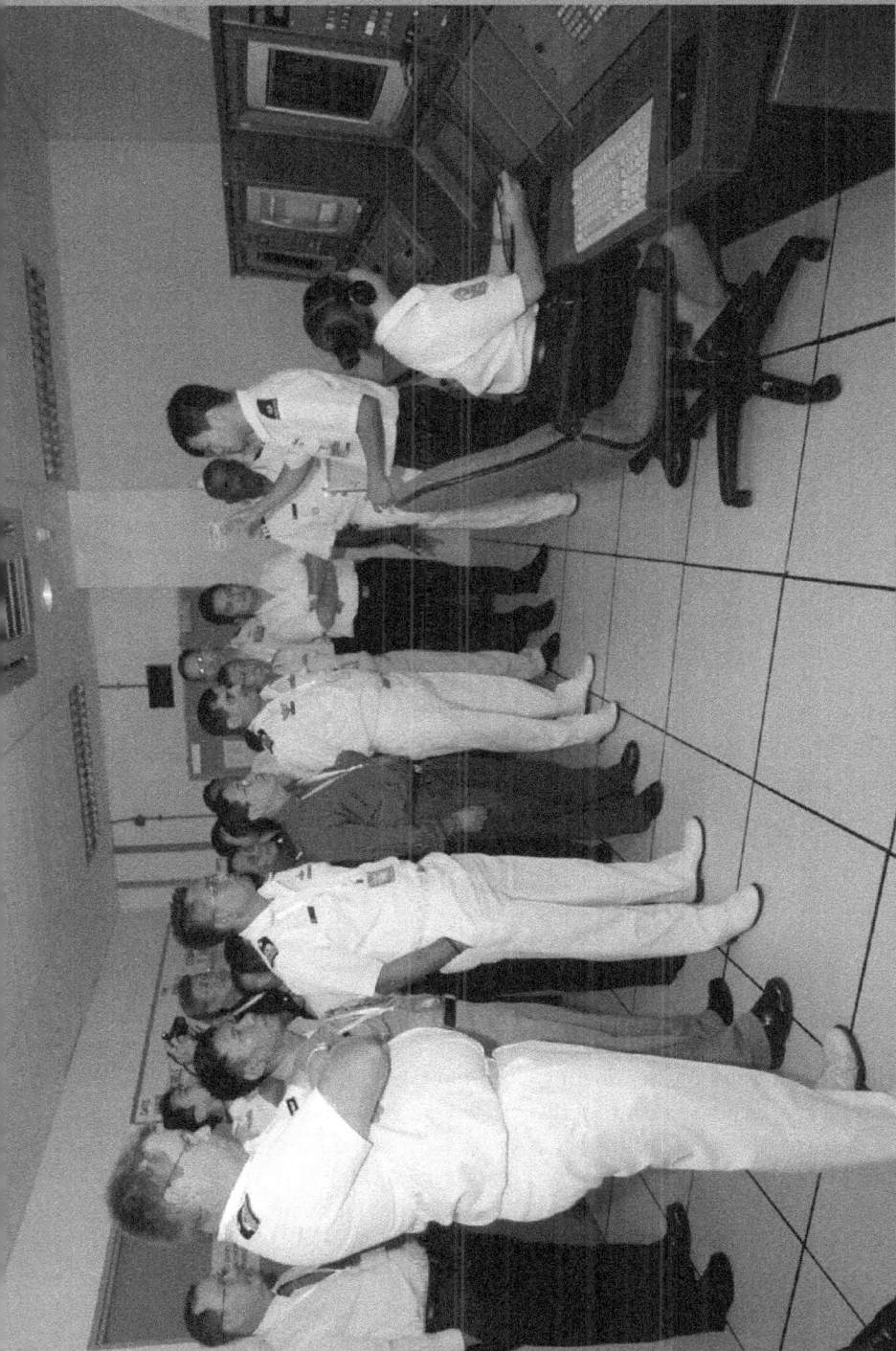

Field visit at the Tactical Training Center Changi during the ARF Maritime Security Shore Exercise Planning Conference. Singapore. 7–8 December 2006. *Source: Reproduced with the kind permission of Ministry of Defence. Singapore.*

would enable ASEAN to pro vide ballast and leadership in East Asia and the Asia-P acific b y achieving a certain lev el of economic weight and competitiveness. The emphasis on energy security was part of this effor t. So were the cultiv ation of ASEAN awar eness among the people of S outheast Asia, the str engthening of regional institutions, and hands-on leadership b y ASEAN's heads of government. The call for the implementation of the Paris Agreements on Cambodia, to which ASEAN had contributed in no small measure, and for the r econstruction of I ndochina was an impor tant way of reaching out to Vietnam, Laos and Cambodia with a view to bringing all of Southeast Asia under the ASEAN r oof.

Many of the decisions proclaimed in Singapore have been carried out; a few others have not. One that has been carried out, and has gone een further in implementation, was the leaders' call on ASEAN to "intensify its external dialogues in political and security matters by using the ASEAN Post-ministerial Conferences".[2] This was meant to addr ess directly the political and security concerns arising from the radical r e-arrangement of the global security configuration that was taking place during that period.

In one sense, the ASEAN leaders ' call on ASEAN and its D ialogue Partners to deal with political and security issues was a modest exhortation, proposing only the intensification of dialogue. I n another sense, it was groundbreaking, being the first time that ASEAN would o vertly, explicitly and formally engage its external partners in activities, no matter how tentative and modest, that had anything to do with security matters.

THE POST-MINISTERIAL CONFERENCES

The ASEAN Post-ministerial Conferences were, at that time, the only forum in which ASEAN engaged its D ialogue P artners in consultations at the ministerial level. The only exception was the regular meeting between ASEAN and European foreign ministers that star ted in 1978. The Dialogue system began with ASEAN's engagement with the European Economic Community through the Special Coordinating Committee of ASEAN Nations, or SCCAN, in 1973. That same year, the ASEAN foreign ministers initiated a "dialogue" with their Japanese counterpart in order to raise the issue of the competition posed by J apanese synthetic r ubber to some ASEAN countries ' expor ts of natural rubber. Not wishing to be left out of developments in Southeast Asia, Australia joined the D ialogue system in 1974, N ew Z ealand in 1975, and Canada and the U nited States in 1977.

The centr epiece of the D ialogue system has been the P ost-ministerial Conferences, in which, immediately following the annual ASEAN Ministerial

Meeting, the ASEAN for eign ministers conduct discussions with their counterparts from the ASEAN Dialogue Partners, together and individually.

Aside from demonstrating its openness to and engagement with the outside world, particular y the developed, capitalist countries, ASEAN initially used the Dialogue system to raise issues r elated to access of their expor ts to developed-country mar kets, inv estments fr om the dev eloped countries in ASEAN, and development assistance to ASEAN countries from the Dialogue Partners. This is why ASEAN' s Dialogue Partners wer e for a long time all developed economies — A ustralia, Canada, the E uropean E conomic Community, J apan, N ew Zealand and the U nited S tates — plus S outh Korea, which became a Dialogue Partner in 1991. South Korea at that time was technically a developing country but, for ASEAN's purposes, had evolved as early as 1991 into a developed economy .

On the other hand, the D ialogue P artners sought engagement with ASEAN in recognition of ASEAN's collective political weight, as demonstrated by its handling of the Cambodian question, its strategic location, its rich resources, and the accelerating economic gr owth of its member-countries.

The 1992 ASEAN S ummit's call for the use of the P ost-ministerial Conferences for political and security dialogues signalled a departur e fr om the dominance of the PMC agenda by economic and development issues. On the eve of the S ingapore S ummit, the Philippines ' S ecretary of F oreign Affairs, the late Raul M anglapus, characterized the pr oposal in the draft summit declaration as a " treme dous br eakthrough", noting that thitherto "nobody even wanted to mention the word security in ASEAN discussions".[3] To be sure, the ASEAN for eign ministers had, in fact, been, in the pr evious year at least, talking about seeking ways to deal diplomatically with the ne w security environment in the Asia-Pacific, but these were informal explorations. Lau Teik Soon, then professor of political science at the N ational University of S ingapore, was later to point out, " Approaches to ASEAN security have tended to be ad hoc in nature and r esponded to specific situations, as when Vietnam invaded Cambodia. There has never been a concerted effor t on a continuing basis to discuss r egional security matters."[4]

Manglapus and Lau may have been overstating their case, though. After all, ASEAN was founded for political and security r easons, although those reasons had to be disguised in economic, social and cultural termsThe Treaty of Amity and Cooperation in S outheast Asia, signed by ASEAN's leaders in February 1976, laid do wn Southeast Asia 's norms for inter-state security relations.[5] The next yea , ASEAN issued the declaration on Southeast Asia as a Zone of P eace, Freedom and N eutrality. Soon afterwards, work began on the tr eaty on the S outheast Asia N uclear Weapon-Free Z one.[6] ASEAN's policy on Vietnam's incursion into Cambodia was not *ad hoc* but arose from strategic considerations. The PMC itself discussed international security issues, mainly questions of nuclear proliferation and disarmament and the situation in the Middle East. However, Manglapus and Lau were right in that what ASEAN's leaders called for in J anuary 1992 w ere ASEAN discussions with the great powers on strategic issues pertaining specifically to Asia-Pacific security, something unpr ecedented in ASEAN's history.

CHANGED SECURITY ENVIRONMENT

In hindsight, it should not have been surprising that a number of people, including ASEAN' s leaders, had thought of holding strategic multilateral discussions with the great powers on political and security issues in the region at that moment in histor y. The ASEAN heads of go vernment — and the world in general — w ere faced with a strategic situation in the Asia-P acific that was altogether different from what had prevailed in their earlier years as political leaders.

The Cold War had ended. S oviet for ces had withdrawn fr om Afghanistan. The S oviet U nion had just br oken up into independent republics, with Russia taking over as its successor state. The Berlin Wall had fallen, and Germany had been r eunited. The countries of Eastern E urope had shaken off Communist rule and Soviet domination. COMECON and the Warsaw P act had been dissolv ed. The M aastricht Treaty deepening European integration and cr eating the E uropean Union had been signed. The withdrawal of Soviet forces from Cam Ranh Bay had been announced. With the emergence of a weakened Russia from the wreckage of the Soviet Union, the U nited S tates had begun to be regar ded as the world 's lone superpower. H owever, in Asia, the U nited S tates had seen its r ole and influence as some what diminished, after its humiliating depar ture fr om Vietnam. The Philippine Senate had refused in 1991 to approve the extension of the U.S. lease on Philippine militar y bases, the largest such U.S. bases outside the continental U nited States.

Remarkably, ASEAN had collaborated closely with both China and the United States in r esisting the Vietnamese invasion of and dominance o ver Cambodia. I n 1991, the P aris confer ence on Cambodia had pr oduced a political settlement and ended the conflict in that county. Two in the series of informal workshops on M anaging P otential Conflicts in the S outh China Sea had taken place, even as the South China Sea disputes continued to simmer. I n China, Deng Xiaoping 's r eforms, which wer e opening the country in economic, social, political and for eign-policy terms, had begun to take hold and had set in train China 's rise as a global po wer. After the uncertainty resulting from the 1989 upheaval centred on Tiananmen Square,

Jiang Zemin, as General Secretary of the Communist Party of China (and Chairman of the Central Military Commission, although not yet President), had returned China to the path of political stability and rapid economic growth, as well as openness to the world. With the Vietnamese withdrawal from Cambodia in 1989 and the political settlement of the Cambodian problem, the healing of Southeast Asia's divide had begun. The ideological gap between the ASEAN members and the Indochinese states had lost its relevance, if not disappeared altogether.

These developments in the global and regional strategic situation had brought about a sense of relief over the presumed easing of international tensions. However, they had also injected a greater sense of uncertainty and unpredictability into perceptions of that situation. The perverse certainties and apparent stability of the ideological division — and balance — between great-power alliances during the Cold War had given way to the ambiguities and perceived instability of nation-states jockeying for strategic position. ASEAN's leaders and other shapers of policy and those of a number of ASEAN Dialogue Partners were evidently determined to make sure that the world's great powers and other countries with interests in East Asia would have a forum, centred on ASEAN, for addressing the new situation in constructive and amicable ways. In ASEAN eyes and in those of other "middle powers", that new situation presented an opportunity to bring about a stable regional environment that was not dominated by a single power or destabilized by great-power rivalries and Cold War-type confrontations.

Moreover, despite the new and improved regional security environment, flashpoints and tensions continued to threaten regional stability. North Korea was developing nuclear armaments, even as its population remained desperately deprived. The South China Sea continued to be the subject of jurisdictional disputes, with China being perceived as becoming more assertive in the area. The situation across the Taiwan Straits remained a cause of regional tension. Territorial disputes and resentments arising from World War II issues were irritating the relations between Japan on the one hand and China and Korea on the other. Within countries, the problems in East Timor and Myanmar were projected by certain states, the media and non-governmental groups as sources of regional instability. The political arrangements worked out in Cambodia were fragile at best.

PATERNITY

Paternity for the idea of a political and security forum for the Asia-Pacific has been claimed by some or attributed to them. The Japanese, the Australians, the Canadians, the Singaporeans — all floated ideas, publicly and in private, for the discussion of political and security issues in Asia and the Pacific in the light of the new — and uncer tain — strategic envir onment in the r egion.

Richard S mith, then D eputy S ecretary in A ustralia's D epartment of Foreign Affairs and Trade, has written:

> There had been some discussion …, in the wake of the ColdWar, about developing new security arrangements in the region. The Canadians and some S ingaporeans had floated some ideas, and the A ustralian Foreign Minister had put up a trial balloon about a possible Asian version of the OSCE (Organization for S ecurity and Cooperation in E urope). While we all saw the unwor kability in the Asian context of some of the ideas that wer e around, ther e was nevertheless a consensus among the mor e active of us that at the least we needed a forum in which regional security matters could be talked about by r egional members.[7]

Gary Smith, a former senior Canadian diplomat, wrote, "At the Government level, Canada and A ustralia pr ovided intellectual spar k and determination which helped launch the ARF ." H e cited fiv e r easons for the two states ' interest — " diplomatic competence; … historical experience and a high comfort level with multilateralism; … a non-threatening nature; no colonial baggage; and … national interest (in) a multilateral grouping as providing the best vehicle for (their) inclusion in the Asian security process on an equal footing with the major po wers".[8]

Then in the Philippines' Department of F oreign Affairs, I published an op-ed piece in an international periodical calling for something in the Asia-Pacific that was analogous to the Conference on Security and Cooperation in Europe (CSCE), which was later to be transformed into the OSCE. Although I dubbed the proposal "Helsinki East" after the process in Finland in the early 1970s that led to the cr eation of the CSCE, I was awar e of the fact — and said so — that the CSCE had been the r esult of a unique bargain betw een East and West. That bargain involved the embracing by all of human rights and democratic freedoms, the interest of North America and Western Europe, in exchange for the affirmation of the permanence of the post-World War II European territorial boundaries, the inter est of the S oviet Union and of the states in Central and Eastern E urope.[9]

In this sense, the bargain that r esulted in the CSCE and was embodied by it was not applicable to the Asia-P acific. After all, ther e were numerous territorial disputes, major and minor , between Asia-P acific states on which neither protagonist was willing to back do wn — between Japan and China, Japan and R ussia, Japan and the K oreas, I ndonesia and M alaysia, M alaysia and S ingapore, Malaysia and the P hilippines, Cambodia and Thailand, Cambodia and Vietnam. And then ther e was the whole question of the overlapping claims to all or par ts of the S outh China S ea. F reezing the borders across the board would obviously not be possible or acceptable, as it was in E urope. Indeed, Japan re ected any analogy with the CSCE, fearing that that would damage its efforts to regain the "northern territories", islands that the Soviet Union had seized at the end of the P acific War.

As for human rights and democracy, the Asia-Pacific states had widely divergent notions of those concepts. There wer e concerns that public commitments on human rights and democracy could provide an excuse for some states to advance their national inter ests by poking into the internal affairs of others in the name of human rights and democracy More broadly, the conditions in Europe and the Asia-Pacific were immensely different in a great number of ways, including the v ast variety of the political systems in the Asia-Pacific. Nevertheless, the proposed security forum for the Asia-Pacific would be similar to the CSCE in that it would, through consultation and dialogue, help build confidence among mutually suspicious states and, perhaps, even pr event conflict between them. That was, in any case, the intention and the hope.

In September 1990, the fore gn ministers of fifteen countries gathered in New York on the occasion of the annual session of the U nited N ations General Assembly in a meeting organized by Indonesian Foreign Minister Ali Alatas and his Japanese counterpart, Taro Nakayama. The countries represented at that meeting were, except for Mongolia, among the founding participants of what was to become the ASEAN R egional Forum. They were Australia, Canada, China, S outh Korea, Laos, Malaysia, M ongolia, the P hilippines, Singapore, the S oviet Union, Thailand, the U nited States, and Vietnam, as well as I ndonesia and J apan. For the first time, a br oad spectr um of states across the Asia-P acific discussed, at the ministerial level, specific security issues, such as the G ulf war, the Korean peninsula, and Cambodia, and the international economic situation, even as the international strategic situation had begun to r oil.

As 1990 and 1991 wore on, the idea took hold that it would be wise to opt for the conser vative — and, as it turned out, the sensible — course of using existing ASEAN institutions and mechanisms — and methods — to meet the generally r ecognized need for a for um to addr ess regional political and security issues. I ndeed, Alatas and other ASEAN officials r ejected the introduction of any ne w institutional structure.

The ideas of ASEAN-ISIS[10] came closest to what was to emerge eventually in the form of the ASEAN R egional Forum, including its participants and some of its procedur es. I n J une 1991, ASEAN-ISIS, meeting in J akarta, produced a set of four proposals for the consideration of the ASEAN Summit that was to take place seven months later, in January 1992, in Singapore. The first of those proposals was for an "Asean Initiative for an Asia-Pacific Political Dialogue". The ASEAN-ISIS paper declar ed:

> We propose that at the end of each PMC an " Asean PMC-initiated conference" be held at a suitable retreat which will allow for the appropriate ambiance for the constr uctive discussion of Asia-P acific stability and peace. It is suggested that the agenda and arrangements for each Asean PMC-initiated "Conference on S tability and Peace in the Asia-P acific" be prepared by a senior officials meeting made up of senior officials of the Asean states and the dialogue partners.

> It is envisaged that such states as the P eople's Republic of China, the Union of Soviet Socialist Republics, the Democratic People's Republic of Korea and Vietnam should be invited to participate on a regular basis.[11]

At the ASEAN P ost-ministerial Confer ence in K uala Lumpur on 22 J uly 1991, Nakayama proposed using the forum for " a political dialogue wher e friendly nations in the region candidly exchange their mutual concerns". He went on:

> I believe utilizing ASEAN PMC as such a political dialogue forum for mutual reassurance is timely and meaningful. I n or der to make such a political dialogue more effective, I think it is also meaningful, for instance, to establish, under the auspices of this confer ence, a S enior O fficials Meeting to pr ovide the conference with feedback on the r esult of the discussion at the meeting. [12]

Michael Richar dson r eported in the *International Herald Tribune* that the United States initially resisted the N akayama proposal for fear that it might undermine Washington's bilateral security alliances, while the ASEAN countries were said to be wary of the initiative out of their concern that it could be seen as a pr oposal for a ne w multilateral alliance. [13] The initiativ e, in fact, was intended to balance both concerns.

Referring to Nakayama's statement, Yukio Satoh, president of the Japan Institute of I nternational Affairs, r ecalls:

> (T)he proposal did not r eceive much pr onounced support on the spot. In hindsight, however, the Nakayama proposal and subsequent Japanese diplomacy arguably made significant contributions to the establishment of the ASEAN R egional Forum (ARF).[14]

As Satoh tells it, the suggestion for a PMC Senior Officials Meeting upset some ASEAN-ISIS personages, who r esented Japan's appr opriation of the ASEAN PMC SOM idea. [15]

Satoh, at that time the D irector-General of the I nformation Analysis, Research and Policy Planning Bureau of Japan's Ministry of Foreign Affairs, was the tireless shaper and advocate of Japanese initiatives and policies on an Asia-Pacific security for um, including the use of the ASEAN PMC for that purpose. These initiatives and policies r eflected the subtle shift in J apanese security policy from one that was totally dependent on bilateral ties with the United States to one favouring "multilateral security cooperation" or "regional security multilateralism" without diminishing the importance of the J apan-U.S. alliance.[16] Satoh pushed his ideas through policy papers, passages in his minister's speeches, and ar ticles for publication or for distribution to policymakers and influential think tanks. H e himself took par t, upon invitation, in the ASEAN-ISIS meeting in Jakarta and in the Manila conference on Asia-Pacific security in June 1991, when proposals for an ASEAN-centred security forum for the Asia-P acific were extensively discussed.

These proposals and the ideas associated with them found authoritativ e expression in the ASEAN leaders' directive to the association to "intensify its external dialogues in political and security matters by using the ASEAN Post-ministerial Conferences". Curiously, the Joint Communiqué of the ASEAN Ministerial Meeting in July 1992 made no mention of the ASEAN Summit's January directive.

PREPARATORY MEETINGS

It was not until 20–21 M ay 1993 that, in compliance with the ASEAN leaders' instructions, wh.ch the D ialogue Partners obviously supported, and as recommended b y ASEAN-ISIS and N akayama, the senior officials of ASEAN and its D ialogue P artners sat do wn in S ingapore for a meeting devoted exclusively to regional security. Singapore was then in the chair of the ASEAN S tanding Committee. A fe w days befor e the meeting, S ingapore's Ministry of Foreign Affairs issued a statement about the event. As reported in the *Straits Times*, the meeting would be another step in str engthening the links between ASEAN and its Dialogue Partners. It recalled that ASEAN had also been seeking closer ties with China and Russia, which had been granted "consultative par tnership" standing in 1991, and with Vietnam and Laos, which had been giv en observer status in 1992. " Taken together", the *Straits Times* reported the M inistry's statement as saying, " these w ere ASEAN' s efforts to evolve a predictable and constructive pattern of relationships in the

Asia-Pacific that would promote optimal conditions for growth and stability after the end of the Cold War."[17] Indeed, as noted above, several officials and academics in ASEAN and its Dialogue system had been discussing the idea of a regional security for um involving ASEAN, its Dialogue Partners, China, Russia and Vietnam.

As the two-day meeting went on, the realization crystallized that, under the prevailing circumstances, it was not possible to hold high-level discussions on regional security without the participation of China, Russia and Vietnam, as well as of ASEAN and its PMC par tners, notwithstanding the apparently more limited scope of the ASEAN leaders' January 1992 directive. Outside the formal sessions, this was the pre-occupation of the participants in the meeting. As ASEAN Senior Official for the Philippines, I was one of those who held this view.

A week before, Singapore's Prime Minister Goh Chok Tong had given the rationale for the new security forum, telling an international gathering in Tokyo, "Following the end of the Cold War, states are already adjusting their relationship with each other. How this process is managed is the basic strategic challenge for the 1990s." He disclosed that "flexible arrangements to bring in China and Russia (into the forum) are also being explored".[18]

Referring to his participation in the May 1993 meeting in Singapore, Richard Smith of Australia recalls:

> The PMC allowed some discussion of (regional security matters), but in an *ad hoc* way and of course neither China, Russia nor Vietnam were members... . (F)or Australia, the role we played in supporting the emergence of the ARF was ... consistent with our objectives of growing a sense of community in the region — a community that is which we could be part of — and of finding ways in which the United States could be kept engaged in Asia after the Cold War. For our part too, we knew that it would be impossible to get an entirely new organization off the ground, and that the only way to get to first base at least would be to work with ASEAN — its members shared our objectives in general, and it carried an automatic six votes, as it were. And so the new forum was grafted on to ASEAN.[19]

Some participants in the senior officials' meeting were of the idea that including China in what was to become the ASEAN Regional Forum would help "socialize" Beijing. These participants viewed China as being outside the international system and needing to be locked into it, and perceived the rising economic and military power as a potential threat. The notion of having to be "socialized" has not sat well with the Chinese, who consider it as patronizing. On the other hand, there is the view that it is China that is "socializing" the ARF.[20]

Another motive was to keep the United States engaged in Southeast Asia despite its traumatic experience in Indochina and the end of the Cold War and despite Washington's misgivings about multilateral security arrangements in the Asia-Pacific, which might tend to undermine its bilateral defence alliances or be perceived as a cover for American withdrawal. Satoh tells of his efforts to reassure the Americans primarily by affirming the high value that Japan continued to place on the Japan-United States security treaty.[21]

As it turned out, President Bill Clinton was to place the United States squarely behind a regional dialogue on security in the context of the ASEAN PMC, telling the South Korean National Assembly on 10 July 1993, "We also need new regional security dialogs. This month's ASEAN post-ministerial conference in Singapore, which the United States will attend, offers an immediate opportunity to further such a dialog." He went on:

> The goal of all these efforts is to integrate, not isolate, the region's powers. China is a key example. We believe China cannot be a full partner in the world community until it respects human rights and international agreements on trade and weapon sales. But we also are prepared to involve China in building this region's new security and economic architectures. We need an involved and engaged China, not an isolated China.

> Some in the U.S. have been reluctant to enter into regional security dialogs in Asia. They fear it would seem a pretext for American withdrawal from the area. But I see this as a way to supplement our alliances and forward military presence, not to supplant them.

> These dialogs can ensure that the end of the cold war does not provide an opening for regional rivalries, chaos, and arms races. They can build a foundation for our shared security well into the 21st century.[22]

ASEAN also saw that "grafting the new forum onto ASEAN" would ensure that Southeast Asians had a voice in whatever arrangements and processes would emerge in the new security environment.

Fourteen years later, Ralf Emmers, associate professor and head of graduate studies at the S. Rajaratnam School of International Studies, Nanyang Technological University, in Singapore, and a leading ARF watcher, recalled:

> ASEAN's decision to establish the ARF resulted from several motivations. It was regarded by ASEAN as a diplomatic instrument to promote a continuing United States involvement in the region and to encourage

China into habits of good international behaviour . The ARF was thus viewed as a means to ... socialise B eijing in a compr ehensive fashion while keeping Washington engaged in the region. F urthermore, the creation of the ARF was meant to ensur e the ongoing relev ance of ASEAN. I ts members needed to avoid being ex cluded fr om a ne w strategic architecture that was chiefly dependent on a Sino-Japanese-US triangle. ASEAN hoped therefore to consolidate its diplomatic position by further developing its stabilising role in Southeast Asia and beyond.[23]

Thus, Peter Chan Jer Hing, Permanent Secretary of Singapore's Ministry of Foreign Affairs and chairman of the May 1993 ASEAN PMC senior officials meeting, issued a statement that, as quoted in the *Straits Times*,[24] welcomed ASEAN's efforts to widen the ambit of the security dialogue so as to include China, R ussia, Vietnam and Laos. The meeting chairman 's statement was worded in this less than categorical way apparently because some delegations, notably the Japanese, still needed more specific instructions from their capitals concerning the composition of the proposed security forum.

In the J oint Communiqué of the ASEAN M inisterial M eeting on 23–24 July 1993, the ASEAN foreign ministers stated:

> The F oreign M inisters w elcomed the successful outcome of the first meeting of senior officials of the ASEAN PMC which was held in Singapore from 20 to 2l May 1993. They noted a convergence of views among the participants on the need to find ways to promote consultations on regional political and security issues. They endorsed the proposal of the senior officials to invite China, Laos, Papua New Guinea, Russia and Viet Nam to meet ASEAN and its D ialogue Partners at the " ASEAN Regional Forum" in B angkok next w eek.[25]

The last phrase was obviously an inadv ertent err or; the ministers meant "next year".

ASEAN settled on the name ASEAN Regional Forum in order to ensure the centrality of the Southeast Asian association's role in it. Agreement on the ARF and on participation in it having been reached within ASEAN, Singapore's Foreign Minister, Wong Kan Seng, later Deputy Prime Minister and Minister for H ome Affairs, conv ened an informal dinner on 25 J uly among the ministers who wer e on hand for the ASEAN for eign ministers' and r elated meetings. As chair of the ASEAN S tanding Committee, S ingapore hosted these meetings. In addition to those of ASEAN, then with six members, and its Dialogue Partners, then numbering seven, the foreign ministers of China, Russia, Vietnam, Laos and P apua N ew G uinea w ere pr esent in S ingapore. Conveniently enough, those countries had already some kind of relationship with ASEAN. China anc Russia (as successor state to the dismember ed and defunct Soviet Union) were "consultative partners" of ASEAN, having been invited to the ASEAN M inisterial M eeting as guests in 1993 and in the previous two years. Vietnam and Laos, in July 1992, had become observers in ASEAN, preparatory to eventual membership, and had acceded to the TAC. Papua New Guinea had been a non-regional ASEAN observer since 1976 and a signator y to the tr eaty since 1989. This circumstance lent an aura of objectivity to the criteria for their par ticipation.

At the end of the dinner , Wong Kan S eng issued a statement, saying, among other things, "This is the first time that the major players in the Asia-Pacific region have had the opportunity to discuss (security) issues collectiely. The dinner was thus a unique occasion and a significant milestone in ASEAN' efforts to promote dialogue on r egional security. The intention is to help build mutual confidence and preserve stability and growth in the Asia-Pacific by ev olving a pr edictable and constructive pattern of r elationships in the region." He reiterated ASEAN's decision to conv ene the ASEAN R egional Forum the next year in Thailand, the incoming chair of the ASEAN Sanding Committee, and invite the ministers to take part in it.The ministers were said to have welcomed that decision. [25]

In what was to become a pattern since then, the ministers ' meeting was preceded by a gathering of senio: officials, labelled ARF SOM for ASEAN Regional F orum S enior O fficials M eeting, in M ay. That annual gathering would be an occasion for the senior officials, normally the top civil ser vants in their foreign ministries, not only to prepare for their ministers' meeting but also to ex change views on their c wn on the outstanding r egional-security issues of the time.

THE FIRST ARF MINISTERIAL MEETING

On 25 July 1994, the first ARF ministerial meeting took place in B angkok, gathering the six ASEAN members, the seven Dialogue Partners, the observers Vietnam, Laos and P apua N ew G uinea, and the " consultative par tners" China and R ussia. I t was held cn the day betw een the annual ASEAN Ministerial Meeting anc the Post-ministerial Conferences. The observers and "consultative partners" were on :and for the public opening and closing of the ASEAN meeting. H owever, they w ere not at the PMC, since they wer e not yet ASEAN members or D ialogue Partners.

The significance of the first ARF was not lost on the participants or on a watching world. I t was the first time that ministers of countries in East Asia and of the major po wers with inter ests in the r egion had sat do wn together to discuss issues having to do with security and stability in the

Asia-Pacific, including measures to strengthen regional security and stability. The idea was to get them to do this in a multilateral setting and to be increasingly comfortable in doing so. This was considered as important for ensuring that r elationships among the leading nations of the Asia-P acific would be managed peacefully in the light of the new security environment in the region.

As the chairman of that meeting obser ved (in his statement), "Being the first time ever that high-ranking representatives from the majority of states in the Asia-P acific r egion came to specifically discuss political and security cooperation issues, the M eeting was consider ed a historic event for the region. More importantly, the Meeting signified the opening of a new chapter of peace, stability and cooperation for Southeast Asia." The statement noted the ministers' recognition of " the need to develop a mor e predictable and constructive pattern of r elationships for the Asia-P acific region".[27]

No one was under any illusion that the ARF would function as a mechanism for resolving disputes between participants, much less for dealing with pr oblems within them. H owever, the confidence built thr ough the forum and the networks formed and str engthened would pr esumably make action on disputes and pr oblems easier, more amicable and mor e likely.

Nor did anyone expect the forum to confront a state that was a common adversary. The ARF participants' strategic outlooks were too diverse for them to agree on one. I ndeed, it was pr ecisely because of these differ ences that it was necessar y for them to engage in peaceful dialogue and consultation. Moreover, all major potential antagonists wer e inside the ARF.

It was also because of the div ergent interests and outlooks of the other participants that it was left to ASEAN, partly b y default and par tly through astute ASEAN diplomacy, to conv ene the for um and manage its pr ocesses. ASEAN, after all, was a loose association of r elatively w eak countries that were friendly to everyone and hostile to no one, representing no threat to or serious strategic disagr eement with any of the other participants — ex cept possibly with China on the S outh China S ea.

With a top for eign-ministry official seated behind each of them, the ministers decided to meet annually fr om then on. They also agr eed to "endorse the purposes and principles of ASEAN' s Treaty of Amity and Cooperation in S outheast Asia (TAC), as a code of conduct go verning relations betw een states and a unique diplomatic instr ument for r egional confidence-building, pr eventive diplomacy , and political and security cooperation".[28] Those principles include the peaceful settlement of inter-state disputes, the r enunciation of the use or thr eat of force in the r elations between states, and non-inter ference in one another's internal affairs. [29]

It was a good and historic start.

SHAPING THE ARF'S NATURE

The second meeting of the ARF ministers, in B   andar S eri Begawan on 1 A ugust 1995, was devoted largely to shaping and defining the forum   's nature, purposes and pr ocesses. These w ere embodied in two documents. One was the Concept Paper drawn up in ASEAN and cleared with the other ARF participants.[30] The other was the Chairman's Statement drafted by the Brunei chair , wor ked out within ASEAN, and negotiated by the then Permanent Secretary of Brunei Darussalam's foreign ministry, Lim Jock Seng, with the other par ticipants.[31]

The Concept Paper observed that, while the region had been "experiencing an unprecedented period of peace and pr osperity", it had also gone thr ough "some of the most disastr ous wars of the tw entieth centur y" and suffer ed from a "residue of unresolved terr.torial and other differences". It pointed out that periods of rapid economic gr wth were "often accompanied by significant shifts in power relations". The Concept Paper noted the region's great diversity in size, level of development, cultur e, ethnic make-up, religion, and history. Because of this div ersity, the ARF participants had differ ent appr oaches to matters of peace and security , which, in turn, r equired what it called " a consensual approach to security issues".

The Concept Paper stressed that, since ASEAN had had "a demonstrable record of enhancing r egional cooperation in the most div erse sub-region of the Asia-Pacific …, fostered habits of cooperation, and pr ovided the catalyst for encouraging r egional cooperation in the wider Asia-P acific r egion", the ASEAN model of cooperation could be emulated b y the rest of that region.

The paper then recommended three stages for the evolution of the ARF — sequentially, confidence-building, the dev elopment of mechanisms for "preventive diplomacy", and, o ver the long term, modalities for conflict resolution. For the initial stage of confidence-building, the document suggested a number of activities in two annex es, one for the immediate futur e and the other for the longer term. The paper called for the activities to be carried out by r esearch institutes and non-gc vernmental organizations (T rack Two) as well as by go vernments (Track One).

The Concept Paper laid down some ground rules for the forum. One was that the ministerial meeting would take place annually on the occasion of the ASEAN Ministerial Meeting, under ASEAN chairmanship. The ARF would not have a secretariat, at least not anytime soon. Decisions would be made by consensus. The forum would progress "at a pace comfortable to all participants".

The chairman's statement of the second ARF r   ecorded cer tain basic understandings about the forum. I t defined the character of the ARF as " a forum for open dialogue and consultation on r egional political and security issues, to discuss and reconcile the differing views between ARF participants in or der to r educe the risk to security ". A ccording to the statement, the ministers adopted many of the pr oposals in the Concept P aper.

They agr eed that the ARF should " move at a pace comfor table to all participants". This was evidently to giv e r eassurance that nobody would railroad or ram thr ough measures that others might deem to be thr eatening to them. With the same objectiv e in mind, the statement affirmed that the principle of decision b y consensus would prev ail.

The ministers were said to have adopted the three stages proposed in the Concept P aper, ex cept that the thir d stage — originally " development of conflict-resolution mechanisms" — would now be "elaboration of approaches to conflicts". The statement went out of its way to declare, "Discussions will continue regarding the incorporation of elaboration of appoaches to conflicts, as an eventual goal, into the ARF pr ocess." These extr emely cautious formulations seem to me to hav e been arrived at as a r esult of the worr y of some delegations, notably the Chinese, that attempts at multilateral conflict resolution would give to certain powers the sanction to get involved in issues like, for example, the S outh China S ea or the Taiwan pr oblem, not to mention internal dissent or separatism.

Now with senior defence or national-security as well as foreign ministry, officials seated behind them, the ministers str essed that the ARF's concept of security was " comprehensive", including "not only militar y aspects but also political, economic, social and other issues ". These issues ar e often called sources of "non-traditional" security threats or, as some prefer, "non-military" issues.

In terms of pr ocess, the ministers noted that " ASEAN under takes the obligation to be the primay driving force" while assuring the other participants of their "active, full and equal participation". They agreed to meet every year, "in the context of" the annual ASEAN Mnisterial Meeting and Post-ministerial Conferences.

The ministers arrived at a consensus that the ARF pr ocess would go on both Track One and Track Two. The participants seem to have been split on the role of Track Two. Some were enthusiastic about it as a fount of ideas and as a sounding board. Others were wary of it because of the lack of government control over some of its component institutions or esponsibility for them, or they were simply unfamiliar with how non-governmental institutions worked. There was also the possibility that unw elcome NGOs might find their way into ARF-related discussions and other activities. The ministers thus came to agree that strategic institutes and "relevant" non-governmental organizations would take part in the ARF process but their activities would have to "result from *full* consultations with *all* ARF participants" (italics mine).

The second ARF decided to set up what it called the I ntersessional Support G roup on Confidence B uilding M easures and the I ntersessional Meetings on Cooperativ e A ctivities as the initial v ehicles for mo ving the inter-governmental process along. Each of their activities was to be co-chaired by one ASEAN member and one non-ASEAN participant. The ministers "encouraged", as initial confidence-building measures, ex changes of security perceptions, the v oluntary issuance of defence policy statements, contacts and exchanges among military academies, staff colleges and training bodies, and participation in the U nited Nations Conventional Arms R egister.

Over lunch at one of the earlier ARF ministerial meetings, the ministers tackled the question of the divis.on of labour betw een the ARF and the PMC. They agr eed that the ARF would deal with political and security issues in the forum's gecgraphic "footprint", while the PMC would continue to discuss non-security matters and security issues outside of the footprint", such as the M iddle East and disarmament and non-pr oliferation. As the ARF ev olved, ho wever, this division of labour came to be blurr ed in concept and ignored in practice.

CONCLUSION

It seems clear that the ARF was founded to build confidence betw een states and to reduce the likelihood of conflict betw een them in the " traditional", military sense. Yet, as early as their second meeting, the ARF ministers — some more than others and some even before that — were already promoting the notion of " comprehensive security", involving political, economic and social dimensions and not just the military one. As the ARF process unfolded over the years, academic and media commentators raised questions as to why the ARF was not inv olved in matters internal to participating states — East Timor, then part of Indonesia, Aceh, Myanmar, and even southern Thailand.

The current ARF participants seem to be determined to keep the for um going for purposes of confidence-building and mutual consultation — and watching one another . At the v ery least, none wishes to be left out of a regional forum that, several times a y ear, talks about the configuration of regional security in the uncer tain envir onment of the Asia-P acific and, throughout the year, works together in numerous security-r elated activities.

As it does so, the ARF finds itself grappling with two existential questions. One is the balance to be maintained between traditional, military-related issues and non-traditional, non-military concerns that are somehow linked to the security of the region broadly defined. The ARF participants seem to have concluded that cooperativ e security and, consequently , preventive diplomacy could most feasibly and fr uitfully be directed at the non-traditional, non-militar y security thr eats, wher e they incr easingly recognize their inter ests to converge. The other question is whether the ARF, especially in its still-inchoate pr eventive-diplomacy function, is to involve itself in some way in conflicts or poblems within states in the name of "human security" and "the responsibility to protect" on the ground that such conflicts or problems ar e today the main sour ces of thr eat to the security and stability of the r egion.

Notes

1. Singapore Declaration of 1992, Singapore, 28 January 1992. See <http://www. aseansec.org/5120.htm>.
2. Ibid., para. 3.
3. *Straits Times*, 25 January 1992.
4. *Straits Times*, 16 May 1993.
5. See Appendix C.
6. See Appendix D.
7. Richard C. S mith, "R egional S ecurity: I s 'Architecture' All We N eed?" (unpublished paper, 19 October 2007), p. 6.
8. Gary J. S mith: "M ultilateralism and R egional S ecurity in Asia: The ASEAN Regional F orum (ARF) and AP EC's G eopolitical Value", P aper N o. 97-2 (Cambridge, Massachusetts: The Weatherhead Center for International Affairs, Harvard University, February 1997).
9. I have not been able to locate a cutting of my ne wspaper article and, therefore, have to r ely on memor y.
10. Established in 1988, ASEAN-ISIS, which stands for ASEAN Institutes of Strategic and International Studies, is a non-governmental organization that is a network of policy research institutes in the ASEAN countries. Its original members were the Centre for Strategic and International Studies of Indonesia, the Institute of Strategic and International Studies of Malaysia, the Center for I ntegrative and Development Studies (later Institute for Strategic and Development Studies) of the Philippines, the Singapore Institute of International Affairs, and the Institute of Security and International Studies of Thailand.
11. ASEAN-ISIS, "A Time for Initiative — Proposals for the Consideration of the Fourth ASEAN Summit" (4 June 1991), pp. 4–5.
12. Quoted in Tamotsu Fukuda, "Japan's Evolving Interests in Multilateral Security Cooperation in the Asia-P acific: A Two-Dimensional A pproach" (Canberra: Australian National University) <http://dspace.anu.edu.au/ manakin/bitstream/ 1885/39965/2/Japan_evolving_interest.pdf>.

13. Michael Richardson, "Seen as Harmful to Direct Alliances: U.S. Wary of Japanese Plan Pacific Security Idea", *International Herald Tribune*, 23 July 1991.

14. Yukio Satoh, "Reflections on the Nakayama Proposal", in *The Inclusive Regionalist*, edited by Hadi Soesastro and Clara Joewono (Jakarta: Centre for Strategic and International Studies, 2007), p. 97.

15. Ibid., p. 102.

16. This shift is discussed extensively by Tamotsu Fukuda, op. cit. The domestic debate on Japan's stance on security policy in general and the ARF in particular is analysed in Tsuyoshi Kawasaki: "Between Realism and Idealism in Japanese Security Policy: The Case of the ASEAN Regional Forum", *The Pacific Review* 10, no. 4 (1997): 480–503. It is analysed in great detail by Takeshi Yuzawa in his book, *Japan's Security Policy and the ASEAN Regional Forum: The Search for Multilateral Security in the Asia-Pacific* (London and New York: Routledge, 2007).

17. *Straits Times*, 15 May 1993.

18. *Straits Times*, 14 May 1993.

19. Smith, op. cit., pp. 6 and 7.

20. The view that China may be "socialising" the ARF was expressed by Kwa Chong Guan, S. Rajaratnam School of International Studies, Nanyang Technological University, in an interview by the author in Singapore, 9 October 2007.

21. Satoh, op. cit., pp. 102–04.

22. <http://findarticles.com/p/articles/mi_m2889/is_n28_v29/ai_14234764>.

23. Ralf Emmers, "ASEAN Regional Forum: Time to Move Towards Preventive Diplomacy" in *RSIS Commentaries*, 112/2007 (Singapore: S. Rajaratnam School of International Studies, 22 October 2007), p. 1.

24. *Straits Times*, 22 May 1993.

25. <http://www.aseansec org/2009.htm>.

26. *Straits Times*, 26 July 1993.

27. <http://www.aseanregionalforum.org/PublicLibrary/ARFChairmans StatementsandReports/ChairmansStatementofthe1stMeetingoftheASE/tabid/ 201/Default.aspx>, paras. 3 and 8.

28. Ibid., para. 6.

29. Treaty of Amity and Cooperation in Southeast Asia <http://www.aseansec.org/ 1217.htm>, Art. 2.

30. See Appendix A.

31. See Appendix B.

2

WHY JOIN THE ARF?

At the official level, the creation of the ASEAN Regional Forum started with the call of the ASEAN S ummit for ASEAN to use the P ost-ministerial Conferences (PMC) to "intensify its external dialogues in political and security matters". The ASEAN Dialogue system, of which the PMC is the centrepiece, had originally been intended to link ASEAN with the leading dev eloped countries for economic purposes — to expand the access of ASEAN products to the markets of the dev eloped economies, attract inv estments fr om the developed countries, and seek development assistance fr om them. Although the Dialogues had not shied away from the discussion of political and security issues in the past, using the PMC to "intensify" such discussions, particularly with respect to the Asia-Pacific, would affirm the altered nature and purpose of the Dialogue system.

As pr eparations got under way for carr ying out the ASEAN leaders ' mandate, it became clear to ASEAN' s officials and those of its D ialogue Partners that discussion of r egional political and security matters would not be effective without the par ticipation of China, R ussia or Vietnam, none of which was at that time an ASEAN member or D ialogue Partner. Without them, a forum on regional security would not be useful in the r egional-security environment that had dev eloped after the br eak-up of the S oviet Union, the fall of the communist r egimes of Eastern Europe, the end of the Cold War, economic reforms in the centrally planned economies, the rise of Chinese power, and the settlement of the Cambodian pr oblem. So, it was quickly decided to bring in ASEAN' s "consultative par tners" — China and Russia — and obser vers — at that time, Laos, P apua N ew G uinea and

Vietnam. Indeed, even before the May 1993 ASEAN PMC Senior Officials Meeting in Singapore, proposals had already been floated about the desirability of their participation in a new Asia-Pacific security forum.[1] Barbara McDougall, Canada's Secretary of State for External Affairs, was quoted after the July 1991 ASEAN Post-ministerial Conferences as expressing the hope that China, the Soviet Union, Vietnam, Laos and Cambodia could join the proposed regional security consultations "at an appropriate time".[2]

The new forum, the ASEAN Regional Forum, would thus include ASEAN's members, Dialogue Partners, observers and consultative partners. Having been, as initially conceived, based on ASEAN's Dialogue system, the ARF had among its original number the European Community (to expand later into the European Union), the only non-state participant in the ARF Its ASEAN Dialogue Partnership formally dates back to 1977, but Europe had been informally engaged with ASEAN since 1973. Europe's massive commercial transactions with East Asia benefit from political stability in the region and require the security of the sea lanes. The EU uses the ARF to share its experience in managing matters related to such "non-traditional" security activities as disaster relief, small arms movements, and border control.

As a minor sidelight, the EU's participation has led to recurrent disputes with the ASEAN hosts concerning seating arrangements at ARF ministerial meetings. ASEAN has insisted that, like the other participants, the EU be entitled to only one seat at the front and two seats behind. The EU, however, has asked for, initially, two seats in front — one for the Council presidency and the other for the European Commission. The request was raised to three seats with the creation under the 1999 Amsterdam Treaty of the position of High Representative for the Common Foreign and Security Policy. The compromise for a number of years was to start out with one EU seat in front, with the two others quietly pulling their seats forward after the meeting had started. In the past few years, upon the presidency's request, the High Representative, Javier Solana Madariaga, former Foreign Minister of Spain, has led the EU delegation to the ARF ministerial meetings.

France and the United Kingdom, early in the ARF's existence, sought to take part in the ARF on their own, separately from the EU. Their claim was based on several factors. They were both permanent members of the UN Security Council. They were both recognized nuclear-weapon states. They both had interests in East Asian security and could contribute substantially to it. France had possessions in the South Pacific. The United Kingdom was a party to the Five-Power Defence Arrangements with Australia, Malaysia, New Zealand and Singapore and, before its handover to China, exercised sovereignty over Hong Kong. However, ASEAN has not been able to reconcile the proposed separate involvement of France and the United Kingdom with the continued par ticipation of the EU, of which they ar e both members.

Perhaps partly to bolster its claim to ARF participation, F rance acceded to the Treaty of Amity and Cooperation in S outheast Asia in J anuary 2007. The EU itself has decided to sign the treaty as an entity, with ASEAN sorting out the legal complications surrounding the signature of a non-state party. At their first meeting, the ARF ministers had endorsed the treaty's "purposes and principles ... as a code of conduct go verning relations between states and a unique diplomatic instr ument for r egional confidence-building, pr eventive diplomacy, and political and security cooperation ".[3]

CRITERIA FOR PARTICIPATION

Almost fr om the beginning, the ARF made it clear that it was open to participation by others in addition to its original composition of ASEAN members, Dialogue Partners, observers and consultative partners. According to ASEAN's Concept Paper for the ARF, "Applications to par ticipate in the ARF shall be submitted to the Chairman of the ARF who will then consult the other ARF participants." [4] Repeating this formulation, the second ARF ministerial meeting, in 1995, r equested the next chairman, I ndonesia, "to study the question of futur e par ticipation and dev elop the criteria for the consideration of the Third ARF thr ough the ARF-SOM".[5]

Pursuant to this mandate, the Indonesian chairman, Foreign Minister Ali Alatas, went on a round of consultations with other ARF participants and produced a paper proposing criteria for admission to the forum. On the basis of the proposals, the ARF ministers, at their thir d meeting, in J uly 1996 in Jakarta, arrived at several decisions go verning future ARF par ticipation.[6]

One was that the pr ospective participant should be admitted " only if it can be demonstrated that it has an impact on the peace and security of the 'geographical footprint' of key ARF activities " and only if it " can dir ectly affect the peace and security of the region". The chairman's statement of that meeting str essed that ther e was "already an implicit consensus among ARF participants" on what the ARF' s " geographical footprint" would co ver — Northeast Asia, Southeast Asia and Oceania (meaning Australia, New Zealand and the island-nations of the South Pacific). Moreover, each new participant would "be admitted on the firm understanding that its par ticipation is necessary for the ARF to accomplish its key goals ".

Another criterion was: "All questions r egarding par ticipation should be decided by consultations among all ARF par ticipants." This was evidently meant to assur e the non-ASEAN par ticipants that ASEAN would not unilaterally decide to admit ne w members. (I n practice, questions of membership are thrashed out within ASEAN befor e the other par ticipants are consulted.) Nevertheless, ASEAN insisted, and the forum agreed, that all ASEAN members would "automatically become participants of ARF". This was clearly intended to ensure that non-ASEAN participants that disapproved of the r egime in M yanmar could not block the admission of that countr y. Indeed, Myanmar was welcomed as a new member of the forum by that same ARF meeting, having, two days befor e, become an ASEAN obser ver on its way to ASEAN membership. India was admitted into the forum on the same occasion. H aving been ASEAN' s " sectoral" D ialogue P artner since 1993, India was about to become a full ASEAN D ialogue Partner. The adopted criteria wer e silent on the automatic par ticipation of ASEAN D ialogue Partners or observers, but this seems to be implicit in the initial composition of the ARF . Cambodia had joined the ARF in 1995, after it became an ASEAN observer preparatory to its eventual membership in the association.

A criterion was inser ted upon China's insistence, namely, that all " new participants" had to be "sovereign states". The reference to "sovereign states" was, of course, meant to ensure the exclusion of Taiwan from the ARF while accommodating, with the wor d "new", the continued participation of the European Union. Taiwan's inclusion in international political forums, as well as a separate national identity for the island, is vigour ously opposed b y Beijing, which insists that the island is par t of China and must someday be united with it. All other ARF participating states subscribe to what is known as the O ne China P olicy, which means officially r ecognizing the P eople's Republic as the sole legal government of China while maintaining commercial and other "non-official" ties with Taiwan.

It was clear as early as in its thir d year that the ARF par ticipants were concerned about any rapid expansion of the forum. P rudently, ASEAN and the other ARF par ticipants agreed, "The ARF should expand car efully and cautiously. As the ARF process is barely three years old, it would be advisable to consolidate the ARF pr ocess before expanding it rapidly…. E fforts must be made to control the number of participants to a manageable level to ensure the effectiveness of the ARF ." As generally interpr eted, this amounted to a moratorium on membership, albeit with gaping loopholes.

Two y ears later, hc wever, in 1998, a new par ticipant, M ongolia, was admitted into the ARF , a month after its formal application.   The U nited States had pressed for mineral-rich Mongolia's admission. At the meeting that admitted Mongolia, the chairman's statement declared, "With the addition of Mongolia in the ARF, the Ministers agreed to allow the ARF to consolidate as a gr oup and to dev elop an efficient pr ocess of cooperation." [7] This was another attempt at a membership moratorium.

NORTH KOREA

In 2000, North Korean Foreign Minister Paek Nam-sun wrote to the ARF chairman, Thailand's Foreign Minister Surin Pitsuwan, seeking participation in the regional forum, an application that was swiftly granted. F rom the beginning, the ARF had been addressing issues pertaining to North Korea. At the time of the first ARF ministerial meeting, the discovery of the construction of nuclear facilities at Yongbyon had been announced, leading to a flurr y of negotiations, which would r esult in the O ctober 1994 Agr eed F ramework between the Democratic People's Republic of Korea (DPRK) and the United States.[8] The Agreed Framework required the DPRK to "freeze" its "graphite-moderated reactors (which w ere capable of pr oducing materials for nuclear weapons) and related facilities" and "eventually dismantle" them. These steps were to be monitor ed by the UN' s I nternational A tomic E nergy Agency (IAEA). Pyongyang would r emain a par ty to the N uclear Non-proliferation Treaty, which it had threatened to quit — and eventually did — "consistently take steps to implement the N orth-South (Korea) Joint Declaration on the Denuclearization of the K orean P eninsula", and " engage in N orth S outh dialogue". In return, the U nited S tates would organiz e a consor tium, later named the K orean Peninsula Energy D evelopment Organization (KEDO), that would build light-water reactors for the North. Much less capable of use for weapons purposes, such reactors would r eplace the graphite-moderated ones at Yongbyon. While the ne w plants w ere under constr uction, the consortium would supply N orth K orea with a cer tain amount of fuel oil. Washington would formally assure North Korea that the United States would not resort to the use or thr eat of nuclear w eapons against it. The two sides would take steps leading, as " progress is made on issues of concern to each side", to "full normalization of political and economic r elations", something that Pyongyang had long wanted.

From 1994 to 1999, the Korean situation had been intensively discussed at the ARF in the absence of N orth Korea. In fact, accor ding to the late Michael Leifer, North Korea had unsuccessfully sought access to the first ARF meeting in B angkok.[9] The chairman's statements of the first six ARF ministerial meetings had been welcoming United States-DPRK negotiations, calling for the resumption of the inter-Korea dialogue, and expressing hope for the implementation of the Agreed Framework and support for KEDO.

The for um had also been upholding the continued v alidity of the 1953 Armistice Agreement that halted the Korean War pending the conclusion of a final peace tr eaty. The formulation of the paragraphs on the K orean situation was influenced largely by the United States, South Korea and, to some extent, Japan.

After North Korea was finally admitted into the ARF, the DPRK Foreign Minister or his deputy attended the 2000 and subsequent ARF ministerial meetings. In the earlier meetings, they mer ely read from prepared texts, but in recent y ears, I am told, they par ticipated mor e activ ely and mor e spontaneously in the discussions.

Since Pyongyang's admission, the ARF has continued to express support for negotiations on the denuclearization of the K orean Peninsula. After the series of Six-Party talks in Beijing began in 2003, [10] the ARF has backed that process. In the presence of the North Korean minister or his deputy, the ARF has indicated its concern o ver that countr y's missile tests and has called on Pyongyang to r everse its decision to withdraw fr om the N uclear N on-proliferation Treaty. On the other hand, the ARF has had to " note" North Korea's positions, without describing them, on issues on which most of the rest of the forum evidently disagr ee with Pyongyang. The ARF's calls for the "full implementation" of the Agreed Framework could be interpreted as being addressed to both N orth Korea and the U nited States.

At their 2001 meeting, the ARF ministers expr essed their appr eciation for "the active participation b y the DPRK in ARF activities in the last y ear and considered this a contribution to wards str engthening the ARF pr ocess and advancing the cause of r egional peace and security ". [11] From 2001 to 2007, N orth K orea cor tributed to no less than fiv e issues of the ARF' s *Annual Security Outlook*. Since its admission into the ARF , the DPRK has taken part in cer tain "inter-sessional" activities, that is, ARF ev ents between ministerial meetings, but not in others. F or example, DPRK r epresentatives attended the two confer ences on security policy and the seminars on alternative development", on " non-traditional security issues " and on small arms and light weapons. They have been at gatherings of heads of Defense Universities, Colleges and I nstitutes. They took par t in an ARF seminar on the non-proliferation of weapons of mass destruction in Singapore in March 2006 and in a seminar on narcotics contr ol in Xian in S eptember 2007. A N orth Korean delegate made an inter vention in a seminar on cyber terrorism in Busan, South Korea, in 2007. A DPRK epresentative was present for the first time at the meeting of the I ntersessional S upport G roup on Confidence Building M easures (r econstituted as the I ntersessional S upport G roup on

Confidence Building Measures and P reventive Diplomacy in J uly 2005) in April 2001. The DPRK was also in attendance at the meetings of the group in December 2001, April 2002, October 2004, February 2005, March 2006, and November 2007, but not in N ovember 2000, N ovember 2002, M arch and N ovember 2003, A pril 2004, O ctober 2005, N ovember 2006, M arch 2007 and A pril 2008.[12]

The ARF has been an interested b ystander in the complex pr ocess of bringing about the denuclearization of the K orean peninsula, with its accompanying threats and counter-threats, diplomatic moves and counter-moves, and mutual accusations of non-compliance with pevious agreements. At the same time, the ARF has managed to bring N orth K orea into a comprehensive multilateral forum on security issues, the only one outside the U nited N ations in which P yongyang sits together with the U nited States, J apan and other dev eloped countries. I n the ARF, the DPRK can state and clarify its positions in a multilateral setting and listen to those of other participants. The ARF also provides an occasion for high-level North Korean officials to hav e informal and quiet contacts with those of the United States, Japan and South Korea without the glare of publicity attending more formal meetings.

PAKISTAN AND TIMOR-LESTE

Ever since ASEAN granted I ndia a S ectoral D ialogue Partnership in 1992, Pakistan had been seeking some kind of r elationship with ASEAN. ASEAN, however, was divided on the point. When in 1996 India was admitted into the D ialogue system as a full par tner and into the ARF , P akistan's effor ts intensified and were rewarded with a Sectoral Dialogue Partnership in 1997. Still, Islamabad was unrelenting, apparently concerned that the ARF and the PMC would be discussing South Asian affairs without its presence. Although South Asia was outside the ARF' s "geographic footprint" — indeed, I ndia itself had been averse to having international forums addr ess the Kashmir problem and other India-P akistan disputes — the ARF " expressed grav e concern over and deplored" the 1998 nuclear tests of both hdia and Pakistan. India was able to give its side of the issue. Pakistan was not present to do so. According to S udhir D evare, a r etired top official in I ndia's M inistry of External Affairs, New Delhi was initially opposed to Pakistan's admission not only because Pakistan was considered to be outside the ARF's "footprint", but also because of concerns that Pakistan might raise "extraneous issues" at ARF meetings, namely, its bilateral disputes with I ndia. India lifted its objections after Pakistan undertook to refrain from raising bilateral issues in the ARF.[13] The ARF finally decided to admit P akistan, in 2003, after ASEAN had resolved the disagreements among its members on the matter .

Upon Mongolia's admission in 1998, the ARF ministers had " agreed to allow the ARF to consolidate as a gr oup and to develop an efficient pr ocess of cooperation." When North Korea joined the forum in 2000, the chairman's statement had re-imposed the implicit moratorium on expansion. It had said, "With r egard to the issue of membership   , the Ministers r eaffirmed the decision taken at the F   ifth ARF and agr eed that with the curr   ent 23 participants, the focus should now be on consolidating the process of dialogue and cooperation among the pr esent participants of the ARF."[14]

However, at their 2003 meeting, the ARF ministers again decided to lift the *de facto* moratorium on additional participation and to admit Pakistan. José Ramos-H orta, then for eign minister of the new nation of Timor-Leste, was in Phnom Penh as a guest at the 2003 ASEAN Ministerial Meeting. He was sorely disappointed in his countr y's continued exclusion from the ARF despite the moratorium being lifted in fav our of Pakistan.[15] In November 2002, six months after its independence, the Democratic Republic of Timor-Leste had begun lobbying for admission into the ARF , even as it remained ambivalent on ASEAN membership. On Timor-Leste, too, ASEAN was divided.

Thus, in 2004, P akistan attended the ARF ministerial meeting for the first time, and the I ndian foreign minister was the first to congratulate his Pakistani counterpart. Timor-Leste had to wait until the next year to gain admission.

BANGLADESH, SRI LANKA AND OTHERS

At the ARF ministerial meetings in 2006 and 2007, the admission of two more South Asian nations, B angladesh and Sri Lanka, respectively, enlarged the ARF participation further to twenty-seven. Bangladesh had started lobbying for ARF admission in D ecember 2002 and S ri Lanka in S eptember 2003. Despite the misgivings of some ASEAN members, other ASEAN states succeeded in pushing the par ticipation of the two S outh Asian countries. A number of non-ASEAN par ticipants r eportedly gr umbled both about the ARF's enlargement and about what they felt w ere insufficient consultations regarding it. P ersons present on both occasions have said that ther e was an understanding within ASEAN and in the ARF that the incr ease of S outh Asian participation from two to four would not enlarge the ARF' "geographic footprint", which would remain Northeast Asia, Southeast Asia and Oceania.

Some ARF watchers ar e of the vie w that it was a bad idea — one has called it "dumb" — to bring in the S outh Asians other than I ndia, which is a rising power that has a strategic interest and role in East Asia. Others think that the inclusion of more South Asians would be helpful so long as the ARF' primary focus remained East Asia, the view being that South Asia should not be r epresented in the ARF by I ndia alone. I t is notewor thy that both the United States and China welcome the expanded South Asian participation in the ARF.[16] Strategically, that par ticipation may r eflect recognition of the reality that, in a sense, the security issues in South Asia had become seamlessly intertwined with those of East Asia.

Still others have joined the line, namely Kazakhstan, with express Russian support, K yrgyzstan and Afghanistan. I ndeed, Kazakhstan applied for admission as early as June 1998. Some ARF countries may at some point find it in their national inter est — regardless of its effects on the forum's efficacy — to push for the par ticipation of one or mor e of these and other aspirant nations. The problem of diffusion and o ver-reach could then worsen.

CONCLUSION

This expansion of the ARF membership , including four countries of S outh Asia, may hav e br ought the for um to the point wher e the par ticipants will have to ask themselv es two questions. O ne is whether the expanded siz e of the for um will not r ender it too unwieldy and thus set back the likelihood, small as that is already, of progress beyond the confidence-building stage.The other is whether the ARF's expansion will not diffuse its attention fur ther at a time when what it needs is precisely a sharper focus on specific problems in the area of its original " footprint".

In a "discussion paper" cir culated at the J uly 2006 ASEAN M inisterial Meeting,[17] the ASEAN Secretariat urged compliance with long-standing ARF guidelines on the admission of ne w members. I t r eminded its r eaders that those guidelines had called for the "consolidation" of the ARF process before its "rapid" expansion and for keeping the ARF' s siz e "manageable" for the sake of the forum's "effectiveness". The Secretariat paper reiterated the previous ARF understanding that the forum should admit only those states whose "participation is necessar y for the ARF to accomplish its key goals ". Bowing to reality , ho wever, the paper pr oposed that the moratorium on futur e participation be kept "flexible", which is what such moratoriums had always been. I t also made the ne w suggestion that the ARF invite "inter ested countries and institutions in a certain capacity other than full participants (i.e. observers) at appropriate lev els of ARF meetings and activities ".

One factor to consider in the matter of ARF par   ticipation is the motivation of the curr ent par ticipants in arriving at their decisions on applications for admission. I n addition to genuine or ostensible concerns about the manageability and effectiveness of the forum, such decisions are invariably driven by a current participant's relationship, actual or potential, with the applicant-countr y or b y br oader foreign-policy considerations. This was clear in the case of   Washington's sponsorship of M ongolia's participation. It was clearly evident in the closed-door ASEAN debate on that of P akistan, with several ASEAN members basing their positions almost solely on the nature of their relations with Islamabad. The decision on North Korea's admission resulted from a convergence of interests among the ARF par ticipants most dir ectly involv ed in K orean matters. The motivations behind the admission of B angladesh and S ri Lanka ar e less clear, but they could have included the realization that the security of South Asia had become inextricable fr om that of East Asia.

In the meantime, the existence of a r   egional multilateral for um that brings together po wer rivals or countries in contention of some kind with each other is, in the view of ARF adv   ocates, of benefit to the peace and stability of the r egion, even if the forum stays at the confidence-building stage. It is only in the ARF wher e they can consult, hold dialogues, network and discuss regional-security issues comprehensively and in a broad setting — China and the United States, China and Japan, Russia and the United States, China and I ndia, N orth and S outh K orea, N orth K orea and the U nited States, and, at the hub of it all, ASEAN and its members.

On the other hand, ARF critics point to the possibility that a r egionally all-inclusive multilateral arrangement would undermine the balance of power on which r egional peace and stability ultimately depend. E ven if this w ere true, however, it may no w be too late to disband the ARF or for any of the current participants to withdraw from it, thus ex cluding itself from a broad forum for regional-security discussions.

Notes

1. See Chapter 1.
2. Michael Richardson, "Seen as Harmful to Direct Alliances: U.S. Wary of Japanese Plan Pacific Security Idea", *International Herald Tribune*, 23 July 1991.
3. "Chairman's Statement: The First ASEAN Regional Forum", in *ASEAN Regional Forum Documents Series 1994–2006* (Jakarta: ASEAN Secretariat, March 2007), p. 4. Also in <http:// wwwaseanregionalforum.org/PublicLibrary/ARFChairmans StatementsandReports/ChairmansStatementofthe1stMeetingoftheASE/tabid/ 201/Default.aspx>, para. 6.

4. See Appendix A, para. 19.

5. See Appendix B, para. 6C.

6. "Chairman's Statement: The Third ASEAN Regional Forum", *ASEAN Regional Forum Documents Series 1994–2006*, pp . 23–25. Also in <http://www .asean regionalforum.org/PublicLibrary/ ARFChairmansS tatementsandReports/ ChairmansStatementofthe3rdARF/tabid/196/Default.aspx>, para. 5.

7. "Chairman's Statement: The Fifth ASEAN R egional Forum", *ASEAN Regional Forum Documents Series 1994–2006*, p. 85. Also in <http://www .aseanregional forum.org/PublicLibrary/ ARFChairmansS tatementsandReports/Chairmans Statementofthe5thMeetingoftheASE/tabid/180/Default.aspx>, para. 4.

8. <http://www.armscontrol.org/documents/af.asp>.

9. Michael Leifer, *The ASEAN Regional Forum: Extending ASEAN's Model of Regional Security*, Adelphi Paper 302 (Oxford and New York: Oxford University Press for the International Institute for S trategic Studies, 1996), p. 34.

10. The six parties are North and South Korea, the United States, China, Japan, and Russia.

11. "Chairman's Statement: The Eighth ASEAN Regional Forum", *ASEAN Regional Forum Documents Series 1994–2006*, p. 188. Also in <http://www.aseanregional forum.org/LinkClick.aspx?fileticket=w%2fMjx3xLGRU%3d&tabid=66& mid=410>, para. 15.

12. I am grateful to the ARF Unit of the ASEAN Secretariat for data on attendance in ARF inter-sessional activities.

13. Interview by the author, Jakarta, 7 D ecember 2007.

14. "Chairman's Statement: The Seventh ASEAN Regional Forum", *ASEAN Regional Forum Documents Series 1994–2006*, p. 159. Also in <http://www.aseanregional forum.org/PublicLibrary/ ARFChairmansS tatementsandReports/Chairmans Statementofthe7thMeetingofASEANR/tabid/115/Default.aspx>, para. 3.

15. Conversation with the author, Phnom Penh, 18 June 2003.

16. Interviews with Yang Yanyi, D eputy D irector-General, Asian D epartment, Ministry of Foreign Affairs, China, Beijing, 21 S eptember 2007, and Elizabeth Phu, D irector for S outheast Asia, N ational S ecurity Council, U nited S tates, Washington, D.C., 23 O ctober 2007.

17. ASEAN Secr etariat, "F uture P articipation in the ASEAN R egional F orum" (unpublished discussion paper, July 2006).

3

DOES THE ARF BUILD
CONFIDENCE?

On the basis of the Concept Paper produced by ASEAN, the second ministerial meeting of the ASEAN Regional Forum, in August 1995, prescribed "three broad stages" for the evolution of the forum: "the promotion of confidence-building, development of preventive diplomacy and elaboration of approaches to conflicts".[1] The Concept Paper had defined the third stage as "Development of Conflict-Resolution Mechanisms",[2] but China and similarly cautious participants insisted that the formulation be watered down to the meaningless terminology eventually adopted.

The second ARF ministerial meeting also adopted the Concept Paper's proposal that the "ARF process shall move at a pace comfortable to all participants".[3] Because some participants have not felt "comfortable" with moving to the second stage — indeed, the participants have not reached a common understanding of "preventive diplomacy" — the ARF has essentially remained in the first stage, that of confidence-building. The eighth ministerial meeting, in 2001, according to its chairman's statement, "emphasized that confidence-building is of essential importance to and remains the foundation and main thrust of the whole ARF process".[4] The 2003 chairman's statement referred to "Continuing work on confidence-building measures as the foundation of the ARF process".[5]

The questions to ask, of course, are: Why seek to build mutual confidence in the Asia-Pacific? How does the ARF help and what more can the ARF do?

The Concept Paper answers the first question in necessarily broad and sweeping terms, in terms of what it calls the key challenges facing the region"

— the "significant shifts in power relations" that result from rapid economic growth and can lead to conflict; the r egion's "remarkable" diversity; and its "residue of unresolv ed territorial and other differ ences". The assumption underlying this proposition is that building mutual confidence — or pomoting mutual reassurance[6] — diminishes suspicions and uncer tainties and thus would help mitigate the potential for conflict.

More specifically , mutual suspicions and uncer tainties arise fr om perceptions of actual or potential strategic thr eats among the nations of the Asia-Pacific. Some in the region see a threat in the rise of China's economic, political, diplomatic and militar y po wer. The United States might see that rise as threatening to its strategic position in the Asia-Pacific. Beijing, in turn, might perceive the United States, with its enormous armaments and bilateral military alliances, as leading an effort to surr ound and "contain" China and prevent it from taking its rightful place in the world.There remain uncertainties over the extent to which China's military capacity is being strengthened and over whether such strengthening is really attributable to the Taiwan problem, as Beijing claims, or to some other motiv e. Another question hangs o ver Tokyo's continuing confidence in the Japan-U.S. security treaty and the U.S. nuclear umbrella and on whether it is solid enough for Tokyo to maintain its policy of abjuring an offensive military capability and its own nuclear deterrent. The perception of rivalry between China and Japan for influence in East Asia could be threatening to regional stability. The conflicting claims in the South China Sea remain a sour ce of insecurity for the r egion. China's and I ndia's strategic aims in Myanmar are at best unclear. The security of commercial sea routes in the Asia-P acific, as well as inv estor perceptions of o verall regional stability, is vital for the r egion's economic r ecovery and future growth. One could say that the ARF can build confidence to the extent that it brings some light and air to these questions and, wher e possible, sor ts them out so as to reduce the mutual suspicions and uncertainties inher ent in a r egion where power relationships are in flux.

However, grappling with these significant but sensitiv e issues could instead heighten mutual suspicions and engender ill will. I n October 1996, citing a r eport in the *Far Eastern Economic Review*, B ryan J. Couchman, a Visiting Fellow at Cambridge University, quoted Izhar Ibrahim, then Director-General of Political Affairs in I ndonesia's D epartment of Foreign Affairs, as noting that, once such specific issues were raised, "the participants concerned would begin attacking each other ".[7]

The ARF pursues confidence-building in several ways. The first involves the definition and clarification of positions on global and regional issues. The second mode of confidence-building is the extension of the "ASEAN way" to

the Asia-P acific on the conviction that that way has foster   ed peace and
stability in Southeast As_a and could do the same for the larger r egion. This
mode may be contradictor y to the first, since part of the " ASEAN way" is
setting aside difficult issues if confronting them would lead to divisiveness or
adversarial confrontation. The th_rd consists of cooperativ e endeavours that
promote transparency, networking, and the notion of shar ed interests.

DEFINING AND CLARIFYING POSITIONS

The first mode of confidence-bui_ding — stating and clarifying policy positions
— is pursued in formal and info_mal contacts among ministers at the annual
ARF ministerial meetings [8] and among officials at the ARF S enior Officials
Meetings. Defence and national-security officials meet among themselves on
these and other occasiors. S uch exchanges and discussions also take place at
the twice-yearly meetings of the Intersessional Support Group on Confidence
Building Measures, or ISG-CBM, recently renamed the Intersessional Support
Group on Confidence Building Measures and Preventive Diplomacy, or ISG-
CBM/PD. These, too, inv olve high-lev el for eign ministr y, defence and
national-security officials. Gatherings of strategic institutes in the Council for
Security Cooperation in the Asia-Pacific (CSCAP) perform a similar function,
albeit of an " unofficial" natur e and, ther efore, in a mor e candid and less
restrained manner. (The member-institutes enjoy a very wide range of degrees
of actual independence fr om their r espective go vernments.) ASEAN think
tanks, organized into ASEAN-ISIS and similarly enjo   ying — or suffering
from — a great diversity of independence from governments, also thrash out
and make r ecommendations on ARF issues.

    As in the D ialogue system, the centr epiece of the ARF process is the
annual ministerial meeting, which takes place on the occasion of the ASEAN
Ministerial Meeting, that is, the yearly gathering of ASEAN foreign ministers
among themselves and with their Dialogue Partners in various configurations.
All these meetings, including that of the ARF   , ar e pr esided o ver b y the
ASEAN chairman, who is also the host, and ar e managed b y ASEAN. The
attendance of a non-ASEAN foreign minister is regarded as an indication of
his or her country's interest and stake in East Asian affairs and the strength of
its relations with ASEAN. The forum pro vides a platform for defining and
clarifying each state's positions and policies on regional and global issues in a
multilateral setting. It g_ves ministers an opportunity to signal to the domestic
and/or international audience their governments' concern over certain issues
of interest to the public. It offers a venue for informal and quiet ministerial-
level consultations between two or mor   e countries inv olved in a specific

problem or issue, such as the situation on the Korean peninsula. The meetings are occasions for discussing ways of building confidence among the participating states. B y these means, the ARF intends trust to be gradually developed and mistrust dispelled.

However, the way the meetings are conducted militates against the more effective fulfilment of these intentions. The agenda items for an ARF ministerial meeting are formulated in extremely broad terms, such as "exchange of views on regional and international security issues ". S uch broad formulations ar e supposed to give the ministers wide discr etion, maximum flexibility and the freedom to air their own concerns; but they also esult in a lack of focus in the discussions, preventing individual issues from being thrashed out thoroughly and in depth. Without such thorough and in-depth discussions, it is possible to expect mutual confidence to be built only very slowly, if at all. Officials of some ARF participating states have privately complained about the insufficient focus that characterizes ARF ministerial discussions. The response obviously would be an agenda of fe wer but mor e specific items. As an important b y-product, a more detailed and specific agenda would pressure ASEAN and the ARF to face the issue of whether the for um should be primarily concerned with "traditional" security or "non-traditional", non-military security or both and, if both, in what pr oportions of relative importance.

As an illustration, if the chairman 's statement of that meeting is any indication, the August 2007 ARF ministerial meeting in Manila is reported to have discussed an extremely large number and variety of subjects — the Korean peninsula, Myanmar, Thailand, the South China Sea, the situation in the Pacific island countries, the Middle East, Iran's uranium-enrichment programme, I raq, Afghanistan, terr orism, the use of and trade in small arms, maritime security , weapons of mass destr uction and the non-proliferation of nuclear w eapons, people trafficking, a potential avian influenza pandemic, and energy security .[9] Even if one takes into account the fact that many of those subjects find their way into the chairman 's statement without being actually discussed at the meeting, it is har d to imagine how ev en one-third of the items mentioned can be dealt with in any kind of depth in one day . Yet, delegations often consider it in their national interest or necessary for domestic political purposes or with an eye to media coverage to raise pet issues at the ARF ministerial meetings, either discussing them at the forum or having them mentioned in the chairman's statement, without expecting the ARF actually to do anything about them. In the pr ocess, the division of labour betw een the ARF and the PMC, agreed upon in the ARF's early days, has become hopelessly blurred. It may be recalled that, ten y ears befor e, at their J uly 1997 meeting, the ARF ministers had declined to discuss drug trafficking and economic crimes like money laundering. They agreed that, in accor dance with the pr evious understanding, such issues were better taken up at the PMC.

In addition, the ministers spend an inor dinate amount of time on matters of procedure and management, matters that, it is noted, are better left to senior officials to decide. Indeed, this is another complaint that some states have raised. At the ARF SOM in May 2007, the EU proposed that, in order to afford the ministers more time for substantive discussions, the ARF senior officials be empo wered to endorse inter-sessional meetings, wor kshops and seminars, ev en as the ministers continue to make decisions on mor   e fundamental questions, including the establishment of new inter-sessional meetings and other initiativ es. The EU also suggested that, in cases of need for urgent decisions, such as in the ev ent of an outbreak of avian influenza, ARF SOM not wait for the next meeting to make such decisions. The ARF chair could receive the urgent proposal for an ARF activity and circulate it to the rest of the ARF senior officials thr   ough diplomatic channels and by electronic means. The proposal would be consider   ed as appr oved if no objection was r eceived by a certain deadline. Yang Yanyi, Deputy Director-General of the Asian Department of China   's M inistry of F oreign Affairs, observed that ARF discussions needed something between a "general debate" and a pr eoccupation with "nuts-and-bolts" matters. [10]

The combination of the lack of focus and the shortness of time may rationalize the failure of the ministers to discuss in depth certain critical issues having to do with Asia-Pacific security. Some of these concerns might be the expansion of "blue-water " navies, including the acquisition and r   ole of submarines; the purpose of the United States' bilateral security arrangements with certain states in the Asia-Pacific from both Washington's and its partners' points of vie w; the implications of the rise of China   's economic, political, diplomatic and military power for the security, traditional or non-traditional, of the Asia-Pacific and of the world; the nature of China's and India's interests in Myanmar; the recurring contretemps on the South China Sea; the security implications of the plans of several East Asian states to expand or initiate the use of nuclear power for the generation of electricity. Zhai Kun, the director of S outheast Asian and O ceanian S tudies at the China I   nstitute of Contemporary International Relations, the think tank of China's State Council, has suggested that the ARF focus on specific issues, like the M alacca Straits, counter-terrorism, and non-traditional security threats. Like Chinese foreign ministry officials, however, he is wary of ARF discussions on the South China Sea disputes. [11] And then there is the need to shed light on some of the other questions cited as examples at the beginning of this chapter   . N o one can reasonably expect the ARF discussions to lead dir ectly to a r esolution of or even an epiphany on such sensitive and complex issues; but at least it should be able to bring par ticipants closer to a clear er understanding of them.

A monograph on the ARF by the I nstitute of D efence and S trategic Studies of Nanyang Technological University, Singapore, urges:

> ARF members should expr ess their concerns and differ ences so that positions may be clarified and a better understanding of divergent perspectives could arise. They should be pr epared to accept div ergent analyses and agree to disagree where there are fundamental differences of views. The pr ocess of engagement and of attempting to understand divergent views is constructive. [12]

CSCAP has stressed, "G reater frankness and candidness (sic) among participants will facilitate improved confidence building and the momentum towards preventive diplomacy."[13] Prince Norodom Sirivudh, founder-chairman of the Council for I nternational Cooperation and P eace and former for eign minister of Cambodia, has complained that ARF discussions ar e not "forthright" enough.[14] On the other hand, M. C. A bad, former head of the ARF Unit in the ASEAN Secretariat, and Termsak Chalermpalanupap, then special assistant to the ASEAN S ecretary-General, have obser ved that ARF discussions have been getting "sharper" of late.[15]

At the same time and just as impor tantly, the ARF par ticipants — the ASEAN chairmanship abo ve all — must ensur e that the thorough and in-depth discussion of sensitive strategic issues does not, contrary to the intention, lead to divisiveness and heighten animosities and suspicions. This would mean trenchantly discussing important issues while maintaining the non-confrontational, non-offensive " ASEAN way". This is a challenge, ev en a dilemma, that faces the ARF.

In order to navigate through and around the dilemma, the ASEAN/ARF chairman might propose, after consultations all around, a few specific subjects. Such subjects could be chosen if discussions on them would have a chance of promoting more candour in the projection of national positions and, perhaps even a narrowing of the gaps between those positions, a chance of fostering greater transparency and thus of encouraging mutual confidence. At the same time, those discussions should avoid the confrontational stances that exacerbate divisions and suspicions. I n achieving this balance betw een for thrightness and mutual confidence, the judicious choice of a fe w agenda items, the management of a focused agenda, and the skillful handling of the discussion of each item would entail an effective ASEAN leadership of the sort required for ASEAN to earn its role as "   driver" of the ARF pr   ocess, as ASEAN repeatedly insists upon.

In broad terms, the July 2008 ARF ministerial meeting was r eported to have "agreed on the need for the ARF to … car efully consider how to focus on those issues most relevant to its mandate, capabilities and membership".[16]

Because of their lo wer, less p- ominent level, the ARF S enior Officials Meeting and the ISG-CBM/PD are able to undertake more focused discussions and produce a number of concrete pr oposals. At least, they used to be. The ARF Senior Officials Meeting, or ARF SOM, is intended as a preparation for the ARF ministerial meeting. N crmally held in M ay, the ARF SOM does discuss the administrative and substantive preparations for the ARF ministerial meeting, but it also conducts its o   wn ex change of vie ws on political and security issues in the Asia-P acific.

The ISG-CBM/PD meets at the dir ector-general or ambassadorial level twice yearly. Each of these meetings is co-chaired by an ASEAN member and a non-ASEAN ARF par   ticipant on a v   oluntary basis. The meetings ar e normally held in the countries of the co-chairpersons.   The first set of Intersessional Support Group meetings took place in the first half of 1996, co-chaired by J apan and I ndonesia in Tokyo and J akarta. If their r eport is anything to go by, the discussions at those meetings focused on a few subjects — bilateral security arrangements, the K orean peninsula, w eapons of mass destruction, the envir onment, dr ug trafficking, and transnational crime. Among the specific confidence-building measur   es pr oposed w ere the publication of defence policy papers, the establishment of contact networ ks among defence officials, ex   changes among defence staff colleges, and participation in the U nited Nations Registry of Conventional Arms.

Upon China's request, I co-chair ed, with China's Assistant M inister of Foreign Affairs, the M arch 1997 ISG-CBM meeting, which was under the co-chairmanship of China and the P hilippines. After affirming the necessity of dialogue and cooperation and the need to settle disputes peacefully   , the meeting, in Beijing, went into an exchange of views on unresolved territorial disputes, the Korean peninsula, the transboundary movement of radioactive waste, environmental pollution, drug trafficking, and illegal immigration. I t cited with appro val bilateral and sub-r   egional defence networ king and confidence-building activities, noting in particular the work of the Shanghai Cooperation Organization. The meeting stressed the importance of discussing the defence policies and statements that had been circulated and the conversion of defence facilities and equipment to civilian uses. It called for participation in the UN Registry of Conventional Arms and accession to the UN conventions on w eapons of mass destr uction. The meeting discussed, but r   eached no consensus on, the observation and notification of joint military exercises and the ban on anti-personnel land mines.

What protracted the meeting for many hours was a rancor ous dispute between China and the United States. The dispute was on the reference in the draft report to the United States' bilateral defence alliances in the region, with New Zealand and others proposing alternative formulations. Because China was directly involved in the argument, I had to chair the meeting at that juncture by myself. At least, the pr olonged discussion was r evealing of the conflicting positions of China and the United States on the issue of bilateral alliances, with B eijing regarding them as r elics of the Cold War meant to encircle and contain China and the U nited S tates insisting on them as essential instruments of its role as guarantor of international security .

Ten years later, in M arch 2007 in H elsinki, the group's discussions, co-chaired by Indonesia and the European Union, had greatly expanded so as to resemble those of the ministers, with their lack of focus and crwded timetable. According to its r eport, the meeting of the gr oup took up a br oad range of subjects. They included the Six-Party Talks on the Korean peninsula, Myanmar, Thailand, F iji and the S olomon I slands, Timor-Leste, Afghanistan, the perceived improvement in the situation in the South China Sea, Iran's nuclear-enrichment programme, the Middle East, and the proliferation of weapons of mass destruction. In addition, it is said to hav e addressed a wide v ariety of "non-traditional" security pr oblems — illegal logging, trafficking in drugs and in persons, natural disasters, the periodic haze over large parts of Southeast Asia, communicable diseases, maritime security, energy security, and terrorism. It reportedly also dealt with trade in small arms and light weapons and money laundering, and with specific measur es to combat those thr eats.

In the light of this record of ARF discussions, one may be forgiven for concluding that, although officials may complain about the lack of focus, depth and concrete outcomes of those discussions, they may feel that it is enough for them to be pr esent and make sure that nothing is done in the forum that would be adverse to their national interests. They may also find it necessary to be part of the networ ks of contacts that ar e formed by the ARF process.

Since 1995, many delegations hav e found it useful to include defence, military and national-security officials. On the occasion of the 1997 ministerial meeting, those officials also met on their o wn, o ver lunch. A t their 1998 meeting, the ministers " encouraged the activ e par ticipation of defense and military officials at appropriate lev els in all r elevant ARF activities".[17] Since March 2003, they have also been holding their o wn dialogues at the time of the meetings of the Intersessional Support Group. With the ASEAN defence ministers meeting in a "retreat" for the first time in March 2007, there is now talk of a possible ARF defence ministers ' for um. If this happens, defence, military and national-security officials will be gathering to pr epare for the forum. M.C. Abad, then head of the ASEAN Secretariat's ARF Unit, pointed out that, in that case, including their dialogue on the occasion of the ARF SOM, those officials would be meeting four times a year , ther eby adding substantially to the networking component of confidence-building in the ARF.[18] The annual meetings of the heads of defence colleges ser ve the same purpose. One can only hope that the increased gatherings of defence ministers and senior defence officials do not attract the suppliers of big-ticket armaments and military equipment.

Since 2003, the foreign ministers have turned their exchange of views on security issues into a " retreat". While this format offers a mor e r elaxed atmosphere and greater opportunities for freer give and take, the defence and other officials ar e unable to follo w the discussions, since each delegation is limited in the retreat to the minister and one other usually the senior foreign-ministry official. N ot even a "listening room " is pr ovided. This has been a source of fr ustration for the defence ministr y people.

The Council for S ecurity Cooperation in the Asia-P acific (CSCAP), founded in 1993, that is, a y ear before the ARF's inauguration, also helps in building confidence among the ARF countries, as its membership encompasses most of the countries represented in the ARF, and its Track Two discussions, papers and r ecommendations cover issues dealt with b y the ARF.

THE ASEAN ROLE[19]

From the beginning, the " ASEAN way", with its informal, non-binding, non-coercive character, has been thought to be essential, at least at the initial stages, for the building of tr ust among the ARF participants. That characteristic ASEAN phrase, "at a pace comfortable to all", which reflects ASEAN's leisurely, cautious progr ess and consensual decision-making, is explicitly applied to the ARF's progression from stage to stage. Indeed, the chairman's statements of the 2006 and 2007 ARF ministerial meetings reiterate this very phrase. To ensure that no participant is o verwhelmed by a majority, decisions ar e made by consensus, as in ASEAN (and in the Organization for S ecurity and Cooperation in E urope and most other regional associations), again a concept r epeated in the 2006 and 2007 statements.[20] ASEAN has been ackno wledged as the convener , hub and driver of the ARF process, if only by default, if only because of the absence of any other countr y or entity that is acceptable to the others for the discharge of that role. As ASEAN' s ARF Concept P aper suggested:

> In promoting confidence-building measur es, the ARF may adopt two complementary approaches. The first approach deriv es from ASEAN's experience, which pr ovides a v aluable and pr oven guide for the ARF . ASEAN has succeeded in r educing tensions among its member states, promoting regional cooperation and creating a regional climate conducive to peace and prosperity without the implementation of explicit confidence-building measures, achieving conditions approximating those envisaged in the Declaration of Zone of Peace, Freedom and Neutrality (ZOPFAN). The concepts of ZOPFAN and its essential component, the Southeast Asia N uclear Weapons-Free Z one (SEANFWZ), ar e significantly contributing to r egional peace and stability. ASEAN's well established practices of consultation and consensus (musyawarah and mufakat) have been significantly enhanced b y the r egular exchanges of high-level visits among ASEAN countries. This pattern of r egular visits has effectiv ely developed into a pr eventive diplomacy channel. In the Asian context, there is some merit to the ASEAN approach. It emphasises the need to develop trust and confidence among neighbouring states. [21]

At its very first ministerial meeting in 1994, the ARF had agreed to "endorse the purposes and principles of ASEAN's Treaty of Amity and Cooperation in Southeast Asia, as a code of conduct go verning relations between states and a unique diplomatic instrument for regional confidence-building, preventive diplomacy, and political and security cooperation".[22] Technically and strictly, the TAC is not an ASEAN agr eement. The signatories to it ar e the states of Southeast Asia and Papua New Guinea. The document makes no reference to ASEAN at all, except to cite, in its preamble, the 1967 ASEAN Declaration, along with the United Nations Charter, the ten principles of the declaration of the 1955 Afro-Asian Conference in Bandung, and the ZOPFAN Declaration of 1971. Nevertheless, the treaty has always been identified with ASEAN and managed in the ASEAN context. Its purposes and principles can be basically summed up as the r ejection of the use or thr eat of force in the r elations among states, the peaceful settlement of inter-state disputes, and non-interference in the internal affairs of nations. I t has been obser ved that the ASEAN countries' adherence to these principles is a key to the promotion of peace and stability in S outheast Asia. The ARF concluded that embracing them would also be the foundation for the building of confidence and enduring stability in the Asia-Pacific. Of the ARF participants, in addition to the ASEAN members and P apua N ew G uinea, China, I ndia, J apan, Pakistan, South Korea, Russia, Mongolia, New Zealand, Australia, Timor-Leste, S ri Lanka, B angladesh, N orth K orea and the U nited S tates have acceded to the TAC. France has already signed on to the treaty separately from the E uropean U nion, which has alr eady signified its intention and readiness to sign the tr eaty.

During her visit to the ASEAN Secretariat on 18 February 2009, Hillary Rodham Clinton, the first U.S. S ecretary of S tate to make such a visit, had announced that "the Obama Administration will launch our formal interagency process to pursue accession to the Treaty of Amity and Cooperation in Southeast Asia". She continued, "This is the first time the U nited States has taken this step . We will wor k through this process to put for ward our concerns, and then work with the countries of ASEAN to r esolve them so that we can achieve our goal of accession." Before the Obama administration, the United States had declined to accede to the TAC for a number of reasons. One was the fear that accession would tie Washington's hands in pursuing its interests in the Asia-P acific. Another was the concern that submitting the treaty to the United States Senate for its advice and consent would stir up an unwanted and uncontrolled public debate on cer tain Asian issues.

Whatever success ASEAN has attained as a r egional association and political entity can be attributed in substantial measur e to the fact that Indonesia, as the largest member , has deliberately adopted a lo w-profile stance, a position of at most that of *primus inter pares*. Projected to the ARF, this position is r eflected in the fact that all ARF par ticipants are formally equal, whether one is China or the U nited S tates or one is Timor-Leste or Laos, with ASEAN as an association at the cor e and no one po wer being dominant. A t the same time, ASEAN is not designed to r esolve conflicts; neither is the ARF.

As par t of ASEAN' s role of being the only acceptable conv ener, hub and driver of the ARF process, the ASEAN chair hosts and presides over the ARF ministerial meeting and the ARF SOM and other wise serves as ARF chair throughout the y ear of its ASEAN chairmanship . In the early y ears, some non-Asian ARF par ticipants chafed at ASEAN' s monopoly on the ARF's leadership. A number of co-chairmanship configurations hav e been suggested. N one has taken hold, mainly on account of the insistence of such countries as China and J apan and of ASEAN itself that ASEAN occupy the " driver's seat " in the ARF . I n a quintessentially ASEAN compromise formulation, the chairman 's statement of the second ARF ministerial meeting stated:

> A successful ARF requir es the activ e, full and equal participation and cooperation of all participants. H owever, ASEAN under takes the obligation to be the primar y driving for ce.[23]

All would be full and equal paricipants, but ASEAN takes on *as an obligation* the role of "primary driving for ce". In another compromise, each session of the Intersessional Support Group on Confidence Building Measures and the Intersessional M eetings on Cooperativ e A ctivities, which the second ARF ministerial meeting established, would be co-chair ed b y an ASEAN and a non-ASEAN member .[24] Other inter-sessional ARF activities wer e to be similarly co-chaired.

ASEAN's leadership of the ARF is now accepted by all, and the "ASEAN way" is the ARF's way. Still, after a decade and a half of the ARF' s existence, a number of par ticipants have become impatient with the measur ed pace of the forum's progress, although there is no clear agr eement as to wher e faster progress should lead. Even as there is no alternative to ASEAN chairmanship, the ARF suffers from the uneven nature of the ASEAN members' intellectual leadership and activism. I n my inter views with them, par ticipants in and observers of the ARF hav e indicated as much.

Carolina H ernández, F ounding P resident of the I nstitute for S trategic and Development Studies at the University of the Philippines, affirmed that, in the ARF , while ther e was no alternativ e to ASEAN leadership , ASEAN must lead.[25] Tan Sri Rastam I sa, Secretary-General of M alaysia's M inistry of Foreign Affairs, said bluntly, "ASEAN should exercise leadership."[26] Pengiran Dato P aduka Osman P atra, P ermanent S ecretary of B runei D arussalam's Ministry of F oreign Affairs and Trade, str essed that, while ASEAN had to "work har der" in managing the ARF pr ocess, it had to supply "intellectual leadership" to it and place its activities in a strategic framework". He observed that few ARF initiatives had come fr om ASEAN.[27] Bounkeut S angsomsak, Deputy Foreign Minister of Laos, deplor ed the fact that no initiativ es come from ASEAN.[28] Some, like two Chinese scholars to whom I spoke, believ ed that ASEAN lacked the " cohesion" r equired to ex ert effective leadership of the ARF.[29] However, one of the Chinese scholars, Liu Xuecheng of the China Institute of International Affairs, pointed out that ASEAN-10 had come into existence only in 1999; China could wait a bit mor e. Nguyen Trung Thanh, former Assistant Foreign Minister of Vietnam and later Vietnamese ambassador to S ingapore, also cited the need for a mor e cohesiv e, mor e integrated ASEAN in order for the association to lead the ARF mor e effectively.[30] Primo Joelianto, D irector-General for Asia-P acific and African Affairs at the

Department of Foreign Affairs of Indonesia, emphasized the need for "ASEAN unity" in the ARF .[31] Before he assumed the position of ASEAN-S ecretary General, Surin Pitsuwan, former Foreign Minister of Thailand, called for the development of common ASEAN positions on ARF issues for the sake of more effective ARF leadership.[32] Unfortunately, however, ASEAN does not seem to prepare adequately for its par ticipation in ARF discussions.

Specifically, M aria Consuelo O rtuoste, then H ead of the Center for International Relations and Strategic Studies at the Foreign Service Institute of the Philippines' Department of F oreign Affairs, declar ed, "To retain the driver's seat, ... ASEAN needs no: only to v oice its concerns or push its agenda, but also to set the example of concr etely putting r egional interests ahead of national inter ests, of implementing some of the pr oposed CBMs even within the ASEAN framewor k."[33]

More fundamentally, in an ar ticle in the O ctober 1997 issue of *Asian Survey*, Shaun Narine, a sharp ASEAN watcher, questioned the applicability of the ASEAN way to the ARF . He pointed out that the ASEAN countries were weak states which had to cooperate when faced b y external threats, citing the Vietnamese incursion into Cambodia as one such thr eat. At the same time, he noted:

> ASEAN has not developed techniques to confr ont conflict dir ectly....
> Its ability to reconcile conflicting objectives or resolve contentious relations
> of states is extremely limited .... Directly and indirectly, it has contributed
> to the alleviation of intra-ASEAN tensions. Again, however, its techniques
> were developed within, and operated under conditions of external threat
> and cannot simply be transplanted to the larger Asia-P acific region....
> Thus, without the p: esence of external thr eat, it is highly unlikely that
> ASEAN would have ev olved .nto its pr esent form, or dev eloped the
> ASEAN pr ocess. M ember states' weakness pr ovided the incentiv e to
> cooperate. This reality is the foundation for the success of ASEAN and
> the ASEAN way.[34]

On the other hand, N arine observed about the ARF:

> ARF is a r egion-wide organization that includes all of the gr eat, and
> potentially great, po wers of the contemporar y international system —
> the U.S., China, Russia, Japan, and India. There is little potential for the
> emergence of an external threa: to the region that would act as a unifying
> force. Moreover, the presence of powerful states within ARF means that
> the intra-ARF dynamic is fundamentally differ   ent than that which
> operated within ASEAN to produce the ASEAN way. Unlike the ASEAN

member states, the gr eat po wers will not cooperate or make difficult compromises out of a sense of mutual weakness. Thus, the two elements most necessary to explaining ASEAN's development and success simply do not fit into the ARF context. [35]

Nevertheless, no substitute for ASEAN leadership or the " ASEAN way" has been plausibly put for ward for building mutual confidence in the ARF system. Indeed, China as well as ASEAN insists on it. Whatever the merits or disadvantages of ASEAN's ARF leadership, the fact is that it is the only one that is acceptable to all. Deploring that fact without pr oposing acceptable improvements for the situation would simply be a waste of time.

In exercising ARF leadership, ASEAN is faced with still another dilemma. ASEAN could be more active in leading the ARF if it — or its chairman of the year— were to take more forthright and clearer positions on the pominent security issues of the times. I ndeed, Kao Kim H ourn, Secretary of S tate at Cambodia's Ministry of F oreign Affairs and I nternational Cooperation, has urged ASEAN to " take positions on issues " and to be mor e " active and creative".[36] However, if it did so, the trust in ASEAN as a neutral, objectiv e and harmless entity might er ode, trust that put and keeps the association in its leadership role in the first place. This point has been made by Kwa Chong Guan of the S. Rajaratnam School of I nternational S tudies at S ingapore's Nanyang Technological University.[37] Dewi Fortuna Anwar, Vice Chairman of the I ndonesian I nstitute of Science (LIP I), ackno wledges that ASEAN' s effectiveness in leading the ARF would diminish if it agr eed on and came forward with "strong ideas". Nevertheless, ASEAN could lead effectiv ely on non-traditional security issues (see Chapter 4). [38]

PROMOTING TRANSPARENCY, NETWORKING AND COOPERATION

The third mode in which the ARF seeks to build confidence is thr ough the promotion of a certain degree of transparency in security affairs, networking, and joint activities in areas of common security concern. The ASEAN Concept Paper for the ARF pr escribed a list of measur es designed to incr ease transparency, str engthen contacts and networ king, and thus bolster mutual confidence. Among these are the issuance of statements on defence policy positions and defence white papers or equivalent documents, participation in the United Nations Conventional Arms R egister, exchanges among defence and military officials, and obser vation at joint militar y exercises.[39]

Since 2000, the ARF has been publishing an *Annual Security Outlook* for the region, to which each participating state is supposed to contribute its own security outlook for itself and for the r egion. Such chapters are intended to shed some light on each countr y's security per ceptions and its strategic outlook and intentions. Mutual understanding is thereby promoted. Although a common format and table of contents ar e still under discussion, each chapter normally outlines the security situation in the countr y and in the region, defining the areas in which that situation is thought to impr ove and those in which it is seen to deteriorate. I highlights the hierarchy of importance and imminence that the state assigns to what the government perceives to be threats to the countr y's security and that of the r egion. I t spells out the policies that the government adopts to deal with those threats. Many chapters treat security in a compr ehensive manner, including non-traditional, as w ell as traditional, security concerns. S ome state general for eign-policy stances.

The voluntary nature of the *Annual Security Outlook* has been repeatedly stressed. It is reflected in the fact that, in most years, the number of contributors to each *Annual Security Outlook* has hovered at only around fifty per cent of ARF par ticipants. Contributions ran to betw een elev en and thir teen in 2002–07. The highest number, sixteen, was r ecorded in 2001. S ignificantly and appropriately, however, the contributions came from the ARF participants whose defence outlooks, strategic postur es and militar y capabilities count most in the security situation in the Asia-P acific. Australia, Canada, J apan, South K orea and the U nited S tates, as w ell as S ingapore and Thailand, contributed to all sev en volumes over 2001–07. R ussia contributed to six, and China, the E uropean Union and N orth Korea to five.

Moreover, A ustralia, China, J apan, R ussia, the U nited S tates, and the larger countries of the E uropean Union, as well as the EU itself, periodically publish their o wn separate " defence white papers ". I n commending this practice for ARF-wide use, the ARF almost from the beginning, has encouraged the exchange of defence white papers or similar documents as a confidence-building measure. In its annex ed list of r ecommended confidence-building measures, the 1995 ARF Concept P aper called for the issuance of "D efence Publications such as Defence White Papers or equivalent documents", taking care, in stressing the voluntary nature of the measur e, to add "as considered necessary by respective governments".[40]

The contributions to the *Annual Security Outlook* — like the " white papers" — r eveal nothing that is not in the public domain.   There are, moreover, repeated strictur es against "editing" them. H owever, they ser ve a useful purpose by presenting, in concise form, the authoritative stance of the government as a whole. In this way they are unlike the "white papers", which are issued in the name only of the defence ministries. The process of drafting the chapters in the *Outlook* compels the different government institutions to forge a government-wide consensus on their perceptions of the regional and national security situations and of the thr eats to them. B ecause they draw from the views of a number of government institutions, rather than from the defence ministry alone, most contributions embody a mor e comprehensive concept of security than the " white papers", including non-traditional and non-military notions of security While they are, of course, not legally binding, the chapters in the *Outlook*, as do the "white papers", state definitive positions that can be invoked by other ARF participants in case of significant departures from them. At the ver y least, the v olumes provide handy and authoritativ e references for scholars and academics, as well as for policy-makers, representing a range of security outlooks that span the Asia-P acific.

ASEAN, however, which is supposed to be in the " driver's seat" of the ARF process, has not been ver y helpful with r espect to the *Annual Security Outlook*. S ingapore and Thailand are the only ASEAN member-countries that hav e been consistent in their contributions. I ndonesia joined them starting in 2004, the year that it chair ed the ARF ministerial meeting, and every year thereafter. The Philippines did so in 2006 and 2007, the y ears of its chairmanship of the ASEAN S tanding Committee and the ARF pr ocess. Cambodia contributed only three times — in 2001, 2002 and 2003, the year that it hosted the ARF ministerial meeting. Vietnam and Brunei Darussalam submitted their sole chapters in 2001 and 2002, respectively, when they were in the ARF chair. Malaysia has made two contributions — in 2001 and in 2006, the year of its ARF chairmanship All in all, the record of ASEAN, with its ten members, has not been very exemplary, a failure of ASEAN's substantive leadership of the ARF. As discussed above, several non-ASEAN participants, including North Korea, have done better.

In 1998, the ARF published a " distillation" of confidence-building measures that had alr eady been agr eed upon. Among these, consider ed implemented were dialogues on security perceptions, exchanges among national defence colleges, a meeting on the role of defence authorities in disaster relief, and the exchange of information on observation and notification of military exercises. Deemed not to hav e been fully implemented w ere: high-lev el defence contacts, the submission of annual defence policy statements and the publication of defence white papers, par ticipation in the UN Conv entional Arms Register, the signing and ratification of international non-proliferation and disarmament regimes, and discussions on defence conversion programmes. The same publication also suggested ne w measures, including the ex change of visits by nav al vessels, cooperation in militar y medicine and militar y law, visits to militar y establishments, the institution of a multilateral communications network, a seminar on the pr oduction of defence policy documents, and a confer ence among defence language schools. [41]

These networking measur es and operational cooperativ e activities are meant to develop both mutual confidence and the channels for building it. Increasing numbers have been undertaken over the years. These measures and activities are discussed in Chapters 4 and 5.

CONCLUSION

Whether the ARF pr ocess is succeeding in actually building confidence is a question whose answer lies in the perception of individual participants and is, therefore, difficult to discern in the short term. However, whatever one thinks of the ARF's efficacy in building confidence and pr eventing conflict, it does seem better to have a forum where the major powers can talk to one another in a multilateral setting about regional security in the Asia-Pacific than not to have one at all. E ven if to har d-nosed obser vers confidence-building and preventive diplomacy in the ARF ar e an illusion, such an illusion does hav e a calming effect. The par ticipation of all the major po wers in security discussions in a r egion wher e po wer r elationships ar e fluid and uncer tain helps to ensure that all hav e a say and none dominates. The publication by the major par ticipants of policy papers on national and r egional security makes available to ev eryone authoritativ e statements of perceptions and intentions that shed some light on policy and give other powers, particularly rival ones, something to invoke in case of substantial depar tures from them. The personal contacts and networ king that the ARF makes possible and promotes are something of v alue in terms of confidence building as w ell as operational cooperation. The gathering of the major powers to discuss regional security at several levels engages them in a benign fashion in S outheast Asia and East Asia as a whole, something that ser ves the inter ests both of the region and of the po wers themselves.

This is a fairly modest assessment of the ARF's significance in terms of the process labelled as confidence-building, particularly when consider ed against the demands that are often made on the for um. In the light of this lowered expectation, demanding that the ARF lur ch beyond the stage of confidence-building and quickly acquir e the ability dir ectly to pr event conflict and resolve disputes between or within states would be doing the forum a disser vice.

On the other hand, there is a view that the ARF is not capable of building confidence between powers with contending interests, a view cogently expressed by Shaun Narine, as noted above. Robyn Lim goes even further, asserting that the ARF actually undermines r egional security. She wrote in 1998:

> The ARF risks undermining security because it distracts attention fr om the r oots of strategic pr oblems. A part fr om pr oblems on the K orean peninsula (which stem from the natur e of the r egime in P yongyang), strategic tensions in East Asia have their origins in the natur e of the regime in Beijing .... The manifestations of strategic tension include the growing clash of interests betw een China and the U nited S tates o ver issues such as maritime passage in the S outh China S ea, and Taiwan's continued ability to r esist enforced integration with China. [42]

In any case, ASEAN, being the " driver" of the ARF pr ocess, has the responsibility to do what it can to str engthen the for um's effectiveness as a confidence-building device. I t could trim do wn the agenda of confidence-building discussions so as to enable them to achiev e focus, a significant clarification of strategic positions, and the ability to thrash out security issues in some depth. At the same time, the ASEAN chairmanship has to ensur e that more focused and mor e thorough discussions do not become counter-productive by exacerbating contention between participants. ASEAN should also contribute mor e substantially to what ar e billed as confidence-building measures wherever it can, such as the *Annual Security Outlook.*

Finally, there is the other type of confidence-building. I is the confidence that the example of the ARF inspir es in other r egions, the example of the world's major po wers and the states in the Asia-P acific sitting together to discuss, in a peaceful and amicable manner , strategic security issues that pertain to a potentially v olatile region of the world.

Notes

1. Appendix B, para. 6.2.3. Also in <http://www .aseanregionalforum.org/ PublicLibrary/ARFChairmans Statementsand Reports/ChairmansStatementofthe 2ndMeetingoftheASE/tabid/199/Default.aspx>, para. 6B.
2. Appendix A, para. 6.
3. Appendix B, para. 6.2.2. Also in <http://www .aseanregionalforum.org/ PublicLibrary/ ARFChairmansStatementsandReports/ChairmansStatementofthe 2ndMeetingoftheASE/ tabid/199/Default.aspx>, para. 6B.
4. "Chairman's Statement: The Eighth ASEAN R egional Forum", in *The ASEAN Regional Forum Documents Series 1994–2006*, p. 185, para. 4. Also in <http:// www.aseanregionalforum.org/LinkClick.aspx?fileticket=w%2fMjx3xLGRU %3d&tabid=66&mid=410>.

5. "Chairman's Statement: The Tenth ASEAN Regional Forum", in *The ASEAN Regional Forum Documents Series 1994–2006*, p. 260, para. 4. Also in <http://www.aseanregionalforum.org/PublicLibrary/ARF> ChairmansS tatements andReports/ChairmansStatementofthe10thMeetingoftheAS/tabid/76/Default.aspx.

6. "Mutual reassurance" was the preferred term of Yukio Satoh, president of the Japan Institute of International Affairs, who was a senior diplomat at the time of the ARF's founding. See Satoh, "Reflections on the Nakayama Proposal" in *The Inclusive Regionalist*, edited by H adi S oesastro and Clara J oewono (Jakarta: Centre for S trategic and I nternational S tudies, 2007), pp. 101–02. H owever, CBM has become the term of choice in the ARF .

7. Bryan J. Couchman, *The ASEAN Regional Forum: Does Reality Match the Rhetoric?* (Johannesburg: East Asia Project, University of Witwatersrand, October 1996), p. 4.

8. See Appendix F.

9. <http://www.aseanregionalforum.org/LinkClick.aspx?fileticket=RbahNhjo2E8%3d&tabid=66&mid=940>, paras. 10–36.

10. Interview by the author, Beijing, 21 S eptember 2007.

11. Interview by the author, Beijing, 20 S eptember 2007.

12. *A New Agenda for the ASEAN Regional Forum*, IDSS Monograph No. 4 (Singapore: Institute of D efence and S trategic Studies, Nanyang Technological University, 2002), p. 62.

13. "The ARF into the 21st Century" (paper presented to the 9th ASEAN Regional Forum Ministerial meeting, Bandar Seri Begawan, 31 July 2002), p. 3.

14. Interview by the author, Singapore, 6 August 2007.

15. Interview by the author, Jakarta, 13 July 2007.

16. "Chairman's Statement, 15th ASEAN Regional Forum, 24 July 2008, Singapore", in <http://www.41amm.sg/amm/index.php/web/info_for_delegates/statements/chairman_s_statement_15th_asean_regional_forum_24_july_2008_singapore, para. 6.

17. "Chairman's S tatement: The Fifth ASEAN R egional F orum", in *The ASEAN Regional Forum Documents Series 1994–2006*, p. 86, para. 6. Also in <http://www.aseanregionalforum.org/PublicLibrary/> ARFChairmansS tatements andReports/ChairmansStatementofthe5thMeetingoftheASE/tabid/180/Default.aspx>, para. 6.

18. Interview by the author, Jakarta, 13 July 2007.

19. For an extended discussion of ASEAN' s role in the ARF, see M ely Caballero-Anthony, *Regional Security in Southeast Asia: Beyond the ASEAN Way* (Singapore: Institute of S outheast Asian S tudies, 2005), pp. 113–56.

20. "Chairman's Statement: The Thirteenth ASEAN Regional Forum", in *The ASEAN Regional Forum Documents Series 1994–2006*, p. 429, para. 6, and <http://www.aseansec.org/20807.htm>, para. 6.

21. Appendix A, para. 8.

22. "Chairman's S tatement: The First ASEAN Regional F orum", in *The ASEAN Regional Forum Documents Series 1994–2006*, p. 4, para. 6.2. Also in <http://www.aseanregionalforum.org/PublicLibrary/ ARFChairmansS tatements andReports/Chairmans S tatementofthe1stMeetingoftheASE/tabid/201/ Default.aspx>, para. 6.

23. Appendix B, para. 6B.

24. Ibid., para. 6E.

25. Interview by the author, Taipei, 30 August 2007.

26. Interview by the author, Putrajaya, Malaysia, 16 August 2007.

27. Interview by the author, Singapore, 28 August 2006.

28. Interview by the author, Singapore, 27 August 2007.

29. Interviews by the author with Professor Su Hao, Foreign Affairs University, and Professor Liu X uecheng, China Institute of I nternational S tudies, B eijing, 19 September 2007.

30. Interview by the author, Singapore, 7 April 2008.

31. Interview by the author, Jakarta, 16 July 2007.

32. Interview by the author, Singapore, 15 October 2007.

33. Maria Consuelo C. Ortuoste, *Reviewing the ASEAN Regional Forum and Its Role in Southeast Asian Security* (Honolulu, Hawaii: Asia-Pacific Center for S ecurity Studies, February 2000), p. 13.

34. Shaun N arine: "ASEAN and the ARF: The Limits of the ' ASEAN Way' ", in *Asian Survey* XXXVII, no. 10 (October 1997): 974.

35. Ibid., pp. 974–75.

36. Interview by the author, Singapore, 28 August 2007.

37. Interview by the author, Singapore, 9 O ctober 2007.

38. Interview by the author, Jakarta, 8 May 2008.

39. Appendix A, Annex A.

40. Appendix A, Annex A, I tem I.4.

41. "Distillation of Agreed CBMs from the First up to the F ourth ARF" and "List of New ARF CBMs", in *The ASEAN Regional Forum Documents Series 1994–2006*, pp. 115–17. Also in <http://www.aseanregionalforum.org/PublicLibrary/ ARFChairmansStatementsandReports/DistillationofAgreedCBMsfromthe Firstuptot/tabid/183/Default.aspx> and in <http://wwwaseanregionalforum.org/ PublicLibrary/ARFChairmansStatementsandReports/CoChairsConsolidated ListofPossibleNewARFCB/tabid/184/Default.aspx>.

42. Robyn Lim: "The ASEAN Regional Forum: Building on S and", *Contemporary Southeast Asia* 20, no. 2 (August 1998): 116.

4

DIPLOMACY TO PREVENT WHAT?

The ASEAN R egional F orum Concept P aper that the Association of Southeast Asian N ations produced had the " development of pr eventive diplomacy" as the second stage in the ARF' s evolution. The second ARF ministerial meeting, in 1995, adopted this notion. The direct provenance of ASEAN's use of the term " preventive diplomacy" was "An Agenda for Peace, P reventive D iplomacy, P eacemaking and P eace-keeping", a r eport issued b y Boutros Boutr os-Ghali, then S ecretary-General of the U nited Nations, on 17 J une 1992. That repor t defined pr eventive diplomacy as "action to prevent disputes from arising between parties, to prevent existing disputes from escalating into conflicts and to limit the spr ead of the latter when they occur". It explained specifically, "Preventive diplomacy requires measures to create confidence; it needs early warning based on information gathering and informal or formal fact-finding; it may also involve preventive deployment and, in some situations, demilitariz ed zones."[1] This was, in fact, an elaboration and updating of the term and concept originated b y one of Boutr os-Ghali's predecessors, Dag Hammarskjöld.[2]

The ARF Concept P aper made it clear that confidence-building was a pre-requisite to preventive diplomacy, pointing out, "Without a high degree of confidence among ARF par ticipants, it is unlikely that they will agr ee to the establishment of mechanisms which ar e perceived to be intr usive and/or autonomous."[3]

Some questions have arisen over the years: Does preventive diplomacy in the ARF context envision only inter-state conflicts, or does it encompass internal conflicts as well? Would it deal only with " traditional" sources of possible military conflicts or also with "non-traditional", non-military problems that threaten "human security "? If both, which of them is to get mor   e attention? When and how should the ARF mo ve from confidence-building alone to the pr eventive-diplomacy stage?

CONFLICTS WITHIN STATES?

The por tion on pr eventive diplomacy in the UN S   ecretary-General's " An Agenda for P eace" concerned itself with intra-state, as well as inter-state, conflict. I t spoke about pr   eventive deplo yment, humanitarian assistance, international help in maintaining internal security , and conciliation effor ts in "conditions of crisis within a country", albeit stressing, "when the Government requests or all parties consent."[4] It declared, "In these situations of internal crisis the U nited N ations will need to r espect the so vereignty of the S tate; to do otherwise would not be in accor   dance with the understanding of M   ember States in accepting the principles of the Charter"[5] That was the United Nations.

On the other hand, the ASEAN Concept P aper for the ARF evidently intended to r estrict preventive diplomacy to inter-state conflicts, at least in the short term. The immediate measures suggested for preventive diplomacy referred to the Treaty of Amity and Cooperation in S outheast Asia (TAC)[6] and the 1992 ASEAN D eclaration on the S outh China S ea, both of which deal with disputes betw   een states. [7] The prev entive-diplomacy measur es proposed for the longer term appeared to be more ambiguous. They called for the exploration of " the idea of appointing S   pecial R epresentatives ... to undertake fact-finding missions at the r   equest of par ties inv olved (in) an issue" and of " the idea of establishing a R   egional Risk R eduction Center"[8] without specifying in what kind of issue the fact-finding mission was to be despatched or what kind of risk was to be r   educed.

The ARF ministerial meeting in H   anoi in J uly 2001 adopted a paper entitled " ASEAN R egional F orum Concept and P   rinciples of P reventive Diplomacy".[9] Originally drafted by Singapore, circulated and discussed at the preceding ARF S enior Officials Meeting, and amended b y suggestions from a number of par ticipants, the paper clarified the point, defining pr   eventive diplomacy in this way:

> PD is consensual diplomatic and political action taken b   y so vereign states with the consent of all dir ectly involved parties:
>
> • To help pr event disputes and conflicts fr om arising *between States* (italics mine) that could potentially pose a thr eat to r egional peace and stability;

- To help pr event such disputes and conflicts from escalating into armed confrontation; and
- To help minimize the impact of such disputes and conflicts on the region.

The 2001 paper gav e examples of steps that could be taken ev en before a crisis arose — confidence-building efforts, adopting norms consistent with the TAC and the UN Charter , enhancing channels of communication, and using the ARF chair . The prev entive-diplomacy measur es that the paper recommended made clear that they applied to r elations between states. "(D)rawn mainly fr om discussions in CSCAP" (Council for S ecurity Cooperation in the Asia-P acific), the eight "key principles " pr oposed for preventive diplomacy wer e clearly aimed at making sur e that PD was not exercised without the consent of the par ties involved or used to inter vene in the internal affairs of nations. One of the principles specified that PD would not include military action or the use of for ce. Another — one that was *not* among the CSCAP r ecommendations — explicitly stated that pr eventive diplomacy "applies to conflicts between and among S tates".

A Track Two seminar on pr eventive diplomacy in P aris in N ovember 1996 had skir ted the issue of whether pr eventive diplomacy would concern itself with intra-state, as well as inter-state, "subject areas of potential crisis". Organized by L'Institut Français des Relations Internationales and the Centre for Strategic and International Studies of Indonesia, the forum was attended by academics and go vernment officials "in their priv ate capacity". Some of the measures discussed w ere an annual security outlook, a r egional research and information centr e, an early warning system, confidence-building measures, the good offices of the ARF chair, a register of experts on preventive diplomacy, a risk-reduction centre, and the establishment of an ARF unit (its functions, location and funding w ere not specified in the seminar r eport). One or more participants succeeded in inser ting in the seminar's report the conditions that pr eventive diplomacy would be subject to the " strict maintenance of consensus amongst all ARF members" and that the proposed ARF unit would operate on the basis of " equal and full par ticipation of all ARF members". The report thus underlined the principle, with the intention of ensuring its practice, that pr eventive-diplomacy measur es would not be carried out over the objections of any participant. They were evidently wary of the potential use of prev entive-diplomacy measur es b y some states to intervene in domestic conflict situations in others. [10]

Some media and academic commentators have heckled the ARF for not doing anything about developments internal to states. For example, an Inter

Press Service story posted on AsiaTimes Online on 1 February 2000 claimed, "Security analysts hav e hit out at the 22-member Asean R egional Forum (ARF), saying it made no contribution to resolving the East Timor conflict in the past, and had little to offer now." It then quoted Richard Tanter, professor of international relations at Japan's Kyoto Seika University, as saying, "Unlike the more sophisticated and tested Organization for Security and Cooperation in Europe, ARF has made no attempt to deal with member states that violate basic international standards of human rights." [11] Obviously, this statement, as quoted, ignor ed the unique natur e of the ARF and the wide differ ence between the ARF and the OSCE and between East Asia and Europe. Nor did the media item proffer any suggestion as to what the ARF could and should have done about the East Timor predicament under the cir cumstances.

There is a view that " today the gr eatest thr eat to r egional stability is internal conflict"[12] and that, therefore, the ARF should seek to pr event and otherwise deal with such conflicts thr ough pr eventive diplomacy. I f it is accepted that internal conflict is today the leading source of regional instability, and the ARF is not equipped with the capacity or the willingness as a body to do something about such conflicts — or is pr evented by the contending interests of its mor e po werful participants from doing so — the for um becomes open to public denigration as a mer e " talk shop ". S uch snide criticisms, of course, imply that nothing is gained by " talk" at several lev els among big and small po wers with stakes in the r egion, by discussions on issues affecting the security of the Asia-P acific, and b y the cultivation of habits of consultation among them. M oreover, it is not clear what the ARF should be doing or what a body made up of po wers with disparate inter ests could do about internal conflicts.

To be sure, as recor ded in the chairman's statements, the ARF ministers have discussed dev elopments internal to countries in the Asia-P acific. F or example, in 1997, the ministers expressed their concern over the situation in Cambodia in the wake of the fighting between the forces of the two co-Prime Ministers, Hun Sen and Prince Norodom Ranariddh. In 1998, they declared their support for ASEAN's and others' help in the r estoration of stability in Cambodia and hailed the peaceful conduct of the elections there. From 2000 to 2004, the ARF supported the territorial integrity of Indonesia, first, in the context of the violence that pr eceded East Timor's eventual separation fr om it and, then, with r eference to the tr oubles in A ceh. S ince 2000, the ARF ministers have hear d briefings from the M yanmar minister on the situation within his country, called for progress in the implementation of its "roadmap to democracy", and urged the release of Aung San Suu Kyi and other political prisoners. As A ustralia pr oposed, the ministers hav e also referr ed to the troubled conditions in the South Pacific island countries, notably those in the Solomon Islands. The ARF's statements on those internal situations were largely positive and encouraging and refrained from calling for any steps to be taken by external powers. In some cases, the statements supported action already taken by individual states or groups of states.

In any case, as noted above, a number of ARF participants, primarily on the Asian side, seem to be determined to hedge against the use of preventive diplomacy to interfere in their internal affairs. Moreover, all are aware of the great likelihood that national interests, particularly those of rival powers, will clash over any proposal for ARF intervention in internal conflicts. Underlying these considerations is the fact that there is no agreement among the big powers or even within ASEAN on where lies the threshold between situations that merely provoke popular revulsion or domestic political posturing and those that are so massive, like genocide, or so chaotic and destabilizing as to make possible an agreement on ARF intervention. This is why the ARF statements of positions on developments internal to participant-states have been mostly positive and invariably bland and why the forum has not called for any kind of action, preventive or otherwise, by the ARF itself or by its participants in response to such developments. Not least, the lack of ARF regional institutions precludes the forum from taking any kind of effective action in conflict situations.

Then, there is the especially complex and sensitive issue of Taiwan. The fundamental Chinese position considers Taiwan as part of China, and any problem involving Taiwan is a matter internal to China. If ARF preventive diplomacy is allowed to apply to domestic conflicts, will that not enable rival powers in the ARF to use preventive diplomacy as a cover for intervening in the Taiwan situation? That seems to be Beijing's main concern with respect to preventive diplomacy.

NON-TRADITIONAL SECURITY

The consideration of preventive diplomacy raises the question: prevent what? The paper that the ARF ministerial meeting adopted in May 2001, "Concept and Principles of Preventive Diplomacy", stressed that the aim of preventive diplomacy had to do with conflicts between states. Indeed, even in the confidence-building stage, the ARF's initial concern was with inter-state conflict. The "distillation of agreed CBMs" and the list of new confidence-building measures that the Intersessional Support Group on Confidence Building Measures (ISG-CBM) adopted in 1998 contained only measures related to traditional, military areas, except only for "counter-narcotics project" in the "second basket" in the list of new measures. [13]

However, the direct relevance of the ARF's preventive-diplomacy phase to conflicts between states may be questioned. O bviously, the ARF can do little directly to prevent a conflict — unlikely at this time — or a confrontation between rival powers — between China and the U nited States, China and Japan, China and I ndia, or I ndia and P akistan. What it can do is to foster conditions, some of which go b y the name of confidence-building, that reduce the likelihood of such conflicts and confr ontations or delay their occurrence. One of those conditions would be the consolidation of the *status quo* to such an extent as to make ev en a great po wer hesitate to upset it. Behind these considerations, however, are the strategic elements that go vern the basic relationships between the major powers, elements from which much of the tension and many of the issues arise in the first place.

The "flashpoints" that curr ently do give rise to " traditional" concerns about possible armed inter-state conflict in the Asia-P acific are the K orean peninsula, the Taiwan S traits, bilateral territorial disputes, and the S outh China Sea. However, although they, except Taiwan, are discussed in the ARF, these sources of concern are being dealt with substantively in forums outside the ARF. The S ix-Party Talks seem to be making pr ogress in pursuing the denuclearization of the K orean peninsula. Through channels that they hav e bilaterally established, Beijing and Taipei are engaged in sporadic discussions about their r elations, including the pr oblems across the Taiwan S traits, negotiating ways of easing tensions between them, improving the atmosphere for their r elationship, and expanding the opportunities for economic and people-to-people interaction. In any case, Beijing insists that its r elationship with Taipei is a matter internal to China, in which no one else has the right to get involved. The states involved in bilateral territorial disputes ar e, with varying degrees of success, working out those problems between them, either through negotiations or through adjudication b y international bodies.

It is deemed to be appr opriate and mor e effective for these issues to be directly handled by forums and mechanisms outside the ARF . The main protagonists like it that way and prefer that the ARF not get involved directly in such issues of potential conflict. The smaller bodies ar e mor e focused, involve only states that ar e directly concerned with the issue, and can negotiate with nimbleness and outside the glar e of public attention. As the Chinese keep insisting, br oadening the discussions — "internationalizing " the issue — would only " complicate" matters. And as Philippine P resident F idel Ramos' National Security Adviser, José Almonte, has pointed out, 'substantive negotiations are best done out of the public ey e — and with as few participants as is possible".[14]

However, in the case of the South China S ea, "internationalizing" the issue served for a while as additional lev erage against China's power. Indeed, a few months after the first ARF ministerial meeting, in February 1995, the Philippines publicly complained about the discovery of Chinese facilities on Mischief Reef, off the Philippine island of Palawan. In April of that year, ASEAN and Chinese officials at vice ministers/permanent secretaries level met for the first time in Hangzhou, a process of political consultation that I had initiated. There, the ASEAN officials raised the issue of Mischief Reef and broader questions about the Chinese claims in the South China Sea. Four ASEAN countries also have claims of different extents and on different bases to land features in and waters of the South China Sea. In the first ARF ministerial meeting, the disputes on the South China Sea had been discussed after dinner, in the dead of night and outside the formal session. After the senior officials' meeting in Hangzhou, the ARF has talked routinely about the South China Sea as a regional-security concern in open meeting, but without addressing the merits of individual claims or the need for other powers to intrude into the disputes.

In fact, since the issuance of the Declaration on the Conduct of Parties in the South China Sea in November 2002, ASEAN and China have by themselves been seeking to reduce the tensions arising from the conflicting jurisdictional claims. They are doing this with reference to the 2002 declaration and the joint activities that it has spawned and in the informal, ostensibly non-official workshops on managing potential conflict in the South China Sea. Or else, individual rival claimants seek to deal bilaterally with specific aspects of the situation. Beijing has made it clear that it opposes the active involvement of the ARF in the South China Sea question. [15]

Discussions in the ARF may have helped restrain China in the South China Sea. On the other hand, Beijing may have succeeded in keeping the non-ASEAN powers from getting involved in the issue by frequent assurances about freedom of navigation in the area and by being seen to be dealing on the subject with ASEAN as a group.

What, then, is there for the ARF to prevent through diplomacy? One answer is the exacerbation of problems that all participants consider as threats to the security — broadly construed — of their peoples and to the stability of the region as a whole, which all seem to value at this time. These might include environmental degradation, communicable diseases, trade in illicit drugs, trafficking in human persons, large-scale transboundary movements of people, international terrorism, other transnational crimes, water problems, and the threat to sea lanes. They all go under the rubric of "non-traditional", non-military security concerns. There is also the danger arising from the possible proliferation of nuclear and other weapons of mass destruction, proliferation not only to states but also to terrorist groups.

As a r eflection of the ASEAN countries ' initially war y stance on the proposal for a ne w regional-security for um, Abdullah Ahmad B adawi, then Malaysia's foreign minister and later P rime Minister, was quoted as str essing that security had to be viewed "in a comprehensive manner".[16] The chairman's statement of the ver y first ARF ministerial meeting proclaimed " the comprehensive concept of security, including its economic and social aspects", as a leading object of the ARF's concern.[17] The statement issued at the end of the second ARF ministerial meeting declared, "The ARF recognizes that the concept of comprehensive security includes not only military aspects but also political, economic, social and other issues." [18] The ARF Concept P aper considered at that meeting had as one of the two principles for confidence-building the " Adoption of compr ehensive appr oaches to security ".[19] Accordingly, at their 1996 meeting, the ARF ministers, appar ently not distinguishing between " comprehensive security " and " non-traditional security", agreed to consider at their next meeting drug trafficking, money laundering, and other "trans-national issues" that "could constitute threats to the security of the countries of the r egion".[20] The N ovember 1996 P aris seminar on preventive diplomacy alluded to earlier in this chapter indicated that preventive diplomacy should encompass both militar y-related and non-military " subject ar eas of potential crisis such as: territorial disputes, proliferation of conventional weapons and weapons of mass destruction, *non-military transnational concerns such as drug trafficking, terrorism, water and other resource problems, smuggling, environmental degradation, maritime safety, piracy and unregulated population movements*" (italics mine).[21]

Years later, recalling the ARF's provenance, Sheldon W. Simon, professor of political science at Arizona S tate University, wrote:

> The ARF emerged from ASEAN in the 1990s. The end of the Cold War left the Asia-Pacific searching for a new organizing principle for security. While traditional alliances remained, including bilateral treaties with the United S tates and the F ive Power D efense Arrangement, these seemed inadequate to deal with security matters of a nonmilitary nature, such as transnational crime, environmental hazar ds, and illegal population movements.[22]

However, as recalled in Chapter 3 of this book, the 1997 ARF ministerial meeting declined to discuss subjects of a non-militar y nature, declaring that "such issues would be mor e appr opriately addr essed, at this time, at the ASEAN P ost M inisterial Confer ences".[23] Nevertheless, effor ts to apply preventive diplomacy to non-traditional, non-militar y matters persisted. An ARF Track Two conference on preventive diplomacy took place in Singapore in S eptember 1997. O rganized by the I nstitute of D efence and S trategic Studies of Singapore's Nanyang Technological University and the International Institute of Strategic Studies, the conference agreed to forward five proposals to the ISG-CBM, the ARF' s equivalent to a wor king group, and the ARF SOM. Among the pr oposals was "M ultilateral co-operation as a form of Prevention (sic) Diplomacy on trans-national issues such as drug trafficking; shipment, storage and disposal of nuclear waste; major mo   vements of population etc, wher e dir ectly linked to security ".²⁴ The subsequent ARF ministerial meeting, in uly 1998, commended the S ingapore confer ence's proposals for the ISG-CBM' s consideration. The report of the gr oup's next pair of meetings, however, gave no indication that the application of peventive diplomacy to the non-traditional issues cited had been discussed in any detail, if at all.

On the other hand, the J uly 1998 ARF ministerial meeting could not avoid extensive discussions on the financial crisis that had for the past y ear been ravaging several parts of the r egion, politically as w ell as economically. After all, the financial crisis had had massive political effects and could hav e an impact on r egional security as w ell. At their meeting in J uly 1999, the "Ministers discussed transbouncar y pr oblems that could have a significant impact on r egional security", specifying the "illegal accumulation of small arms and light w eapons", piracy, and illegal migration. ²⁵

Mely Caballero-Anthony, head of the Centre for Non-traditional Security Studies at the S. Rajaratnam School, suggested to me that the change had been occasioned at least partly by the repercussions of the 1997–98 financial crisis on people 's liv es.²⁶ The crisis had led to heightened pr   essures for environmental destr uction, illegal migration, and transnational crime. This coincided with and r einforced the evolution in official and academic cir cles of the concept of non-traditional security fr   om the established one of "comprehensive" securi:y, meaning the political, economic and social pots of inter-state conflict, to that of "human security ", that is, the need to pr otect human beings, wherever they might live, from threats to their liv es or well-being, whatever and fr om wher ever these might be. S uch thr eats would include matters like energy , water r esources, large-scale migration, and pandemic diseases. The financial crisis, too, had triggered a chain of events in Indonesia that started with the fall of President Soeharto, which, in turn, led to the decision by his successor, B.J. Habibie, to subject the question of East Timor's autonomy or independence to a popular consultative process among East Timor's population. The violence that follo wed the consultations manifested the need to protect the East   Timorese people from it.   These developments in East Timor had intensified suppor t for the notion of the "responsibility to protect " propagated in the UN and else   where in the international community. However, some ARF participants, including some in ASEAN, r emain suspicious of the possible motiv es behind the use of preventive diplomacy even in this limited way.

As a demonstration of their concern for non-traditional, non-militar y security issues and their embrace of the expanded concept of "comprehensive security", the ARF ministers hav e, fr om 2000 onwar ds, added maritime piracy, illegal migration, trafficking in persons, the illicit production of and trafficking in dr ugs, the illicit trade in small arms, money laundering, computer crime, and ev en corruption to the subjects of their discussions. The exceptions were the 2002, 2003 and 2004 ministerial meetings, which, according to their chairman's statements, were dominated by terrorism and related subjects. This was clearly a result of the dramatic terrorist attacks on the United States in September 2001. Following those attacks, the United States felt it necessary to raise the subject of terrorism at every international opportunity. In 2005, 2006 and 2007, however, the chairman's statements mentioned the possibility of an avian influenza pandemic in addition, in 2005 and 2007, to people smuggling and human trafficking. I n 2007, energy security was discussed for the first time. h 2008, the ministers listed a number of "challenges facing the Asia-Pacific region" — "counter terrorism, non-proliferation, disaster r elief, maritime security , avian and pandemic influenza, human and drugs trafficking ".[27] Just befor e this enumeration, the chairman stated the ministers ' agreement to step up cooperation on "both traditional and non-traditional security challenges confr onting the region". However, the chairman's statement also indicated some participants' concern over the possible use of non-traditional security measues to advance the interests of others at their expense by stressing in the same sentence "the importance of the basic principles of decision-making b y consensus and non-interference".[28]

An ARF Track Two wor kshop on pr eventive diplomacy in Tokyo in March 2004 had " emphasized the importance of achieving common understanding of and r ecognizing the impor tance of 'N ew Threats', with focus on transnational problems, *inter alia*, international terr orism, illicit trafficking in arms, dr ugs and persons, and diseases such as HIV/AIDS, piracy and proliferation of weapons of mass destruction, which require global and regional cooperation and r esponse". It recommended "that the focus of ARF work should co ver security in a compr ehensive manner , including traditional and non-traditional security issues, and explor e practical ways to accelerate the ARF' s r esponse to ne w security thr eats, and to r einforce its preventive diplomacy efforts".[29]

In March 2005, China hosted an ARF seminar on " non-traditional security issues". The seminar provided an idea of the nature of such issues by citing examples of them in its r eport — "illicit dr ugs, infectious diseases, HIV/AIDS, people smuggling and human trafficking, corr uption, money laundering, cyber crime, piracy, environmental degradation, corruption and illegal logging", as w ell as terrorism. The report str essed that these wer e "transnational and transregional in nature, which requires (sic) regional and international cooperation". I t hinted at continuing differ ences among the participants in what to emphasiz e in dealing with such thr eats. While the meeting called for r espect for national so vereignty, territorial integrity and non-interference in internal affairs, " some participants" w ere said to hav e pointed to the need to observe humanitarian, human rights and refugee laws. Participants were also reported to have stressed the need both for sustainable economic and social dev elopment and for " near-term actions ... to meet immediate threats". The meeting recommended some broad steps, but there is no record of any of them being carried out. [30]

The newly re-named International Support Group on Confidence Building Measures and P reventive D iplomacy (ISG-CBM/PD) met in H onolulu in October 2005. I t categorically observed in its summar y report[31] that "Non-Traditional Security Challenges are among the most amenable issues for the application of P reventive Diplomacy in the ARF context". The report cited maritime security, international terrorism, pandemic influenza, trafficking in persons, arms smuggling, dr ug trafficking, money laundering, smuggling of goods, illegal fishing, and illegal trade in natural esources as among the "non-traditional security threats" that the meeting had discussed. I t went on:

> Participants also discussed the development of Preventive Diplomacy in the ARF, particularly as it might be applied to N on-traditional Security Threats. This discussion included consideration of a possible way to move further on Preventive Diplomacy, starting with a "soft approach", which could include: (1) tasking the ARF EER to examine how the ARF could implement PD, (2) tasking the ARF Unit to undertake studies on PD, and (3) compiling a list of best practices including on traditional/non-traditional security issues, drawn fr om other bilateral/multilateral experiences.

Evidently at the behest of the moe cautious participants, the summary report stressed "that any future proposals must take full account of the so vereignty of individual countries and that any futue implementation of these proposals will take place at a pace comfortable to all ".

While the second of the pair of ISG-CBM/PD meetings for the inter-sessional year, in March 2006, apparently discussed non-traditional security threats extensiv ely, the ARF ministerial meeting of J uly 2006 was not as forthright in str essing the need for prev entive diplomacy to focus on such threats. N evertheless, that need has been gradually accepted.   The gr owing prominence of non-traditional security issues in ARF discussions at various levels attests to this. Three factors seem to lie behind this ev olution. One is the gro wing r ecognition that the ARF has little dir   ect r ole in pr eventing armed conflict of the traditional kind, that is, betw   een states, and must, therefore, turn its attention to other kinds of thr   eat in terms of pr eventive diplomacy. Another is the "securitization" of the political as well as economic impact of the 1997–98 financial crisis.   The thir d is the surge in the preoccupation with terrorism, generally consideed as a non-traditional security threat. Moreover, the fact that non-traditional security pr oblems are a threat common to all and pr esent less potential gr ound for strategic disagreement has made pr eventive diplomacy mor e acceptable than if it w ere applied to issues of the traditional kind. By September 2007, Liu Xuecheng, professor at the China Institute of International Studies, was able to state baldly "Preventive diplomacy should deal with non-traditional security issues."   [32] Zhai K un, director of S outheast Asian and O ceanian studies at the China I nstitute of Contemporary International Relations, the think tank of China's State Council, urged that non-traditional security pr   oblems be accor ded " priority" in preventive diplomacy.[33]

However, there is another view, the view that the ARF was conceived and formed for the expr   ess purpose of dealing with inter-state conflict and traditional security threats, and turning its attention to non-traditional security issues would distract the forum from that basic objectiv e. Taking this view, Kwa Chong Guan of the S. Rajaratnam School has noted that the ARF is not meant to deal with non-traditional security threats.[34] Surin Pitsuwan, former Thai for eign minister, made much the same point befor e he assumed the position of ASEAN S ecretary-General.[35]

The effective application of preventive diplomacy to security issues of the non-traditional kind would r equire for ceful ASEAN leadership in making clear that preventive diplomacy in the ARF was all about such issues. ASEAN leadership would also have to r esult in r eassuring all ARF par ticipants that preventive diplomacy would not be used to adv   ance any one countr y's foreign-policy agenda. S o far, ASEAN has not wielded its leadership of the ARF for this purpose, perhaps because the association itself is divided on or uncertain of it. Even if it did, without regional institutions to take initiatives and under take action, it would not be possible to carr   y out pr eventive diplomacy in any substantial way.

Nevertheless, discussions on non-traditional security issues at v   arious levels foster the acceptance of "human security" as a fit subject for the ARF's attention and r egional cooperation and str engthen the networ ks among personnel and institutions involved. This helps to promote mutual confidence, transparency, cooperation, and a sense of common purpose, as w ell as networking, among such personnel and institutions, and thus conceiv ably helps to reduce the likelihood of conflict, a function that could contribute indirectly to conflict pr evention.

Simon S.C. Tay and Obood Talib, as early as 1997, pointed to what they consider as a problem in ARF pr eventive diplomacy, that of asymmetr y between the status of ARF participants:

> Members may be differ entiated on the basis of whether they lie within the ARF's area of concern, or "geographical footprint", or outside of it. If they ar e inside, they may be subject to preventiv e diplomacy, even potentially for matters which they hold to be within their domestic jurisdiction. On the other hand, if they lie outside the ARF' s footprint, like Europe and North America, they are not subject to such scrutiny.... Such asymmetry will tend to strain mutual trust and confidence. This is especially if those urging pr eventive diplomacy will themselv es not be subject to it. [36]

This asymmetry has led M. Jawhar Hassan, chairman of Malaysia's Institute of S trategic and I nternational S tudies and a long-time spar k plug of both CSCAP and ASEAN-ISIS, to complain that "some in the ARF are objects of others". He has urged that the ARF also discuss South Asian problems, since four countries from that r egion already participate in the for um. [37] Tan S ri Ahmad Fuzi Abdul Razak, former Secretary-General of Malaysia's Ministry of Foreign Affairs and later ambassador-at-large, has said much the same thing. [38]

FROM CONFIDENCE-BUILDING TO PREVENTIVE DIPLOMACY

Over the years, the ARF has struggled with the very definition of preventive diplomacy. Some participants seek to move the ARF process forward towards the pr eventive-diplomacy phase accor ding to their conception of it, while others cautiously hold it back. Some Western participants have tended to be more activist and eager to get on to the next stage of the ARF' s progression. Many of the Asians, par ticularly the Chinese, seem to be content with the ARF remaining in the confidence-building phase, contending that confidence-building measures are themselves a form of and a tool for preventive diplomacy. Indeed, in the M arch 2004 seminar on pr eventive diplomacy in Tokyo, the Chinese participant was reported to assert that "keeping the nature of ARF as a political and security dialogue" and "having ASEAN playing a leading role in developing preventive diplomacy" are " concrete measures" of preventive diplomacy.[39] Chinese academics have openly expressed their concern that preventive diplomacy might be used as a pretext to "interfere" in the Taiwan issue, apparently referring to the United States and, perhaps, Japan.[40]

As early as the second ARF ministerial meeting, in August 1995, the ministers recognized that the distinction between confidence-building and preventive diplomacy was somewhat artificial, acknowledging the potential for and the actuality of overlap between the two stages. The measures involved in the overlap were to proceed "in tandem".

This notion of overlap between confidence-building and preventive diplomacy was reiterated in the fourth ARF ministerial meeting, in 1997, with the ministers instructing the ISG-CBM to identify areas in which the two phases overlapped. Noting that the distinction between confidence-building measures and preventive diplomacy was "blurred", the ISG-CBM of 1997–98 identified four "areas of overlap": an "enhanced role" for the ARF chair, a register of Experts and Eminent Persons, an annual security outlook, and background briefings on regional security issues. [41] The chairman's statement at the 1999 ARF ministerial meeting " noted the common understandings reached" on the four proposals.

ROLE OF THE CHAIR

The 1998–99 ISG-CBM envisioned four functions of the ARF chair in its enhanced role: providing good offices, liaison with " external parties", coordination between Tracks One and Two, and inter-sessional work, including the convening of special sessions and the issuance of statements on behalf of the forum between ministerial meetings. At the same time, some in the ISG placed constraining conditions on the exercise of these functions, innocuous though they might already seem. They insisted on "prior consultations" with all ARF participants in every case. In the exercise of good offices, the ARF chair would have to base its actions on " respect for sovereignty and non-interference in the internal affairs of other states" and take such actions only with the consent of the " parties concerned". In undertaking liaison with "external parties" or participating in other forums, the chair would not be representing the ARF. In conducting coordination between Tracks One and Two, the ARF chair would not be endorsing any position of any Track Two body or forum or be compromising its integrity and independence. The same ARF ministerial meeting that agreed on the paper on the Concept and Principles of Preventive Diplomacy in July 2001 also adopted a set of "shared

perspectives" on the Enhanced R ole of the ARF Chair .[42] Embodying the
prescriptions and restrictions worked out by the ISG-CBM, it stressed, "The
paper is mainly focused on the role of the ARF Chair in the CBM stage...."

In seeking to discharge the " enhanced role " of the ARF chair , S urin
Pitsuwan, when he was foreign minister of Thailand, visited the headquarters
of the Organization of American States and the United Nations and met with
their secretaries-general. His successor in the ARF chair, Nguyen Dy Nien of
Vietnam, did the same thing and also made contact with the N on-Aligned
Movement. Cambodian Senior Minister Hor Namhong, Minister of Foreign
Affairs and International Cooperation and ARF chairman for 2002–03, paid
a visit to the headquarters of the European Commission in Brussels, where he
met with Chris Patten, then Commissioner for External Relations, and Javier
Solana Madariaga, High Representative for the Common Foreign and Security
Policy of the E uropean U nion. H e also under took consultations with the
Organization for S ecurity and Cooperation in E urope (OSCE).

During his ARF chairmanship , H or N amhong visited Pyongyang in
December 2002 in order, he said, to understand better the situation on the
Korean peninsula. A ccording to a ne ws release by Cambodia's M inistry of
Foreign Affairs and I nternational Cooperation, dated 5 F ebruary 2003, the
minister told then J apanese Foreign Minister Yoriko Kawaguchi in a visit to
Tokyo that the ASEAN for eign ministers "had asked him to continue his
consultations as Chairman of the ASEAN Regional Forum (ARF) with all its
members to set up a small group of foreign ministers from the ARF membership
in order to help reduce the tension in the Korean peninsula". Ms. Kawaguchi
was reported to have "praised Senior Minister H or Namhong for his efforts
in his capacity as Chairman of the ASEAN R egional F orum to reduce the
tension in North Korea issue".[43] A Kyodo despatch from Tokyo on 6 February
2003 quoted H or Namhong as telling the J apanese wire service, "Maybe in
the very, very near future, I will consult ARF members to see if we can set up
a small group of what we call 'friends of the chair' in order to try to see how
we could contribute to defuse (the nuclear) crisis of N orth K orea." I n the
same inter view, the Cambodian minister informed K yodo that Py ongyang
had r ejected two draft ARF declarations on the situation on the K orean
peninsula, thus pr eventing a consensus. [44] In April 2003, he met with S yed
Hamid Albar and Surakiart Sathirathai, the foreign ministers of Malaysia and
Thailand, as "friends of the chair", primarily on "the current situation in the
Korean peninsula".[45] According to an 11 A pril 2003 K yodo r eport fr om
Bangkok, the Thai for eign ministry announced that H or Namhong would
make another visit to N orth Korea later that month, this time accompanied
by Thai, as w ell as Cambodian, officials. The r eport quoted Thailand's

Surakiart as emphasizing that "the ARF chairman's mission to Pyongyang is part of the ARF' s effor ts on pr eventive diplomacy in defusing r egional tensions as agreed upon by the 2001 ARF ministerial meeting".[46] Apparently, little came from this mission as well other than the opportunity to undertake "consultations". I ndeed, accor ding to its chairman 's statement, the J une 2003 ARF ministerial meeting in Phnom P enh mer ely " noted" H or Namhong's consultations with the EU, the OSCE and the DPRK and "expressed their appreciation ... for the initiativ es that he had under taken in accordance with the provisions and spirit of the paper 'Enhanced Role of the ARF Chair'...." Without a regional ARF institution to follow through from y ear to year , how ever, it is difficult to tell what, if anything, these contacts did for the for um.

As early as its second ministerial meeting, in A ugust 1995, the ARF had designated the chairman as " the main link betw een Track One and Track Two".[47] Track Two in this case has meant principally CSCAP and ASEAN-ISIS. R ecommendations of r egional Track Two bodies have been formally offered to Track One, and some of them have been actually adopted. However, much of the influence of Track Two on Track One thinking is exerted at the national level, and such influence, as well as the general relationship between national Track O ne and Track Two institutions, varies considerably fr om country to countr y — from the complete independence of Track Two from Track One to total contr ol by Track One of Track Two.

Some advances have been made in getting Track Two, particularly CSCAP, involved in official ARF activities. H owever, no special ARF meetings hav e been called for the purpose of pr eventive diplomacy or ev en confidence-building. With respect to statements by the chair between ministerial meetings, Prince Mohamed Bolkiah, foreign minister of Brunei Darussalam, issued one as ARF chair on 4 O ctober 2001 condemning the 11 S eptember terrorist attacks on the United States. The statement called for "concerted action" and for the use of " all necessar y and av ailable means to pursue, captur e and punish those responsible for these attacks and to prevent additional attacks". At the same time, it str essed the impor tance of addr essing "the underlying causes of this phenomenon ".[48] Similarly, H or N amhong, as ARF chair , put out a statement on 16 O ctober 2002 condemning the terr orist bombing on 12 October of two popular nightclubs in Bali, declaring, "These most criminal acts of bombing have no justification whatsoev er ...."[49] The ARF chair has issued other statements, but on the occasion of the annual ministerial meeting and presumably with the clearance of the other ARF participants.

At their 2007 meeting in M anila, the ARF ministers appr oved the terms of reference of the "friends of the chair" as an *ad hoc* advisory group made up of the previous and incoming ARF chairs and the foreign minister of a non-ASEAN ARF participant. So far, the group has not been convened or otherwise used.

EXPERTS AND EMINENT PERSONS

The second measure identified as straddling confidence-building and preventive diplomacy was a roster of "experts and eminent persons" on whom the chair, in the exercise of its "enhanced role", or the ARF as a whole would draw for advice. The 2001 ARF ministerial meeting adopted the " terms of reference" of the EEPs, which had been drawn up by the 2000-01 ISG-CBM co-chaired by Malaysia and South Korea. The terms of reference defined the "Scope and Procedure for Activities of the EEP s":

a) The EEP s may pr ovide non-binding and pr ofessional views or recommendations to the ARF participants, when they ar e requested to under take in-depth studies and r esearches or ser ve as r esource persons in ARF meetings on issues of r elevance to their exper tise.
b) The ARF Chair or any ARF par ticipant may propose to activate the EEPs for the abo ve-mentioned tasks ....
c) The activities and findings/results of the EEPs should be reported to the ARF Chair which would shar e it with all ARF par ticipants. In this regard, the EEPs should be informed in advance on the way their findings/results will be used by the ARF Chair or ARF participants.[50]

In July 2004, the ARF ministers adopted " guidelines" that r efined the prescribed role of the EEPs and the procedures for their activities and meetings. The guidelines seemed to narrow the focus of the EEPs' work even further to "issues and subjects which ar e relevant to the inter ests and concerns of the ARF not being adequately addr essed elsewhere and to which their expertise is directly applicable". They specified, "The work of the EEPs should directly support activities to take the ARF fur ther forward ...." They cited the nine recommendations drawn up b y Brunei Darussalam and adopted *in toto* by the July 2002 ARF ministerial meeting as 'good examples of those subjects in which the exper t study, analysis and r ecommendations of the EEP s may be required". The guidelines further circumscribed the scope of the EEPs' work by specifying, among other things, that their " findings/results will not be publicized outside the ARF". [51]

By the July 2004 ARF ministerial meeting, a r egister of EEPs had been compiled and circulated. I was among the five (the maximum number) EEPs whose names the Philippine government had submitted for the register.[52] As the ministers had agr eed in 2005, the EEP s met for the first time on 29-30 June 2006 on J eju Island in K orea. That meeting, initially billed as a " trial meeting", pr oduced eight r ecommendations, including commissioning the EEPs as a " vision group", integrating them into the " ARF mechanism" as advisers, utilizing them in fact-finding missions or as special env oys, and getting them to conduct planning ex ercises in such ar eas as international terrorism, maritime security , disaster management, pandemics, and peace-keeping operations. Unsure of our role and functions, the EEP also asked the participant-states to "(d)istinguish the r ole and functions of the EEP s from those of Track I (e.g. ISG) and Track II (e.g. CSCAP and ASEAN-ISIS)". [53]

The ASEAN EEP s had met in K uala L umpur in October 2005 to prepare for ASEAN participation in the EEP plenar y meeting in Korea. We agreed to form an ASEAN caucus in the ARF EEP, draw up a concept paper on the ARF' s futur e direction, and initiate studies on contagious diseases, disaster management and ASEAN-ARF linkages with respect to the TAC'and the ASEAN Security Community Plan of Action. None of this has happened.

At the Jeju meeting, I suggested that the EEP draw up papers on specific changes to the ARF structure and process that the EEP themselves proposed, including alterations of the concept and principles of pr eventive diplomacy, an ARF action plan to deal with each kind of non-traditional security threat, and possible alternatives to ASEAN leadership of the ARF. I asked, "Who is to do all this?" I went on:

> When I was nominated as a Philippine EEP , I had the impr ession that the idea was to set up a r egister of EEP s from among whom the ARF chair would seek advice or studies. H owever, ther e seems to be an evolution in thinking on the natur e of the EEPs, an evolution reflected in the terms of r eference of the EEP s and the guidelines subsequently developed for them. Now, the EEPs are being considered as a body that meets periodically.
>
> This raises a fur ther question: will studies and r ecommendations come from the EEPs as a body or from individual EEPs? This is not clear in the terms of r eference or in the guidelines.
>
> The ASEAN EEP caucus has proposed that the EEP s be allo wed to volunteer studies to assist the ARF chairman and other ARF paticipants; in other wor ds, to give unsolicited advice. I f so, should the EEP s do so as a body or as individuals, or either way?
>
> What does "activation" of the EEP s mean? [54]

These questions have not been answ ered.

The ARF EEPs met for the second time in Manila in February 2007. The meeting, which I did not attend, concentrated overwhelmingly on Northeast Asia, commending non-traditional security concerns as offering "opportunities for regional cooperation". It gave as examples of such concerns environmental security, energy security, infectious diseases, counter-terrorism, maritime security, and r efugees. The meeting made four r ecommendations: the encouragement of regional dialogue and cooperation in the peaceful settlement of disputes; the strengthening of r egional capacity in conflict pr evention, crisis management, and post-conflict stabilization; the organization of small EEP working groups for the discussion of important security issues; and the use of ARF meetings as oppor tunities for the par ticipants in the S ix-Party Talks to hold separate meetings on N ortheast Asian security issues. [55] The foreign ministers of the six participants did meet on the occasion of the ARF ministerial meeting in S ingapore in July 2008.

There does not seem to be any connection betw een the first and second meetings of the EEP s. On the ministers' request, the ARF SOM under took assessments of the " practicability" of the r ecommendations from the EEP s' two meetings. The 2007 and 2008 ministerial meetings subsequently adopted the assessments, which, however, have not been made public. I n any case, it may be too early to tell which, if any, of the EEPs' recommendations will be carried out and ho w.

ANNUAL SECURITY OUTLOOK AND MUTUAL BRIEFINGS

The *Annual Security Outlook* embodies the public, official security perceptions of about half of the ARF participants, including the militarily po werful ones. It lends a bit of transpar ency to their security stances. I t can provide something to inv oke in case a go vernment significantly deviates from the claims that it makes in its contribution. I n this way, the *Annual Security Outlook* can be said to contribute to confidence-building or mutual reassurance. However, it is difficult to see its effectiv eness for or r elevance to preventive diplomacy beyond small confidence-building steps, which ae an indirect form of conflict pr evention.

As for mutual briefings, the four th listed ar ea of o verlap betw een confidence-building and preventive diplomacy, these are conducted to some extent at the ministerial and senior officials meetings, the sessions of the ISG-CBM/PD, and the informal gatherings of defence, militar y and national security officials. They ar e also under taken, explicitly or incidentally, in certain inter-sessional confer ences, seminars and workshops. H owever, the briefings cannot go into any kind of detail or depth on account of these meetings' shortage of time and expanding participation. They are generally more effectively carried out in the bilateral consultations on security questions that take place regularly between many ARF participants but outside of the ARF framework.

CONCLUSION

From its early years, the ARF has been under pressure to move towards "preventive diplomacy", the second stage that the 1995 ARF Concept Paper prescribed for the forum 's development. The question that this begs is: prevent what? The general answer is conflicts and situations that could threaten regional peace and security. But what kind of conflicts and situations? On this no clear and definitive consensus has been reached.

There are specific " flashpoints" of conflict in the Asia-Pacific: North Korea's nuclear weapons programme, the conflicting jurisdictional claims in the South China Sea, the Taiwan question, and bilateral territorial disputes. However, in the light of the demands of realism and the understandable preferences of the principal protagonists, these issues are dealt with outside the ARF.

Some states participating in the ARF specifically those whose governments are responsive to media projections and public perceptions of events inside other countries, urge that the ARF be open to action on events internal to countries in the forum's " geographic footprint ". Such actions would be carried out in the name of the " responsibility to protect" or "humanitarian intervention" in cases in which the state is unable or unwilling to protect persons within its jurisdiction from egregious atrocities. They would be taken on the ground that internal conflict or turmoil is today the main threat to regional peace and security , the principal source of regional tension and instability. Other participant-states are wary of the possible use of these concepts — the "responsibility to protect" and "humanitarian intervention" — as a pretext for seeking to influence events in their countries in the pursuit of the intervening states' foreign-policy agendas or domestic political points. The effect of these conflicting positions on the scope of the ARF's role is that any statement that the forum produces on the domestic affairs of nations is mostly positive and quite tepid and does not call for any kind of action by the ARF itself — for good reason, in the light of the divergent interests of the ARF membership.

ARF ministers, officials and academics often proclaim themselves to be adherents of the " comprehensive" notion of security . Such a notion would encompass not only the thr eat of militar y conflict but also the political, economic, social and cultural dimensions of such thr eats. The idea of non-traditional security is being incr easingly promoted. This pertains to dangers to human security of a non-militar y natur e. Those dangers might include contagious diseases, er.vironmental degradation, transnational crime, international terr orism, natural disasters, energy insecurity , water scar city, piracy and robbery at sea, cyber crime, and even corruption. These are threats not of conflict betw een states but ones that confront all in common. I n practice, however, the ARF, as distinct from its individual participants, has not been involved in operational cooperative actions to deal with such theats beyond training and planning sessions.

Nevertheless, goaded by some participants to move towards the preventive-diplomacy phase, the ARF has z eroed in on measur es wher e confidence-building and pr eventive diplomacy ar e said to o verlap. Such measures have been identified as the enhancement of the role of the ARF chair , the compilation of a register of Experts and Eminent Persons, the publication of an annual security outlook, and mutual backgr ound briefings on security perceptions. These measures, innocuous as they are, have so far been ineffectie. The forays of the ARF chair have produced no identifiable results other than to raise the ARF's international profile somewhat. The EEPs' recommendations have been largely ignored thus far. The annual security outlook is useful but cannot be said to serve, except very indirectly, as a tool of preventive diplomacy. Background security briefings of any substance take place outside the ARF . The ARF is ev en far ther away than ever befor e fr om permanent r egional institutions like a Regional Risk-R eduction Centre or an ARF secr etariat.

Thus, the ARF has essentially stayed at the confidence-building stage. A number of participants seem to be happy with this situation. Others will have to be. The "flashpoints" of conflict ar e being addr essed outside the ARF . Clashing strategic positions, mutual suspicions, and the common inter est in respecting the sovereignty and territorial integrity of nations prevent the ARF from intervening in internal conflicts. Non-traditional, non-military security threats are common concerns and ar e frequently discussed in the ARF , but operational action takes place outside the forum.   The plodding, gradual development of some ARF institutions could some day esult in the participant-states enabling and allowing the ARF to become mor e active as a body; but one should not hold one's breath for it.

Meanwhile, the ARF has undertaken some symbolic changes that demonstrate its commitment to mo ving towards the pr eventive-diplomacy stage. One such change was the reconstitution in July 2005 of the Intersessional Support G roup on Confidence-B uilding M easures (ISG-CBM) into the Intersessional S upport G roup on Confidence-B uilding M easures and

Preventive Diplomacy (ISG-CBM/PD), as recommended by the ISG itself. The first meeting of the group under its new name took place in Honolulu in October 2005.

The ARF's confidence-building function can be said to be a means of preventive diplomacy insofar as it engages almost all countries in the Asia-Pacific, particularly the major powers, and provides hope that this particular forum of engagement will mitigate to some extent the tensions and suspicions between the participants and thus contribute in some measure to the region's stability. Yang Yanyi, a senior official in China's Ministry of Foreign Affairs, has declared that she considers confidence-building as the " foundation" of preventive diplomacy.[56]

Ralf Emmers neatly summarizes the difficulty that the ARF faces in moving towards its preventive-diplomacy phase:

> The ARF is still today primarily a confidence-building exercise. The initiative to move beyond the promotion of confidence-building measures has been painfully slow. In contrast to confidence-building, preventive diplomacy is meant to focus on specific security issues and to adopt measures to reduce the risks of open conflict. Progress towards the second stage of development has been undermined by disagreements over the definition and scope of PD. Some participants regard preventive diplomacy as a more threatening form of cooperative security, as it might in some instances lead to a breach of national sovereignty. Consequently, many analysts have legitimately questioned whether the ARF will ever succeed to move towards the next stage of development ....
>
> To maintain its relevance, the ARF should move beyond definitional and conceptual discussions and seek instead to implement PD efforts in an attempt to reduce the risks of open conflict in specific areas .... A first area of implementation could for instance be the South China Sea. The recent de-escalation of the Spratly dispute offers an opportunity for the ARF to discuss and put in place mechanisms to prevent possible clashes of arms among the claimant states.[57]

The problem is that China, for reasons indicated by Emmers, would most probably object to any ARF involvement in the South China Sea issue. Indulging in "definitional and conceptual discussions" is not the real obstacle. It is actually a cover for preventing preventive diplomacy from being used by rival powers against China's and others' perceived interests. Again, conflicting national interests get in the way of ARF activism. This is, of course, not insurmountable, but it requires time — and probably some crisis — for things to move.

Notes

1. "An Agenda for Peace, Preventive Diplomacy, Peacemaking and Peace-keeping" (New York: United Nations, 17 June 1992), paras. 20 and 23.
2. See Joel Djibom, " An Analysis of Hammarskjöld 's Theory of P reventive Diplomacy" (thesis paper in partial fulfillment of the r equirements for the Certificate-of-Training in United Nations Peace Support Operations, 2008), in <http://www.peaceopstraining.org/theses/djibom.html>. S imon S.C. Tay and Obood Talib also cite H ammarskjöld's coinage of the term in " The ASEAN Regional Forum: Preparing for Preventive Diplomacy", *Contemporary Southeast Asia* 19, no. 3 (1997): 253.
3. Appendix A, para. 13.
4. "An Agenda for Peace, Preventive Diplomacy, Peacemaking and Peace-keeping", para. 29.
5. Ibid., para. 30.
6. Appendix C.
7. Appendix A, Annex A, II.
8. Appendix A, Annex B, II.
9. "ASEAN Regional Forum Concept and Principles of Preventive Diplomacy", in *The ASEAN Regional Forum Documents Series 1994–2006* (Jakarta: ASEAN Secretariat, March 2007), pp. 213–16. Also in <http://wwwaseanregionalforum.org/PublicLibrary/TermsofReferencesandConceptPapers/tabid/89/Default.aspx>.
10. "Seminar on Preventive Diplomacy", in *The ASEAN Regional Forum Documents Series 1994–2006*, pp. 77–78. Also in <http://www .aseanregionalforum.org/PublicLibrary/ARFChairmansStatementsandReports/SeminaronPreventiveDiplomacyParis78Novemb/tabid/193/Default.aspx>.
11. <http://www.atimes.com/se-asia/BB01Ae01.html>.
12. Gerry van Klinken, ed., "Inside Indonesia", posted in F ebruary 2001 on *Asian Analysis*, website of ASEAN F ccus Group at Australian National University.
13. "Distillation of Agreed CBMs from the F irst to the F ourth ARF" and "List of New ARF CBMs", in *The ASEAN Regional Forum Documents Series 1994–2006*, pp. 115–17. Also in <http://www .aseanregionalforum.org/PublicLibrary/ARFChairmansStatementsandReports/DistillationofAgreedCBMsfromtheFirstuptot/tabid/183/Default.aspx> and in <http://www .aseanregionalforum.org/PublicLibrary/ARFChairmansStatementsandReports/CoChairsConsolidatedListofPossibleNewARFCB/tabid/184/Default.aspx>, respectively.
14. José T. Almonte, "H ow ar e We to Keep ARF R elevant to the R egion?" (unpublished notes cir culated at the wor kshop of ASEAN ARF Exper ts and Eminent Persons, Kuala Lumpur, 9–10 O ctober 2005), p. 2.
15. Interview with Yang Yanyi, Deputy Director-General, Asian Department, Ministry of Foreign Affairs, China, Beijing, 21 S eptember 2007.

16. Michael Richardson, "Seen as Harmful to Direct Alliances: U.S. Wary of Japanese Plan Pacific Security Idea", *International Herald Tribune*, 23 July 1991.
17. "Chairman's Statement: The First ASEAN Regional Forum" in The ASEAN Regional Forum Documents Series 1994–2006, p. 4, para. 7.2. Also in <http://www.aseanregionalforum.org/PublicLibrary/ARFChairmans StatementsandReports/ChairmansStatementofthe1stMeetingoftheASE/tabid/201/Default.aspx>.
18. "Chairman's Statement, the Second ASEAN Regional Forum" in The ASEAN Regional Forum Documents Series 1994–2006, p. 7, para. 6.1.3. Also in <http://www.aseanregionalforum.org/PublicLibrary/ARFChairmans StatementsandReports/ChairmansStatementofthe2ndMeetingoftheASE/tabid/199/Default.aspx>.
19. Appendix A, Annex A, I.2.
20. "Chairman's Statement: The Third ASEAN Regional Forum", in *The ASEAN Regional Forum Documents Series 1994–2006*, p. 30, para. 18. Also in <http://www.aseanregionalforum.org/PublicLibrary/ARFChairmansStatementsand Reports/ChairmansStatementofthe3rdARF/tabid/196/Default.aspx>.
21. "Seminar on Preventive Diplomacy", in *The ASEAN Regional Forum Documents Series 1994–2006*, p. 77. Also in <http://www.aseanregionalforum.org/PublicLibrary/ARFChairmansStatementsandReports/SeminaronPreventive DiplomacyParis78Novemb/tabid/193/Default.aspx>.
22. Sheldon W. Simon, *ASEAN and its Security Offspring: Facing New Challenges* (Carlisle, Pennsylvania: Strategic Studies Institute, August 2007), p. 20.
23. "Chairman's Statement: The Fourth ASEAN Regional Forum", in *The ASEAN Regional Forum Documents Series 1994–2006*, p. 52, para. 10. Also in <http://www.aseanregionalforum.org/PublicLibrary/ARFChairmans StatementsandReports/ChairmansStatementofthe4thMeetingoftheASE/tabid/186/Default.aspx>.
24. "Conference on Preventive Diplomacy", in *The ASEAN Regional Forum Documents Series 1994–2006*, p. 122. Also in <http://www.aseanregionalforum.org/PublicLibrary/ARFChairmansStatementsandReports/ConferenceonPreventive DiplomacySingapore91/tabid/185/Default.aspx>.
25. "Chairman's Statement: The Sixth ASEAN Regional Forum", in *The ASEAN Regional Forum Documents Series 1994–2006*, p. 128, para. 15. Also in <http://www.aseanregionalforum.org/PublicLibrary/ARFChairmans StatementsandReports/ChairmansStatementofthe6thMeetingoftheASE/tabid/177/Default.aspx>.
26. Interview by the author, Singapore, 10 July 2008.
27. "Chairman's Statement of the 15th ASEAN Regional Forum, Singapore, 24 July 2008", in <http://www.aseansec.org/21816.htm>, para. 6.
28. Ibid., para. 5.
29. "Co-Chairs' Summary of ARF Workshop on Preventive Diplomacy", in *The ASEAN Regional Forum Documents Series 1994–2006*, pp. 331–32. Also in

<http://www.aseanregionalforum.org/PublicLibrary/ARFChairmans
StatementsandReports/CoChairsSummaryofARFWorkshoponPreventiveD/tabid/
74/Default.aspx>.

30. "Co-Chairs' Summary Report of ARF S eminar on Enhancing Cooperation in
the Field of N on-traditional S ecurity I ssues", in *The ASEAN Regional Forum
Documents Series 1994–2006*, pp. 380–82.

31. "Co-Chairs' Summary Report of the F irst M eeting of the ARF I nter-sessional
Support Group on Confidence B uilding Measures and P reventive Diplomacy,
Honolulu, Hawaii, USA, 17–19 October 2005", in *The ASEAN Regional Forum
Documents Series 1994–2006*, pp. 496–97. Also in <http://www .asean
regionalforum.org/PublicLibrary/ARFChairmansStatementsandReports/tabid/
66/Default.aspx>.

32. Interview by the author, Beijing, 19 S eptember 2007.

33. Interview by the author, Beijing, 20 S eptember 2007.

34. Interview by the author, Singapore, 9 O ctober 2007.

35. Interview by the author, Singapore, 15 October 2007.

36. Simon S. C. Tay and O bood Talib, op cit., p. 261.

37. Interview by the author, 15 A ugust 2007.

38. Interview by the author, 16 A ugust 2007.

39. "Co-chairs' S ummary of ARF Workshop on P reventive D iplomacy, Tokyo,
Japan, 16–17 M arch 2004", in *The ASEAN Regional Forum Documents Series
1994–2006*, p. 331. Also in <http://wwwaseanregionalforum.org/PublicLibrary/
ARFChairmansStatementsandReports/CoChairsSummaryofARFWorkshop
onPreventiveD/tabid/74/Defau_t.aspx>, para. 5(5).

40. Interview with Professor Su Hac, Foreign Affairs University, Beijing, 19 September
2007.

41. "Co-chairmen's S ummary R eport of the M eetings of the ARF I nter-sessional
Support Group on Confidence Building Measures, Bandar Seri Begawan, Brunei
Darussalam, 4–6 November 1997, Sydney, Australia, 4–6 March 1998", in *The
ASEAN Regional Forum Documents Series 1994–2006*, p. 106. Also in <http://
www.aseanregionalforum.org/PublicLibrary/ARFChairmansStatements
andReports/CoCha rmensSummaryReportoftheMeetingsofth/tabid/182/
Default.aspx>.

42. "Enhanced R ole of the ARF Chair (S hared P erspectives among the ARF
Members), in *The ASEAN Regional Forum Documents Series 1994–2006*,
pp. 217–19. Also in <http://www .aseanregionalforum.org/PublicLibrary/ARF
ChairmansStatementsandReports/EnhancedRoleoftheARFChairEEPs/tabid/112/
Default.aspx>.

43. <http://www.mfaic.gov.kh/regiondetail.php?contentid=997>.

44. <http://findarticles.com/p/articles/mi_m0WDQ/is_2003_Feb_10/ai_
97399963>.

45. <http://mfaic.gov.kh/e-visa/Bulletin.aspx?Title=+'Friends+of+ARF+Chair'+

Meeting+in+Siem+Reap+%0A+&M_WebContent_BulletinDir=Asc&M_Web ContentDir=Asc&Category1=2004&Grid1Dir=Asc>.

46. <http://findarticles.com/p/articles/mi_m0WDQ/is_2003_April_14/ai_ 100127378>.

47. "Chairman's Statement: The Second ASEAN R egional Forum", op. cit., p . 8, para. 6.4.3.

48. "Statement b y the Chairman of the ARF on the   Terrorist Acts of the 11ᵗʰ September 2001", in *The ASEAN Regional Forum Documents Series 1994– 2006*, p . 253. Also in <http://www .aseanregionalforum.org/PublicLibrary/ ARFChairmansStatementsandReports/StatementbytheChairmanofthe ASEANRegionalFo/tabid/108/Default.aspx>.

49. "Statement b y the Chairman of the ARF on the   Tragic Terrorist Bombing Attacks in Bali", in *The ASEAN Regional Forum Documents Series 1994–2006*, p . 306. Also in <http://www .aseanregionalforum.org/PublicLibrary/ARF ChairmansStatementsandReports/StatementbytheChairmanoftheASEAN RegionalFo/tabid/100/Default.aspx>.

50. "Co-Chairs' P aper on the Terms of R eference for the ARF E xperts/Eminent Persons (EEPs)", in *The ASEAN Regional Forum Documents Series 1994–2006*, p . 221. Also in <http://www .aseanregionalforum.org/PublicLibrary/ARF ChairmansStatementsandReports/CoChairsPaperontheTermsofReferenceforthe/ tabid/114/Default.aspx>, para. 4.

51. "Guidelines for the Operation of the ARF EEB", in *The ASEAN Regional Forum Documents Series 1994–2006*, pp. 348–49. Also in <http://www .aseanregional forum.org/LinkClick.aspx?fileticket=7CZjUqEWIsA%3d&tabid=89& mid=453>.

52. The other four are former Philippine President Fidel V. Ramos, Ramos's National Security A dviser J osé T. Almonte, I nstitute for S trategic and D evelopment Studies President Carolina G. Hernández, and National Defense College of the Philippines President Carlos L. Agustin.

53. "Co-chairs' S ummary R eport of the I naugural M eeting of the Experts and Eminent Persons, the ASEAN Regional Forum, Jeju Island, 29–30 June 2006".

54. Rodolfo C. Severino: "The Role of the EEB in the ARF Process: Some Questions" (unpublished transcript of a presentation at the first plenary meeting of Experts/ Eminent P ersons of the ASEAN R egional F orum, J eju, R epublic of K orea, 30 June 2006).

55. "Co-chair's Summary Report of the Second Meeting of the Experts and Eminent Persons, the ASEAN Regional F orum, M anila, the P hilippines, 5–6 F ebruary 2007" in <http://www .aseanregionalforum.org/LinkClick.aspx?fileticket= UKUrXkAOt84%3d&tabid=66&mid=940>.

56. Interview by the author, Beijing, 21 S eptember 2007.

57. Ralf Emmers: " ASEAN R egional F orum: Time to M ove Towards P reventive Diplomacy", *RSIS Commentaries* (Singapore: S. Rajaratnam School of International Studies, 25 October 2007), pp . 2–3.

Meeting+in+Siem+Reap+%0A–&M_WebContent_BulletinDir=Asc&M_Web
ContentDir=Asc&Category1=2004&Grid1Dir=Asc>.

46. <http://findarticles.com/p/articles/mi_m0WDQ/is_2003_April_14/ai_ 100127378>.

47. "Chairman's Statement: The Second ASEAN Regional Forum", op. cit., p. 8, para. 6.4.3.

48. "Statement by the Chairman of the ARF on the   Terrorist Acts of the 11th September 2001", in *The ASEAN Regional Forum Documents Series 1994– 2006*, p. 253. Also in <http://www .aseanregionalforum.org/PublicLibrary/ ARFChairmansStatementsandReports/StatementbytheChairmanofthe ASEANRegionalFo/tabid/108/Default.aspx>.

49. "Statement by the Chairman of the ARF on the   Tragic Terrorist Bombing Attacks in Bali", in *The ASEAN Regional Forum Documents Series 1994–2006*, p. 306. Also in <http://www .aseanregionalforum.org/PublicLibrary/ARF ChairmansStatementsandReports/StatementbytheChairmanoftheASEAN RegionalFo/tabid/100/Default.aspx>.

50. "Co-Chairs' Paper on the Terms of Reference for the ARF Experts/Eminent Persons (EEPs)", in *The ASEAN Regional Forum Documents Series 1994–2006*, p. 221. Also in <http://www .aseanregionalforum.org/PublicLibrary/ARF ChairmansStatementsandReports/CoChairsPaperontheTermsofReferenceforthe/ tabid/114/Default.aspx>, para. 4.

51. "Guidelines for the Operation of the ARF EEB", in *The ASEAN Regional Forum Documents Series 1994–2006*, pp. 348–49. Also in <http://www .aseanregional forum.org/LinkClick.aspx?fileticket=7CZjUqEWIsA%3d&tabid=89& mid=453>.

52. The other four are former Philippine President Fidel V. Ramos, Ramos's National Security Adviser José T. Almonte, Institute for Strategic and Development Studies President Carolina G. Hernández, and National Defense College of the Philippines President Carlos L. Agustin.

53. "Co-chairs' Summary Report of the Inaugural Meeting of the Experts and Eminent Persons, the ASEAN Regional Forum, Jeju Island, 29–30 June 2006".

54. Rodolfo C. Severino: "The Role of the EEB in the ARF Process: Some Questions" (unpublished transcript of a presentation at the first plenary meeting of Experts/ Eminent Persons of the ASEAN Regional Forum, Jeju, Republic of Korea, 30 June 2006).

55. "Co-chair's Summary Report of the Second Meeting of the Experts and Eminent Persons, the ASEAN Regional Forum, Manila, the Philippines, 5–6 February 2007" in <http://www .aseanregionalforum.org/LinkClick.aspx?fileticket= UKUrXkAOt84%3d&tabid=65&mid=940>.

56. Interview by the author, Beijing, 21 September 2007.

57. Ralf Emmers: "ASEAN Regional Forum: Time to Move Towards Preventive Diplomacy", *RSIS Commentaries* (Singapore: S. Rajaratnam School of International Studies, 25 October 2007), pp. 2–3.

5

COOPERATING ON THE GROUND

Media and public attention to the ASEAN Regional Forum is most intensively, almost exclusively focused on the annual ministerial meeting, par tly because of the high-profile personalities in attendance and partly in anticipation of some breakthrough — which often never comes — in the headline issue of the day. A large media entourage inv ariably accompanies the U nited States' Secretary of S tate. Most of them not specialists on East Asia, the American journalists often train their co verage on issues pertaining to U.S. domestic politics, to the situation in the M iddle East or to some crisis unfolding in another region of the world. Large numbers of Japanese media personnel also cover Japan's foreign minister and, like their American colleagues, ae focused on domestic politics and international headline material.   What the public generally does not know and the media often ignore are the many meetings, seminars, workshops and exercises that the ARF conducts between ministerial meetings throughout the y ear. Such activities, described as "inter-sessional " — that is, between ministerial meetings or sessions — contribute to netwoking and, at their best, to confidence-building and the capacity to wor k together at the operational level. Although not the stuff of headlines, they can be building blocks for the security " architecture" of which the ARF is a par t.[1]

These activities may be categoriz ed into:

- arms control or management;
- military cooperation;
- essentially civilian endeavours that use mainly military assets and personnel and civil-military relations;

- civilian undertakings not involving anything military but meant to respond to dangers that are increasingly regarded as security threats, the so-called "non-traditional", non-military security issues;
- the exchange of security perceptions; and
- the ARF process.

ARMS CONTROL AND MANAGEMENT

Almost from the beginning, the ARF has expressed its concern over the issue of proliferation of w eapons of mass destr uction, particularly of the nuclear v ariety. The second ministerial meeting, in 1995, w elcomed the commitment of all parties to the Treaty on the Non-proliferation of Nuclear Weapons (NPT) to conclude a Compr ehensive Test Ban Treaty (CTBT) by 1996, called for the cessation of all nuclear-w eapons tests, and endorsed nuclear weapons-free zones,[2] positions reiterated by the July 1996 meeting.[3] The ARF' s constant pr eoccupation with N orth K orea's nuclear weapons programme reflects its participants' concern over nuclear proliferation, as well as over the broader tensions on the Korean peninsula, which have long been widely considered as a thr eat to the r egion's stability.

The CTBT was adopted in September 1996. India and Pakistan, which, together with I srael, had declined to join the NPT , hav e not, logically enough, signed the test-ban tr eaty either. Neither have N orth Korea, Saudi Arabia, Syria, and a few other countries. China and the U nited States have signed but not ratified the CTB T. Egypt, I ndonesia, I ran, Israel, Myanmar, Sri Lanka and Thailand are among the other countries that hav e signed but not ratified it.

The region's contribution to the global nuclear non-proliferation regime, the S outheast Asia N uclear Weapon-Free Z one (SEANWFZ) tr eaty was signed in December 1995 and enter ed into for ce in M arch 1997.[4] In the treaty, the ten par ties, now all ASEAN member-states, r eassure one another, in a legally binding way , that none of them will acquir e or deplo y nuclear weapons in their territories, continental shelves or exclusive economic zones. They make stringent commitments on the dumping or disposal of nuclear material or waste and on concluding safeguar ds agreements with the U nited Nations International Atomic Er ergy Agency (IAEA). H owever, four of the five recogniz ed nuclear-w eapon states ar e still negotiating with the tr eaty signatories, that is, the ASEAN countries, on the pr otocol that would bind them to the tr eaty.[5] The points at issue ar e those per taining to the tr eaty's application to the continental shelves and the exclusive economic zones, areas outside the territorial limits of nations, and the so-called " negative security assurances". The pr ovision on the latter point states, "Each S   tate P arty undertakes not to use or thr eaten to use nuclear weapons against any S tate Party to the Treaty. It further undertakes not to use or threaten to use nuclear weapons within the … Zone."[6] The United States, in particular, has objected vigorously to this article in the draft protocol, arguing that adopting it would undermine its treaty obligations to its allies.

Pursuant to a European Union proposal, endorsed by the ARF ministers, a seminar on non-pr oliferation was organized in J akarta in December 1996 by the Centre of Strategic and International Studies of Indonesia, the Peace Research Centre of A ustralia, and the S tiftung Wissenschaft und Politik of Munich. The seminar set out to discuss the challenge of non-proliferation of weapons of mass destruction, the adequacy of current instruments for meeting that challenge, and measur es to str engthen the barriers to proliferation and encourage disarmament. The statement issued by the seminar asserted, "There was consensus that the stability and prosperity of the Asia-Pacific region have flowed at least in part from the widespread adherence by regional countries to the non-proliferation norms and r egimes."[7]

The unintended irony of this claim burst into public view in May 1998, when India conducted three underground nuclear-weapons tests on 11 May, and two on 13 M ay, the first such I ndian tests since 1974. As might be expected, Pakistan followed suit, carrying out five tests, also underground, on 28 May and one on 30 M ay.

In similar statements issued on the day after the second set of Indian tests and the day after the first of the P akistani tests, the UN S ecurity Council "strongly" deplored the tests, called for restraint on the part of the two South Asian rivals, urged each of them to refrain from conducting further tests, and declared that the tests w ere " contrary to the de facto moratorium on the testing of nuclear w eapons or other nuclear explosiv e devices ".[8] The five permanent members of the Security Council met in Geneva on 4 June 1998 "to coordinate their r esponse to the grav e situation cr eated by the nuclear tests" of I ndia and P akistan. I n their joint communiqué, which was later circulated as a Security Council document, the five — China, France, Russia, the United Kingdom and the U nited States — " condemned" the tests and called on the two countries to "stop all further such tests". Significantly, they stressed, "Notwithstanding their recent nuclear tests, I ndia and P akistan do not have the status of nuclear weapons states in accordance with the Treaty on the N on-proliferation of N uclear Weapons."[9] Referring to the joint communiqué that its five permanent members had issued in Geneva, the UN Security Council two days later adopted R esolution 1172 condemning the tests, demanding that I ndia and P akistan refrain from further nuclear tests, urging maximum restraint on their par t, and calling on them to stop their nuclear weapons development programmes. The resolution encouraged "all states to prevent the export of equipment, materials or technology that could … assist programmes in India or Pakistan for nuclear weapons or for ballistic missiles capable of delivering such weapons".[10]

The U nited S tates imposed sanctions on both countries, terminating economic aid, go vernment and commercial loans, militar y sales, and the export of dual-use items. A number of other countries, sev eral of them belonging to the ARF, denounced or deplored the tests with varying degrees of strength.

The denunciations of the tests continued in the J uly 1998 ARF ministerial meeting. R ecalling the ARF' s welcome of the adoption of the CTBT and UN Security Council Resolution 1172, the chairman's statement of that meeting declared:

> The M inisters, ther efore, expr essed grav e concern o ver and str ongly deplored the r ecent nuclear tests in S outh Asia, which exacerbated tension in the region and raised the specter of a nuclear arms race. They called for the total cessation of such testing and urged the countries concerned to sign the Treaty on the Non-Proliferation of Nuclear Weapons and the Comprehensive Nuclear Test Ban Treaty without delay, conditions, or r eservations. They asked the countries concerned to r efrain fr om undertaking weaponization or deplo ying missiles to deliv er nuclear weapons, and to prevent any transfer of nuclear weapon-related materials, technology and equ pment to thir d countries. I n the inter est of peace and security in the region, the Ministers called on the countries concerned to resolve their dispute and security concerns though peaceful dialogue.[11]

At that ARF ministerial meeting, India received much pointed criticism of its nuclear tests, as did Pakistan. Having joined the ARF two years before, India was able to respond to the barbs then and there. Pakistan, which at that time stood six years away from membership , was not.

However, the ARF' s and its par ticipating countries' concern o ver the South Asian nuclear tests quickly dissipated into apparent resignation to and acceptance of yet another confirmation of the continued dev elopment of nuclear weapons in a volatile part of the world. This quick change in mood was appar ently made easier b y the moratoriums on fur ther weapons tests announced separately by India and Pakistan soon after the M ay 1998 tests. The chairman's statement of the 1999 ARF ministerial meeting, just a little over a y ear since the S outh Asian explosions, mer ely said, " The M inisters noted suppor t for encouraging states that had tested nuclear w eapons last year to exercise restraint, including by adhering to the Compr ehensive Test Ban Treaty, and to r evive the Lahor e process."[12]

After that, the ARF fell silent on the I ndian and P akistani tests. I t has continued to support the NPT and call for its "universalization" and that of other non-proliferation and disarmament agr eements without naming India or P akistan. I t has also urged the conclusion of a F issile M aterial C ut-off Treaty and mo vement towar ds the elimination of nuclear w eapons. This consistent, almost ritualistic invocation of the NPT and other established nuclear arms-control conventions and the pursuit of the quix otic vision of a world without nuclear arms hav e been increasingly defied b y the changing strategic realities on the gr ound.

The NPT had enshrined and legalized the division of the world, in terms of nuclear weapons, into nuclear hav es and have-nots, between the officially recognized nuclear-weapon states — China, France, the Soviet Union (Russia as its successor state), the U nited Kingdom and the U nited States — which also happen to be the fiv e v eto-wielding permanent members of the UN Security Council, and the rest of the world. Essentially under this arrangement, the nuclear have-nots for eswore dev eloping or other wise acquiring nuclear weapons. At the insistence of leading nuclear have-nots, the nuclear haves, in turn, committed themselves to negotiating the r eduction and eventual elimination of their nuclear w eapons. A t the same time, the international community assumed the obligation to assist the non-nuclear states in acquiring the technology for the peaceful uses of nuclear energy while pledging to keep from them anything that would help them dev elop or acquire nuclear arms.

From the beginning, the tr eaty has been vitiated not only b y the lack of seriousness of the nuclear-weapon states in fulfilling their commitment to negotiate the abolition of their nuclear arsenals but also by the fact that India, Israel and Pakistan refused to be par ties to the treaty, which they consider ed to be constraining their strategic options. I n 2003, N orth Korea withdr ew from the NPT after mo ving ahead with its nuclear-w eapons dev elopment programme. This particular process culminated in its announcement that it was enriching uranium to w eapons grade and its conduct of a test nuclear explosion in O ctober 2006. N orth Korea had also been accused of sharing missile technology with Pakistan in return for uranium-enrichment equipment and technology. The allegedly rogue Pakistani nuclear scientist, A. Q. Khan, had been charged with sharing w eapons technology not only with N orth Korea but with Iran and Libya as well. Israel is universally believed to possess nuclear weapons but has not officially admitted it. I ran may or may not, depending on whom one believes, hav e a pr ogramme of developing such weapons. On the other hand, the former Soviet Republics outside Russia that had nuclear arms on their soil gave them up soon after the break-up of the Soviet Union. South Africa did so in the early 1990s. In 2003, Libya announced the cessation of its nuclear programme. The denuclearization of North Korea has proceeded in fits and starts.

In September 2001, just after the terrorist attacks on the United States, President George W. Bush lifted all U.S. nuclear-related sanctions on both India and Pakistan — those imposed in reaction to the 1998 weapons tests and those decreed earlier in response to the two countries' non-accession to the NPT.[13]

In a joint statement issued during a visit by Indian Prime Minister Manmohan Singh to Washington in July 2005, Bush committed the United States to "full civil nuclear energy cooperation" with India. For this purpose, he promised to work for the adjustment both of U.S. laws and policies and of international regimes, "including but not limited to expeditious consideration of fuel supplies for safeguarded nuclear reactors at Tarapur".[14] These commitments were reiterated and elaborated upon during President Bush's visit to India in March 2006. [15] As Prime Minister Singh told the Indian Parliament immediately after the Bush visit, the new U.S. policy spelled the end of India's "nuclear isolation" as well as the dawn of a " new partnership" between the two countries. [16]

In return, India would develop a plan to separate civilian and military nuclear facilities and programmes and place the civilian facilities under IAEA safeguards. India and the United States eventually approved the Separation Plan. India would continue its moratorium on nuclear tests, refrain "from transfer of enrichment and reprocessing technologies to states that do not have them", and support "international efforts to limit their spread".[17] There was the fear, however, that the international supply of nuclear fuel for civilian use would free domestically generated fuel for military purposes.

On 1 August 2008, the IAEA Board of Governors approved an agreement with India that would apply IAEA " safeguards" to India's civilian nuclear facilities. The IAEA and India then started a " dialogue" on an " additional protocol" to the safeguards agreement. An additional protocol gives IAEA inspectors expanded access to nuclear information and facilities of the state party to it. [18] Early in September the chairman of the House Foreign Affairs Committee of the U.S. Congress disclosed a " secret" letter from the State Department to Congress asserting that the United States would stop the supply of nuclear fuel to India should the latter conduct another nuclear-weapons test, a condition that members of India's ruling party challenged. The Indian Ministry of External Relations huffily dismissed the resulting controversy by invoking a policy of not commenting on internal communications between agencies of a foreign government. On 6 September, the forty-five-nation Nuclear Suppliers Group, an informal forum formed, ironically, in reaction to the first Indian nuclear-weapons test in 1974, lifted its ban on nuclear trade with India — reluctantly, it is reported, on the part of some members, which are said to have succumbed to pressure from the United States.[19] Even as the deal stirred fierce controversy in Indian politics, particularly on the ground that it would limit India's strategic options, the U.S. Congress in October 2008 passed legislation to carry out the arrangements, legislation that President Bush signed into law on 8 October 2008. That cleared the way for U.S. Secretary of State Condoleezza Rice and Pranab Mukherjee, India's Minister for External Affairs, to sign the formal agreement three days later. What, if anything, the ARF will say about the whole issue, considering its composition, remains to be seen.

Four years before, on the occasion of the ARF ministerial meeting in July 2004, the ARF chair (Indonesia) had issued a statement on non-poliferation. Evidently cleared with the rest of the forum, the statement made the usual call for the prevention, by national means and through international cooperation, of the proliferation of weapons of mass destruction and their means of delivery. This time, however, the statement was clearly aimed at the spread of such weapons to terrorists and terrorist groups. It expressed strong support for Resolution 1540, which the UN Security Council had adopted three months before.[20] That resolution explicitly applied agreements on non-proliferation to "non-State actors", referring to terrorists and terrorist groups.[21]

Thenceforth, ARF attention to non-proliferation issues has been focused largely on the implementation of Resolution 1540 and other measures to prevent terrorists from getting hold of weapons of mass destruction, as well as, in general, on the growing potential for the spread of such weapons and materials related to them. This is in line with the ARF's preoccupation with terrorism issues following the terrorist attacks on the United States in 2001.

In March 2006, China, Singapore and the United States organized an ARF seminar on non-proliferation. The seminar featured country perceptions of the proliferation threat in general and emphasis on the need to comply with the NPT and other, related agreements; it also highlighted the implementation of Resolution 1540. It paid particular attention to controls on the export of materials related to weapons of mass destruction. Export licensing experts had met in November 2005 under ARF auspices, producing a paper on "Best Practices in Export Control". The seminar also focused on the Proliferation Security Initiative (PSI). Introduced by the United States in 2003, the PSI is a measure for the interdiction of shipments of nuclear, chemical and biological weapons and of related technology. The seminar was said to be useful for the development of domestic systems for the control of the export of such weapons and technology. Some countries offered assistance for the development of expertise for non-proliferation purposes.

In reporting on the ministers' discussions on the threat posed by the proliferation of weapons of mass destruction and their delivery systems, the 2005, 2006 and 2007 ARF chairman's statements emphasized their potential use by terrorists and the need to prevent their spread to "non-state actors" in relation to Resolution 1540.[22] The 2007 meeting issued an "ARF Statement Supporting National Implementation of United Nations Security Council Resolution 1540 (2004)'. An ARF workshop on the implementation of Resolution 1540 had taken place in February 2007 in San Francisco. In 2008, the ministers set up an Intersessional Meeting on Non-proliferation and Disarmament, "with a particular focus on UNSCR 1540 regional implementation".[23] China, Singapore and the United States had proposed the move a year earlier, jointly chairing the first meeting.

At their August 2007 meeting, the ARF ministers urged states to accede to the International Convention for the Suppression of Acts of Nuclear Terrorism, which the UN General Assembly had adopted in April 2005, and the Amendment to the Convention on the Physical Protection of Nuclear Material, adopted in July of the same year.[24]

Beyond weapons of mass destruction, the ARF has carried out intersessional activities on other arms-related issues. A seminar on missile defence took place in October 2005. Two different issues can be discerned in the seminar's report. One is the threat of the proliferation of missiles as possible delivery vehicles for weapons of mass destruction. The other is the purportedly de-stabilizing effect of defence systems against oncoming missiles. Although no consensus seems to have been reached on these issues, the participants are said to have agreed that the seminar had contributed to transparency and thus to a measure of mutual confidence among them.

The traffic in small arms and light weapons has of late been a matter of concern for some participants in the ARF as well as at the United Nations, again largely in relation to international terrorism. The ARF conducted a seminar and a workshop on the subject in Phnom Penh in November 2005 and December 2007, respectively. Between them, in October 2006, a workshop was organized in Bangkok on both small arms and light weapons and man-portable air-defence systems, or MANPADS, which are considered to be a threat to civil aviation, particularly in the hands of terrorists.

For a while, starting in 1996, the ARF called for "universal participation" in the UN Register of Conventional Arms. There was also some discussion of having a similar register for the region, but that initiative has died down, with almost all ARF states having joined the UN R   egister. ASEAN-ISIS has proposed that the ARF wor k towards a multilateral agr eement on avoiding naval accidents.

The discussions on w eapons of mass destruction and the changes in stances towards the NPT and other arms-contr ol agreements have giv en ARF participants a first-hand look at the tectonic shifts in the major-power relationships involving the United States, India, and, indirectly, China and Russia — and the dilemma that they pose for J apan and others. The focus of inter-sessional talks on the implementation of UNSC R esolution 1540 has sharpened par ticipants' consciousness of the potential for w eapons of mass destruction to fall into the hands of terrorists. The ones on small arms and light w eapons, including MANP ADS, illuminate similar concerns, while the seminar on missile defence has shed light on the issues inv olved in such weapons systems. It would, however, be misplaced — and unrealistic — to expect the ARF to achiev e br eakthroughs on pr oblems of arms control and management that hav e taxed the faculties of the international community for decades.

MILITARY COOPERATION

The ARF considers no nation as an actual or potential adv ersary. The ARF has no common enemy against which to make operational plans for war It is not a military alliance. Indeed, its inclusiveness encompasses all powers in the Asia-Pacific, big and small, that could possibly get involv ed in an armed conflict or strategic confrontation. Inclusiveness is one of the ARF's objectives. Nevertheless, ARF participants have undertaken military-related cooperative activities. These are not directed against any one country or group of countries but are useful for networ king, capacity building, mutual understanding, confidence-building, and, conceivably, operational coordination. Among these are meetings of heads of defence colleges and similar institutions and networking and training for peacekeeping operations.

The heads of ARF defence colleges met for the first time in M anila in October 1997. They have been convening ev ery y ear since then. I n these meetings, they normally exchange national-security perceptions, discuss matters of security education, and explore ways of cooperation among the defence educational institutions. At least since 2004, they have been paying attention to "non-traditional" security matters, including terr orism, natural disasters and communicable diseases. While such gatherings may not result in anything concrete by way of cooperation, they have been useful for networking and for some degr ee of illumination of national-security positions as w   ell as for mutual learning.

Peacekeeping opera:ions hav e been one militar y ar ea that has been subjected to ARF scr utiny almost fr om the beginning. As early as M   arch 1995, B andar S eri B egawan hosted a seminar on P eacekeeping Challenges and O pportunities for the ASEAN R   egional F orum. I n 1996 and 1997, Intersessional Meetings (ISM) o: peacekeeping operations took place twice in K uala Lumpur and once in A   uckland, N ew Zealand. The focus of the discussions in these early gatherings was on str engthening UN peacekeeping operations, including the S tandby Arrangements, and training for peacekeeping. A "train the trainers" workshop and a peacekeeping training course were held in con;unction with the March 1997 ISM in Malaysia, and a workshop on training with the A pril 1997 ISM in N ew Zealand. Training courses w ere also condu.cted in D   ublin and Tokyo in O ctober 1998 and March 1999, respective:y. New Delhi hosted an ARF peacekeeping seminar on "best practices and lessons lea:ned " in M arch 2002 and one on "UN peacekeeping challenges and prospects" in April 2007. Peacekeeping experts' meetings took place in Port Dickson, Malaysia, in 2007 and in S ingapore in 2008. The sharing of expertise a.d insights has been consider   ed to be particularly useful in view of the fact that many ARF par ticipants have had extensive experience in internaticnal peacekeeping operations.

Some ARF participants mai:tain peacekeeping training institutions. Brunei D arussalam hos:ed an ARF Track Two seminar on them in M arch 1995, after which ISIS-Malaysia conducted a survey on those institutions. In 1997, Canada, whose international peacekeeping training centre serves as the secretariat for the International Association of Peacekeeping Training Centres, invited ARF par ticipants to join the association.

In recent years, with the danger of inter-state conflict calling for international peacekeeping r eceding in the Asia-P acific, peacekeeping operations hav e been incr easingly r egarded as being applicable mainly to internal conflicts under the rubric of the "responsibility to protect", as in the cases cited in the follo wing paragraph.[25] The UN-adopted "responsibility to protect" principle goes into operation when a state is unable or unwilling to protect people within its bor ders from massiv e atrocities. I n any ev ent, the conduct of peacekeeping operations in an ARF context in the Asia-P acific, whether in conditions cf inter-state or internal conflict, is subject to the acquiescence of the major powers, whose geo-strategic interests often clash, a circumstance hospitable to inaction. N evertheless, ARF activities related to peacekeeping can be useful for countries contributing tr   oops and other personnel to UN peacekeeping operations in scatter ed places around the world and for sensitizing ARF par ticipants to the many issues surr ounding international peacekeeping operations.

An ARF seminar in Tokyo in March 2005 discussed, with appr oval, the growing tendency in peacekeeping and other post-conflict operations to combine militar y and civilian elements in what wer e called "hybrid " arrangements. It looked into the cases of Cambodia,Timor-Leste, the Solomon Islands, Afghanistan, Haiti, and sev eral places in Africa. The par ticipants touched upon the similarities between peace arrangements and disaster relief in terms of civilian-militar y cooperation.[26]

CIVILIAN USE OF MILITARY ASSETS AND CIVIL-MILITARY COOPERATION

Many measur es on behalf of the security of persons, communities or ev en entire nations in the Asia-P acific today ar e essentially civilian in natur e. However, they almost always r equire the heavy par ticipation of the military, either because only the militar y possesses the necessary equipment or because only the militar y has the organizational stucture and the appropriate training and skills or both.

Nowhere is this mor e evident than in the ar ea of disaster r esponse. The Asia- Pacific is exceptionally prone to natural disasters. Some countries in the region or par ts of countries ar e on the so-called ring of fir e, which r enders them vulnerable to volcanic eruptions, or ar e on geologic faults that make them susceptible to massive earthquakes. Some are on the path of typhoons, cyclones or hurricanes. S ome are in all thr ee situations.

Faced with this challenge to human security , the ARF has conv ened Intersessional M eetings on disaster r elief, star ting in 1997 in Wellington. Subsequent ones took place in 1998 in B angkok, 1999 in M oscow, 2000 in Hanoi, 2005 in Bandung, Indonesia, 2006 in Qingdao, China, and 2007 in Helsinki. I n addition, an exper ts gr oup on disaster r elief met in 1999 in Bangkok, where a " train the trainers " seminar took place a y ear later. A training session and a seminar on humanitarian assistance and disaster r elief were conducted in S ingapore in 2000 and 2002, r espectively. In September 2005 Manila hosted a workshop on civil-military operations in disaster relief. These gatherings focused on training, early warning, public information, and the maintenance of databases. The reports of these meetings, seminars and workshops lay par ticular emphasis on national so vereignty, the v oluntary nature of assistance, and the responsibility of the state concerned for emergency response. Thus, one can sense in them a degree of unease over the possibility of the use of disaster relief for the advancement of the foreign-policy objectives of assisting countries.

In July 2006, one and a half y ears after the massive D ecember 2004 tsunami hit a number of ARF participating countries and others in the Asia-Pacific, the ARF ministerial meeting issued a statement on disaster management and emergency r esponse. The statement pr escribed certain measures to be undertaken nationally or through international cooperation. O ne had to do with risk identification, for ecasting, monitoring and information-sharing. Others called for the formation of a virtual task force on disasters, the establishment of a database of contacts, assets and capabilities, and the compilation of ARF par ticipants' disaster procedures and manuals. Another urged ARF par ticipants to integrate disaster risk-r eduction measur es into their national laws, policies and strategies. Another prescribed the enhancement of networking and coordination among national search-and-rescue and relief agencies. Other measures had to do with training, research and the sharing of expertise. The statement called for the regular review of the "progress" of the efforts called for.[27]

In May 2008, the ARF conducted a "desktop" exercise in disaster relief and emergency procedures in Jakarta after an initial planning conference in Darwin, A ustralia, eight months befor e. After some hesitation on the conduct of an actual ex ercise as pr oposed b y the Philippines and the United S tates, the ARF ministers finally appr oved the ex ercise at their meeting in July 2008.

Without referring to the 2006 ARF declaration on disaster management and emergency response, the chairman's statement of the July 2008 meeting devoted an unusually lengthy and detailed passage to disaster-relief cooperation. Emphasizing " training, technical assistance and coor dination among ARF participants in adv ance of disasters ", as w ell as information-sharing and multinational exercises, the statement called for wok to continue on the ARF Strategic Guidance for H umanitarian Assistance and D isaster Relief and an ARF disaster-relief work plan.[28]

These statements and activities have been meant to demonstrate the ARF governments' responsiveness to natural disasters and the heavy casualties and severe damage that they often inflict, attracting bursts of media attention and stirring international compassion. The inter-sessional activities also ser ve to upgrade skills, offer oppor tunities for mutual learning, and impr ove coordination. H owever, they hav e evidently *not* been intended to lead to cooperation in actual disaster relief and emergency response on the part of the ARF as a whole. Whether the joint ex ercise appro ved in J uly 2008 and scheduled for 2009 will change this r emains to be seen.

In any case, responses by ARF par tners to disasters that have visited the Asia-Pacific — most r ecently, the D ecember 2004 tsunami, the M ay 2008 cyclone that devastated wide swaths of Myanmar, and the May 2008 earthquake that destr oyed parts of China 's Sichuan pr ovince, all of which killed or rendered miserable large numbers of people — hav e been carried out as national contributions rather than as ARF effor ts. Indeed, ARF documents on regional responses to natural disasters emphasize their bilateral and voluntary nature. The closest that such responses have been to a regionally cooperative endeavour is the ASEAN-brokered effort at coordination among ASEAN, the UN and the Myanmar government in organizing the international assistance to the victims of Cyclone Nargis in Myanmar. The ARF was totally out of it. This was not because of the policies to   wards M yanmar of a fe w ARF participants, but because, in disaster r elief, the ARF as a gr   oup conducts discussions and training but not actual operations.

The ARF participants are clearly aware of the importance of civil-military cooperation in disaster r esponse and similar endeav ours. The chairman 's statement of the 2008 ARF ministerial meeting r   eported, " The M inisters called for greater civil-military coordination for major, multinational disaster responses through training, information sharing, and multinational exercises. They recognised that military assets and personnel, in full support and not in place of civilian r esponses, have played an incr   easingly impor tant r ole in regional disaster r esponses."[29]

In September 2005, the Philippines and Australia co-chaired a workshop in M anila that examined in gr   eater detail the role of the militar   y in the response to natural disasters. A S eptember 2006 ARF seminar in H anoi was even dev oted to civilian-militar y cooperation in dealing with SARS, avian influenza and other communicable diseases.These deliberations and discussions have offer ed the opportunity for the par   ticipants and their agencies to understand mor e clearly the incr   easing imperativ es and r equirements of civilian-military cooperation in mor e and mor e areas.

Like disaster r elief or the outbr eak of epidemics or pandemics, sear ch-and-rescue is an emergency undertaking that is essentially civilian in character but often requires military assets. It is a response to human predicaments that know no national boundaries and often calls for international cooperation. As in disaster relief, participants use the ARF to help build their capabilities and demonstrate the forum's utility for human security Intersessional Meetings on search-and-rescue were conducted in Honolulu in 1996 and in Singapore in 1997, but they stopped there. Again, as in disaster r elief, cooperation in actual operations has been carried out on the basis of national endeavours or bilateral arrangements, although discussions within the ARF have been helpful for networking and mutual understanding and could lead to operational coordination between two or more countries.

The global trading community and the international community in general have for a long time been deeply concerned with the vulnerability of international trade to piracy and robbery at sea. [30] Ninety per cent of the world's trade is carried by sea transport. Because of this concern, the International Maritime Bureau (IMB) was established in 1981 as a division of the International Chamber of Commerce (ICC) to carry on the fight against maritime crime and other malpractices at sea. Based in the United Kingdom, the IMB has been endorsed by the International Maritime Organisation (IMO), a UN specialized agency. It has concluded a memorandum of understanding with the World Customs Organization and has observer status with Interpol. In 1992, the IMB set up a Piracy Reporting Centre, with headquarters in Kuala Lumpur, in response to the sharp rise in the number of cases of piracy and armed robbery of commercial vessels. The ICC's website says, "The IMB Piracy Reporting Centre (PRC) is the only organization of its kind anywhere in the world, offering ship masters the ability to report attacks of piracy from any location at any time. In addition to compiling reports and issuing warnings PRC provides emergency advice to ships under attack and coordinates medical assistance and support through local authorities."[31]

While armed patrols, interdictions and other measures against piracy on the high seas are usually carried out by naval units with long-range reach, crimes committed against ships within the jurisdiction of littoral states are, strictly speaking, a matter of law enforcement and are, therefore, normally the responsibility of the marine police, the coast guard or an equivalent civilian law-enforcement agency. However, the fight against maritime crimes that are technically not piracy often uses military assets as well.

It was not until their 2003 meeting that the ARF ministers took official cognizance of maritime security, particularly of piracy and armed robbery at sea, as a subject for its attention. To be sure, the late 1990s saw an ARF Maritime Specialists Officers Meeting under the joint chairmanship of Thailand and the United States. The March 1998 ISG-CBM in Sydney, Australia, had discussed the subject extensively in terms of maritime safety, law and order at sea, and the marine environment as well as maritime cooperation. An ARF anti-piracy workshop had taken place in October 2000 and one on "maritime security challenges" in the first quarter of 2003, both in Mumbai, India. However, it was only in June 2003 that a ministerial statement on maritime security was issued. It called on ARF participants to implement UN agreements and resolutions on suppressing piracy and "other threats to maritime security" and to step up cooperation for that purpose. [32]

Citing reports in the *Straits Times*, Amitav Acharya had stated that piracy cases in Southeast Asia had risen fr om 3 in 1989 to 60 in 1990 and 203 in 1991 and that, in 1992, the region had accounted for 73 of the 106 incidents of piracy around the world. [33] The P iracy R eporting Centr e (PR C) had received reports of 143 instances of piracy and armed robbery against ships in 2001 in the r egion that it categoriz es as "S outh East Asia, I ndian S ub-continent and Far East". That number had risen to 218 in 2002 in the same area and was to increase again to 276 in 2003. I then steadily dropped to 202 in 2004, 168 in 2005 and 105 in the first thr ee quar ters of 2006. [34] Adam Young and Mark Valencia in 2003 cited a report that acts of piracy or armed robbery at sea in Southeast Asia alone had increased from 22 in 1967 to 164 in 2002. For further emphasis, they cautioned that ship owners and operators had a tendency to under-report acts of piracy or armed attack, which led to understatements in IMB statistics. [35] On the other hand, I ndonesia has questioned the accuracy of IMB data, particularly with r espect to r eports of "piracy" in its territorial or archipelagic waters.

In any event, in its annual r eport released in J anuary 2009, the PR C noted that only 28 incidents of piracy and armed robber y at sea had been reported in Indonesian waters in 2008, as against 121 in 2003. A ccording to the report, there were only two in the Malacca Straits, down from seven in 2007. [36]

The intensification of the ARF' s concern o ver maritime security may have received impetus not only from the incr easing incidence of maritime crimes in the Asia-Pacific up to 2003, but also from the rapid expansion of international trade and the increased share of the dynamic economies of the ARF countries in that trade. G lobal ship-borne trade is estimated to have quadrupled since 1965. According to Joshua Ho, an officer in the Singapore Navy, more than 63,000 commercial v essels transit the S traits of M alacca alone ever y y ear, including in their cargo about 80 per cent of the oil destined for N ortheast Asia. S ome twenty-six oil tankers no w go through the Straits of Malacca every day, he affirms. [37] Barry Desker, dean of the S. Rajaratnam School, points out that the flo w of oil through the S traits is three times the v olume that goes through the S uez Canal and S umed pipeline and fifteen times the amount that transits the Panama Canal, that two-thirds of the tonnage through the Straits is accounted for by crude oil bound for Northeast Asia, and that more than half of the world's shipping tonnage passes through the S traits. [38]

In addition to piracy and armed robbery at sea, there is the threat of maritime terrorism. Some analysts of terrorism regard vulnerable sea-borne vessels as tempting targets for terrorist attacks in the light of the dramatic nature of such attacks and the enormity of their economic consequences and political impact. Thus, warships, oil tankers, cruise ships and passenger ferries have all been victims of maritime terrorism. The hijacking of the cruise ship *Achille Lauro* in the Mediterranean in 1985, the suicide bombing that killed 17 American seamen and tore a gaping hole in the hull of the U.S. destroyer *USS Cole* while moored at Aden in October 2000, the attack on the French supertanker *Limburg* in the Arabian Sea in October 2002, and the destruction in February 2004 of *Superferry 14* in Philippine waters, killing 116 persons, are among the most notable instances of maritime terrorism.

Joshua Ho of the Singapore Navy wrote in 2005:

> They (Indonesia's National Intelligence Agency) revealed that detained members of Southeast Asian Islamic terror group Jemaah Islamiah, which is linked to al-Q'aeda, admitted that shipping in the Malacca Strait had been a possible target. The discovery of plans detailing vulnerabilities in US naval fleets on Al-Qaeda linked terrorist suspect Babar Ahmad also puts beyond a shadow of doubt that Al-Qaeda terrorist groups have been looking at the maritime domain as a possible mode of attack.[39]

However, Martin N. Murphy of the University of Reading in England pointed out in 2007, "The number of terrorist attacks at sea has been minuscule as a proportion of terrorist attacks overall."[40]

In the wake of the September 2001 terrorist attacks on the United States, there have been suggestions of a potential link-up between piracy and anti-ship crime on the one hand and terrorism on the other. For example, IMO Secretary-General Efthimios Mitropoulos is reported to have praised Singapore "for having taken the threat of piracy being used as a form of terrorism very seriously".[41] However, some other Southeast Asian authorities, notably those in Malaysia, consider such a linkage to be unlikely. In any case, Young and Valencia point out that, although piracy and terrorism are different in their motivations, they are similar in the tactics that they use and in some of the conditions in which they thrive. Moreover, they note that governments have "conflated" piracy and terrorism and "fused" them into a general threat to maritime security in order to gain public support for measures against either of them, including international cooperation for that purpose.[42]

Although casting doubt on the "tactical nexus ... between pirates and extremist groups" and pointing to the differ ence between their objectives, a Reuters ar ticle in N ovember 2008 invited attention to the heightened vulnerability of maritime vessels, as well as major ports and shipping lanes, to attack by either group — and the consequent rise in insurance pemiums for them.[43]

ARF activity in the ar ea of maritime security has gather ed momentum since the 2003 statement. I n S eptember 2004, K uala L umpur hosted a workshop in which national per ceptions of and r esponses to threats to maritime security were exchanged, and the impor tance of bilateral, trilateral and multilateral cooperation and intelligence-sharing was emphasiz ed. The workshop consider ed the lack of cer tain necessar y elements as hindering regional cooperation on maritime security: a common definition of maritime crimes, a shared understanding of the thr eats to maritime security , mutual trust, and r esources.

In March 2005, the ARF conducted in S ingapore what was labelled as a confidence-building measure of regional cooperation in maritime security In that exercise, Singapore gave an "operational demonstration" of how it handled maritime-security thr eats, including potential terr orist attacks. This was followed by a " maritime-security shor e ex ercise" in J anuary 2007, also in Singapore. Meant to help build " capacity for inter-operability", the ex ercise covered border protection, search and rescue, inter-agency information-sharing, the definition of maritime security, and coast guar d cooperation. A ccording to the chairman's report, the par ticipants "agreed that while the (' table-top exercise') may not hav e pr ovided definitiv e solutions, its v alue was in the broadening of perspectives made possible by the presence of different agencies and countries".[44]

In the last quar ter of 2005, the ARF conducted training sessions for cooperative maritime security in K ochi, India, and a wor kshop on capacity-building in Tokyo. These activities cited the need for coordination within and between countries in terms of training methodologies, a common database, and a register of contact points. They highlighted the v alue of bilateral and multilateral exer cises. The I ndian Coast G uard hosted and conducted a maritime-security training workshop in Chennai in M arch 2008. It covered search and rescue, smuggling, piracy , hijacking and armed r obbery, port security and ship security, the confiscation and r epatriation of ships, fishing rights, drug trafficking, and nar co-terrorism.

On Singapore's proposal, the ARF ministers in J uly 2008 welcomed the decision to set up an Intersessional Meeting on maritime security. Indonesia,

Japan and New Zealand offered to co-chair the first meeting in the first half of 2009.

Progress has been made in regional cooperation, involving two or more countries, in dealing with threats to maritime security in the Asia-Pacific. However, it is difficult to tell how much of this cooperation or any improvement in it can be credited to the intensified ARF exchanges on the subject. Some observers do not see the ARF as achieving anything useful in this area. However, one could say that, at the very least, the ARF has served as a framework and a multilateral forum for mutual and common awareness and understanding. It has conferred international legitimacy and bestowed regional sanction on cooperation in maritime security. Training in the ARF context may also have been useful. In any case, the chairman of the August 2007 ARF ministerial meeting declared in his statement, "The Ministers noted that incidents of piracy in the region and the Straits of Malacca have decreased substantially in recent years, in large part due to cooperation among the littoral states." [45]

In the meantime, differences in views persist among ARF participants on certain issues related to dealing with maritime security. One is where to find the right balance between the interests of the users of the maritime channels for commercial and military vessels and the concerns over national sovereignty on the part of littoral states. Su Hao, a professor at the Foreign Affairs University in Beijing, affirmed the sovereign rights of the littoral states. However, he said, some of them lacked capacity, which the users could help them acquire.[46] Another issue is whether to conduct *joint* or simply *coordinated* maritime patrols. Joint patrols may operate under a common command and would allow "hot pursuit" by the assets of one country into the partner-country's territorial sea, while in coordinated patrols each country conducts patrols in its own territory but in coordination with the partner-country or countries. A third issue pertains to the measures taken at the port of origin to ensure the security and legitimacy of goods being shipped to a port in another country. There are also differences in the very definition of maritime security. One definition is a comprehensive one, going beyond piracy, armed robbery at sea and maritime terrorism to extend to the marine environment, shipboard-generated waste, oil spills, illegal fishing, and maritime law.

In August 2007, the ARF organized in Bali a "roundtable" discussion to "take stock" of maritime-security questions. Recognizing maritime security as a non-traditional security issue, the roundtable cited the main threats to it: sea piracy, armed robbery, overlapping maritime claims, territorial disputes, terrorism, environmental degradation, and the smuggling of goods and persons.

It took note of the lack of a common understanding of maritime security and the different national interests in it. In doing so, it laid emphasis on the need for respect for state sovereignty and adherence to international principles and laws when engaging in international cooperation and using technology   . I t cited the importance of information-sharing; inter-agency cooperation; mutual understanding, training, and capacity-building

Contending armies or warring factions within a country have often sown anti-personnel mines in battlefields. Many unexploded mines are left hidden in the soil long after the conflict, inter- or intra-state, has ended.   The v ast majority of the victims of explosions of mines in peacetime hav   e been civilians, including many children. Cambodia, an ASEAN member and ARF participant, has been among the most mine-infested nations in the world. To address this post-war scourge, the international community concluded the Convention on the P rohibition of the U se, S tockpiling, P roduction and Transfer of Anti-P ersonnel Mines and on their D   estruction in S eptember 1997. The document, called the O ttawa Convention after the city wher e most of the negotiations took place, was opened for signatur e in December of that y ear and enter ed into for ce in M arch 1999. ARF states have widely different policies on the convention and its purposes. S   etting aside the European Union, almost all, if not all, the members of which ae parties, only thirteen of the other twenty-six ARF participants ae parties to the convention. These differences had clearly emerged in the national statements on the issue made at the A pril 1997 ARF seminar on demining in P   almerston N orth, New Zealand.

More than eleven years after the conclusion of the O ttawa Convention, the ARF conducted in A pril 2008 a seminar on anti-personnel mines in Penang, Malaysia, expressly in order "to encourage more countries to become parties to the 1997 Ottawa Convention". With eighteen, or only two-thirds, of the ARF' s tw enty-seven par ticipants in attendance, [47] the seminar hear d presentations b y r epresentatives of the UN and of non-go   vernmental organizations, including the G eneva International Centre for Humanitarian Demining, the I nternational Campaign to B   an Landmines, and the International Committee of the R ed C ross, as well as appeals fr   om ARF parties for the participants that had not done so to accede to the convention. Evidently, the seminar succeeded neither in gaining mor e accessions nor in reconciling the differences among the ARF par ticipants. Its summary record claimed that " the seminar has fulfilled its objectiv es", but all it could say in support of this asser tion was that it had " opened up ways to continue the exchange of experiences initiated by this meeting".[48] The efforts of some ARF participants to gain further accessions to the anti-personnel mines conention failed because of the basic policy differences that persisted between them and the hold-outs on the issue of anti-personnel mines.

CIVILIAN UNDERTAKINGS AND NON-TRADITIONAL SECURITY

The ARF has been turning increasing attention to the so-called non-traditional, non-military security problems, as it has become clearer that the forum does not have a substantive r ole in dealing with the mor e traditional sour ces of conflict and political instability in the Asia-P acific, like the nuclear pr oblem in N orth Korea, the Ta wan question, the conflicting claims on the S outh China S ea, and bilateral territorial disputes. The gr eater attention to non-traditional, non-military security has come with the gro wing acceptance of the notion of "human security " as transcending inter-state conflict. I n ARF practice, the non-traditional, non-military security threats include international terrorism, transnational crime, contagious diseases, illicit drugs, and, most recently, energy shor tages.

Most ARF par ticipants regar d terr orism generally as a matter of law enforcement for the police and other civilian authorities to deal with rather than as an " enemy" against which a " war" is to be waged b y the militar y. Nevertheless, military personnel, equipment and institutions play important roles in some of the larger measur es against terr orism.

Not surprisingly, the ARF gav e intense attention to terrorism as an international and regional security threat after the 11 September 2001 terrorist attacks on the U nited S tates. To be sure, there had been befor e then serious acts of terrorism in the world, including in the Asia-Pacific, since the forum's formation. Yet, until S eptember 2001, the r ecords of the ARF ministerial meetings and of the ISG-CBM sho w no mention of terr orism as a security threat, not ev en in the context of transnational crime. I ndeed, the ARF Experts G roup M eeting (EGM) on Transnational C rime, convened in Singapore in April 2000, in Seoul in October 2000 and in Kuala Lumpur in April 2001, did not seem to have discussed terrorism at all, although the ISG-CBM in April 2001 mentioned it as one of the transnational crimes that the ARF would deal with in a different format in the future. (The ARF officially disbanded the EGM on Transnational Crime in J uly 2001,[49] only to set up another body, the I ntersessional M eeting on Counter-terr orism and Transnational Crime, less than a y ear later, that is, after the terrorist attacks on the U nited States.[50])

The extraordinary significance of the events of 11 S eptember 2001 in terms of security perceptions clearly arose from those events' dramatic nature, their sheer scale, the siz e and po wer of the nation assaulted, the number of victims, and the variety of their nationalities, as w ell as the sense that they aroused of lurking danger in one 's midst. The transnational and largely anonymous character of terr orism has added to this sense of hidden peril.

Three and a half weeks after 11 S   eptember 2001, P rince M ohamed Bolkiah, for eign minister of B runei D arussalam and ARF chairman at the time, issued a short statement on behalf of all ARF participants condemning the terrorist attacks in the U nited States. It also called for " concerted action to protect and defend all peoples and the peace and security of the world   " against the "threat of international terrorism", while addressing "the underlying causes of this phenomenon".[51] This had been preceded by a similar statement jointly issued on 12 S eptember 2001 (still 11 S eptember in the Western Hemisphere) by the European Union's Trade Commissioner and the ASEAN Economic Ministers, who had been meeting in Hanoi at that time. [52]

The ARF statement was follo wed by a flurr y of terr orism-related inter-sessional activities. These have included wor kshops on financial measur es against terr orism in M arch 2002, on the pr evention of terr orism the next month, and on counter-terr orism measures in October; the issuance b y the chair (Brunei Darussalam) in July 2002 of an ARF statement urging specific measures against terr orist financing; another ARF statement issued by the chair (Cambodia) condemning the terrorist attacks in Bali in October 2002; and a "CBM workshop" in J une 2003 on "managing the consequences of a major terr orist attack ", including " structural collapse ", urban sear ch and rescue, medical treatment of casualties, forensic investigation, and the challenges posed by chemical, biological and radiological w eapons. These activities ran in parallel with similar ones in ASEAN, APEC and the Shanghai Cooperation Organization, among other forums.

The vulnerability of information-technology systems and physical infrastructure to terr orist " cyber" attack has been a subject of particular concern to ARF par ticipants. E very year since 2004 an ARF seminar or workshop — in J eju, South Korea, in Cebu, the P hilippines, in New Delhi, and in Busan, South Korea — has been devoted to " cyber terrorism". These gatherings considered "cyber" both as a target and as a tool, with national and international "cyber" systems and physical infrastructure being vulnerable to terrorist attack and with terrorists using "cyber" tools as weapons of terrorism. The participants discussed national programmes for the use of technology for "cyber" security and advocated international cooperation for this purpose. Issues of cooperation and coordination, internationally and within countries, were examined. A common definition of " cyber terrorism", ho wever, has continued to be elusive. The 2007 seminar in Busan proposed the establishment of a "virtual working group ... to facilitate the r eal time ex change of thr eat and vulnerability assessments" and for "substantial cooperation" against "cyber terrorism". The 2008 ARF ministerial meeting "welcomed the establishment of the Virtual Meeting of Experts on Cyber Security and Cyber Terrorism", as it was eventually named. However, it stressed that participation in it would be voluntary, thus signifying a continuing discomfor t on the par t of some ARF participants with the notion of " cyber terrorism".[53]

On the occasion of the 2006 ARF ministerial meeting, the M alaysian chair had issued a statement on " cooperation in fighting cyber attack and terrorist misuse of cyber space ". The statement urged ARF participants to enact laws and adopt policy framewor ks on cyber crime and cyber security and to cooperate among themselv es in this r egard.

After the 2001 terrorist assault on the United States, the ARF created the Intersessional Meeting cn Counter-terrorism and Transnational Crime (ISM-CTTC). By folding terrorism into transnational crime, the forum highlighted the civilian nature of anti-terrorist measures and the character of terrorism as a matter of law enfor cement. Indeed, ASEAN bodies hav e been listing terrorism as a transnaticnal crime and as a " non-traditional security issue " with increasing frequency. Convened annually since 2003, the ISM-CT TC has ser ved as a venue for ex changing perspectives on terr orism and other transnational crimes and for sharing experiences and national measues in the fight against them. Terrorism, however, has been the ISMs central and almost exclusive pre-occupation.

Each ISM-CTTC has had a dominant theme and subject, all of them having to do with terrorism. The first one, in 2003, dwelt on bor der security, dealing with the mo vement of people, the mo vement of goods, and document security. The second, in 2004, focused on securing transpot facilities — land, sea, air and multi-modal — against terr orist attacks without obstructing international trade. The 2005 ISM-CT TC called for the sharing of information and intelligence. S ome participants pointed to the sensitiv e natur e of such ex changes, suggesting that they begin with bilateral arrangements at the strategic, as distinct fr om the tactical, lev el. That meeting also stressed the impor tance of international cooperation in law enforcement, including particularly among the police forces. The 2006 ISM covered the question of "root causes", counter-terrorism strategies and measures, capacity-building for emergency r esponse, and information sharing. The 2007 ISM in S ingapore, in effect, took on the natur e of an inter-civilization dialogue, with non-governmental personalities taking part, and was billed as such. Although it was obser ved that such dialogues normally involved only those who alr eady believed in them, undertaking them was r egarded as useful for impro ving inter-civilization r elations, for sending the right messages to outside gr oups, and, not least, for understanding one's own civilisation, and thus helping to combat terrorism. The 2008 ISM, in S emarang, I ndonesia, br ought transnational crimes other than terrorism into the pur view of the body, its theme being "social participation in countering terr orism and transnational crime ". Social participation meant the inv olvement of the media and the public.

Each ISM-CTTC also drafted a statement on terr orism (except for the drugs-related one in 2008) that the subsequent ARF ministerial meeting adopted — Cooperative Counter-terrorist Action on Border Security, which the ministers issued in 2003, S trengthening Transport S ecurity Against International Terrorism in 2004, I nformation S haring and I ntelligence Exchange and D ocument Integrity and Security in E nhancing Cooperation to Combat Terrorism and Other Transnational Crimes in 2005, Promoting a People-centred Approach to Counter-terrorism in 2006, Promotion of Inter-civilization Dialogue in 2007, and Promoting Collaboration on the Prevention of Diversion of P recursors into I llicit Drug Manufacture in 2008.

More broadly, the ISM-CTTC has stressed certain principles that r un through ARF discussions on terrorism. O ne of them is that, while acts of terrorism are to be condemned and ar e never justified, their "root causes" must be addressed, "root causes" being a code phrase for the grievances and conditions that are considered to give rise to terrorism, usually in reference to I slamic terr orism. I t is pointed out, ho wever, that ther e is no ARF consensus on the nature of the " root causes": ar e they r eligion, po verty, injustice, alienation, the U.S. policy on the M iddle East, or all of them at once? Nor is there agreement on whether and how they are to be taken into account. At the same time, terr orism is not to be associated with any religion or ethnic gr oup.

At the F ebruary 2008 ISM-CTTC, the U nited States proposed a work plan for counter-terrorism and transnational crime to build regional capacity in counter-terrorism and to focus the ARF effor ts on concrete cooperation". After other par ticipants had giv en their comments and the U nited S tates revised the pr oposal, the ministers expr essed their support for the proposed work plan at their July 2008 meeting and asked the senior officials to flesh it out. The wor k plan should giv e gr eater coherence and purpose to ISM-CTTC activities; having been initiated b y the U nited S tates, it might be expected to featur e anti-terrorist elements pr ominently.

Like other ARF inter-sessional events, the gatherings to pr omote anti-terrorist cooperation hav e helped to r efine the participants ' grasp of the problem and its complex facets and sharpen their appreciation of one another's perceptions. They have pr ovided a regional framewor k for less-than-region-wide operational cooperation. S uch cooperation seems to have been largely effective in dealing with terrorism in Southeast Asia, although it is undertaken outside the ARF.

In expanding its concerns to non-traditional security issues, par ticularly in relation to pr eventive diplomacy, the ARF has v entured into ar eas that neither par take of a militar y or quasi-militar y natur e nor involv e militar y equipment or personnel. Among such areas in which the ARF has organized inter-sessional activities have been health, narcotics and energy .

As early as N ovember 1998, Beijing hosted a symposium on tr opical hygiene and tr opical infectious ciseases. H owever, that was the ARF' s only purely civilian inter-sessional foray into the health field and has not been repeated since then. As recalled above, a seminar was organized in September 2006 in Hanoi on SARS, avian influenza and other contagious diseases; but that was in terms of civilian-military cooperation. It is to be noted that when the SARS epidemic actually struck several ARF participants, including Canada, China, Singapore and Vietnam, in 2003, the ARF was not inv olved at all in the cooperation that took place among the ASEAN countries and China with the support of the World Health Organization and of individual countries.

Another non-traditional security thr eat that the ARF has faced is that posed by illicit dr ugs — their manufactur e, the traffic in them, and the addiction to them. China has hosted two seminars on this subject. The first, in September 2004 in Kunming, Yunnan, China, was on "alternative development", meaning the cultivation of crops as alternatives to what are called "drug crops" like opium poppy, its benefits, and the difficulties attendant to it. A seminar on narcotics control followed three years later, in Xi'an, Shaanxi, China. It pursued the subject of alternative development, but this time in the br oader context of countries' economic and social dev elopment. I t also dealt with cooperation among law enforcement agencies, demand reduction, and public awareness of, education on and participation in dr ugs-related programmes.

The ARF ventured into another civilian area, that of energy security, by holding seminars on it in Brussels in October 2006 and in Singapore in April 2008. The wide-ranging discussions co vered such elements as the safety of energy transport, diversification of the energy mix, and the dev elopment of alternative sources of energy.

SECURITY PERCEPTIONS

On a broader scale, the ARF has organized conferences and workshops on security perceptions and security policy, which are pertinent to both civil and militar y sectors and often requir e cooperation and coor dination between them.

China hosted in November 2004 the first ARF Security Policy Conference. It highlighted certain policy principles governing security cooperation in the Asia-Pacific. While acknowledging that traditional security issues, notably the Korean situation and the proliferation of weapons of mass destruction, continued to pose threats to an otherwise stable regional security environment, the conference called for stepping up cooperation on non-traditional security concerns. The chairman's statement of that conference listed some of these concerns as "terrorism, ... small arms smuggling, trafficking in drugs and persons, illegal immigrants, smuggling, maritime security, and money laundering", highlighting the need for cooperation on terrorism and maritime security. The conference was said to have discussed "non-traditional security threats as a common ground to build concrete cooperation" and the use, "within national legal frameworks", of national armed forces in combating such threats.[54]

Subsequent security-policy conferences, held annually since they were initiated in Beijing, pursued these principles, with each having a distinct focus. The 2005 conference, in Vientiane, discussed the link between terrorism and weapons of mass destruction. Drawing lessons from the 2004 tsunami, it examined the role of armed forces in disaster response. The 2006 conference, in Karambunai, Sabah, Malaysia, dwelt on maritime security and peacekeeping operations. The Manila conference in 2007 went over the role of armed forces in non-traditional security issues in general and the legal frameworks for participation in international peacekeeping operations. The one in Singapore in 2008 focused, according to its report, on "practical cooperation in areas of common interest", giving as an example "disaster preparedness and emergency response". It discussed energy security and maritime security. Significantly, the Singapore conference looked into the linkage between the availability of energy and access to energy sources on the one hand and regional peace, stability and security on the other.

In the meantime, a workshop had taken place in June 2005 in Uleanbaatar, Mongolia's capital, in which the participants discussed specifically the evolution of the Asia-Pacific countries' security perceptions in response to significant changes in the international and regional security environment. The workshop's summary report, however, indicated continuing disagreement on what constituted "non-traditional security issues".

THE ARF PROCESS

Some ARF inter-sessional events have dealt with the development of the ARF itself. The annual ARF ministerial meetings, with the advice of the ARF

Senior Officials Meeting and the ISG-CBM/PD, make the decisions on the nature, pace and manner of the ARF's evolution. However, inter-sessional gatherings, including those on Track Two, provide ideas and proposals. Most have had to do with the progression towards preventive diplomacy.

Three ARF Track Two seminars on preventive diplomacy took place in three successive years before the issuance of the paper on the ARF Concept and Principles of Preventive Diplomacy in 2001. The seminars did not dwell narrowly on the ARF process but consisted of wide-ranging discussions on the very concept of preventive diplomacy.[55]

In May 1995, less than a year after the first ARF ministerial meeting, a seminar on preventive diplomacy was convened in Seoul, reflecting the eagerness of some participants in both Tracks One and Two to move on to the second stage of the ARF's evolution, as envisioned in the ARF Concept Paper,[56] or at least to anticipate it. Mely Caballero-Anthony summarized the results of the seminar:

> The Seoul meeting generated specific proposals on measures of preventive diplomacy and these included, among others: (1) the establishment of a Conflict Prevention or Risk Reduction Centre; (2) the establishment by the ARF of a register of experts; (3) official discussion on the principles of peaceful dispute settlement; and (4) the use of Eminent Persons in mediation efforts.[57]

The Seoul meeting was followed a year later by the seminar in Paris discussed in Chapter 4 of this book. In addition to the measures proposed in Seoul, which it embraced, the Paris seminar recommended the publication of an annual security outlook, the organization of a regional research and information centre, the setting up of an early warning system, confidence-building measures, the good offices of the ARF chair, and the establishment of an ARF unit.

A third conference took place in Singapore in September 1997. According to its summary, the conference made two points:

- Confidence-building measures are an element of preventive diplomacy and have the best prospect of success in the near term. Efforts, therefore, should be focused on them.
- Preventive diplomacy is, in fact, taking place in Southeast Asia, with the workshops on the South China Sea and ASEAN diplomacy on the Cambodian situation (featuring armed skirmishes between the forces of the then co-Prime Ministers, Hun Sen and Prince Norodom Ranariddh) as examples.

The difficulty of moving to the preventive-diplomacy phase of the ARF was illustrated at the confer ence when the par ticipants could not ev en agree on the application of pr eventive diplomacy to maritime-navigation issues.

Following the adoption by the ARF ministers in J uly 2001 of the paper on the ARF Concept and P rinciples of P reventive Diplomacy, a Track Two workshop in Tokyo in M arch 2004 discussed the concept of pr eventive diplomacy and " concrete measur es to wards (its) implementation ". The co-chairs' summary specified these measur es as the enhancement of the role of the ARF chair, the creation of the ARF U nit in the ASEAN S ecretariat, the role of the Experts and Eminent Persons, and strengthened links with Track Two. The workshop stressed the impor tance of "transnational problems" as "new threats", listing among them international terr orism, trafficking in arms, drugs and persons, contagious diseases, piracy, and the proliferation of weapons of mass destruction, although none of them was really so "new". In a r evealing pr esentation, China expr essed its prefer ence for the ARF to remain as a venue for " political and security dialogue " and for ASEAN to retain its lead part in developing preventive diplomacy, stressing that these are themselves "concrete measures in pr eventive diplomacy".[58]

The record of adoption and implementation of the recommendations of these Track Two meetings on preventive diplomacy is mixed. The ARF Unit is in place in the ASEAN S ecretariat, although on a small scale. The compilations of r egional-security outlooks have been issued annually . Confidence-building measures have been pursued. Attention has been shifted to non-traditional, non-militar y security thr eats. H owever, no conflict-prevention or risk-r eduction centre has been established. N o early-warning system has been set up . The "good offices" of the ARF chair have not been exercised. A register of E xperts and Eminent P ersons has been put together, but their ser vices have not been used.

The apparent reality is that, as pointed out in Chapter 4, ARF participants are willing to engage in cooperativ e activities that deal with non-traditional, non-military security issues that are thr eats to all, but cannot be dir ected at anyone in par ticular, and on which geo-strategic inter ests do not clash and may even converge. However, some seek to bar the application of preventive diplomacy beyond confidence-building measures to, say, mediation in possible inter-state conflicts or internal turmoil.

CONCLUSION

Media co verage of and, hence, public attention to the ARF ar e almost exclusively devoted to the annual meeting of ARF foreign ministers, held on the occasion of the mid-y ear ASEAN for eign ministers' meeting. This is because of the presence of the American and, to a lesser extent, the Japanese, Chinese, I ndian, A ustralian and N orth K orean for eign ministers and the expectation, often generated by the media themselves, of some breakthrough in the "hot" issue of the day When the expectation is disappointed, as it often is, the ARF is derided as nothing but a conclav e of ministers sitting ar ound in easy chairs and talking among themselv es. The media and the public ar e then treated to a bland 'chairman's statement" that says little, at least to those too impatient to analyse it.

In fact, much ARF activity goes on betw een ministerial meetings throughout the y ear. The ARF senior officials meet two or thr ee months before the ministerial meeting to pr epare the gr ound for the ministers. The ISG-CBM/PD convenes twice a year The senior defence officials get together on several occasions during the y ear. The heads of defence educational institutions convene on their o wn every year. CSCAP also meets as a Track Two institution. All these bodies discuss security issues similar to those covered by the ministerial meeting, only in greater detail. They analyse issues, state positions, shar e insights, and make r ecommendations. Confer ences, seminars and workshops are conducted on specific security issues, which have increasingly come to include those of the non-traditional kind.

The subjects of these gatherings co ver an enormous range. E ither they present themselves as ob vious objects of regional security policy and cooperation, like nuclear pr oliferation, terr orism and maritime security , or they are proposed by a cer tain ARF participant or par ticipants for for eign-policy or domestic political considerations. The topics hav e ranged fr om nuclear proliferation, in general or in terms of the possible use of nuclear weapons by terr orists, to missile defence, fr om the traffic in small arms and light weapons to anti-personnel mines. Peacekeeping operations, responses to natural disasters, and search and r escue have been the subjects both of discussions and of training and desk-top ex ercises. So have various elements of maritime security and anti-terrorism measur es. Increasingly, the ARF has gone into purely civilian, non-traditional security areas like infectious diseases, drug trafficking and " alternative dev elopment", and energy security . Conferences have also taken place on security policy and on the ARF process itself, mainly its pr ogression to the pr eventive-diplomacy stage.

An examination of these inter-sessional activities in their temporal setting reveals cer tain patterns. O ne is the steady incr ease in the sheer number of such activities. S etting aside the policy-making for ums — the ministerial meeting, the ARF SOM, the ISG-CBM/PD, and the defence officials meetings (which star ted in 2001–02) — two inter-sessional activities took place in each of the years 1995–96 and 1997–98 and three in 1996–97, while 14 were carried out in 2007–08. Another is that the ARF has continued to work together, or at least hold discussions, on military-related matters — not those that have to do with actual or potential conflict, but those in which the ARF participants have interests in common — maritime security capacity-building for peacekeeping operations, disaster response, the proliferation of weapons of mass destruction, international terrorism, small arms and light weapons, and civilian-military cooperation. The third pattern reflects the apparently growing acceptance of non-traditional, non-military problems as proper subjects for the ARF's attention. Thus, as early as 1998–99, a symposium on tropical hygiene and infectious diseases took place. Since then, similar activities dealing with economic security, energy security, illicit drugs, and other transnational crimes have been carried out.

One finds that the ARF as a body does not get involved in the operational phase even of accepted regional security cooperation, like responding to natural disasters, search and rescue, counter-terrorism and law enforcement, securing maritime trade and travel, and the control of infectious diseases. Such involvement requires a certain level of mutual trust and the regional institutions that mutual trust makes possible. Mutual suspicions will persist as long as the major powers perceive their strategic interests as substantially divergent. Thus, operational matters are invariably left, at least so far, to bilateral or trilateral cooperation. The ARF's non-involvement in operational activities has elicited for the forum the dismissive characterization of being just a "talk shop".

What the ARF as a forum does do, however, is give international legitimacy and a regional framework, context and sanction to operational-level security cooperation. The expositions of positions and the exchanges of perceptions and insights should help to develop mutual understanding and build a degree of mutual confidence. The personal networks that form in the frequent interactions of ARF participants, whether on Track One or on Track Two, should also help. The ARF statements and declarations issued on individual concerns project common positions arrived at by the worlds great powers and their associates in the Asia-Pacific, sending powerful messages to the international community. The increasing attention to non-traditional security issues as common threats should contribute to the development of a sense of common purpose among the participants. The ARF process and ways of doing things could serve to cultivate habits of consultation and dialogue as the preferred method of managing, if not resolving, disagreements. The training that some inter-sessional activities provide and the technical assistance that others offer should be useful to those who seize the opportunity.

As a for um on r egional security that inv olves all the countries of the region and all the major powers of the world, the ARF is a unique phenomenon. It should not be asked — and cannot be expected — to change its character abruptly as an association of gr eat, medium and small so vereign po wers whose interests do not necessarily coincide. The grounds for agr eement and common inter ests, ho wever, should gradually expand, as they ar e, in fact, doing in the only way they can — slo wly.

Notes

1. The ARF Unit of the ASEAN S ecretariat has on its Web site a compr ehensive, up-to-date, although not necessarily exhaustiv e, list of such activities. S ee <http://www.aseanregionalforum.org/PublicLibrary/ARFActivities/ ListofARFTrackIActivitiesBySubject/tabid/94/Default.aspx>. Rizal S ukma, Deputy Ex ecutive of the Centr e for S trategic and I nternational S tudies in Jakarta, in an interview with the author in Jakarta on 13 July 2007, urged more effective outreach to the media on the part, presumably, of the ARF Unit in the ASEAN S ecretariat. Ibnu H adi, D irector for Intra-R egional Cooperation of Asia-Pacific and Africa at I ndonesia's Department of Foreign Affairs, made the same point in an inter view with the author in J akarta on 16 J uly 2007, while pointing to the ARF's lack of institutions for following through on its decisions. Ralf Emmers of the S. Rajaratnam School of I nternational Studies at Nanyang Technological Unive rsity in S ingapore did the same in an inter view with the author on 12 N ovember 2007.
2. "Chairman's S tatement: The S econd ASEAN R egional F orum, B andar S eri Begawan, Brunei Darussalam, 1 August 1995", in *The ASEAN Regional Forum Documents Series 1994–2006* (Jakarta: ASEAN Secretariat, March 2007), p. 11, para. 11.4. Also in A ppendix B and in <http://www .aseanregionalforum.org/ PublicLibrary/ ARFChairmansStatementsandReports/ChairmansStatementofthe 1stMeetingoftheASE'tabid/201/Default.aspx>, para. 11.
3. "Chairman's Statement: The Third ASEAN Regional Forum, Jakarta, Indonesia, 23 J uly 1996", in *The ASEAN Regional Forum Documents Series 1994–2006*, p. 25, para 7(ii). Also in <http://www .aseanregionalforum.org/PublicLibrary/ ARFChairmansStatementsandReports/ChairmansStatementofthe3rdARF/tabid/ 196/Default.aspx>.
4. Appendix D.
5. The four ar e France, Russia, the U nited Kingdom and the U nited S tates. The fifth, China, has expr essed its r eadiness to sign the pr otocol at any time, knowing that ther e will be nothing to sign until the other four r ecognized nuclear-weapon states have agreed with the Southeast Asian parties on its terms.
6. <http://www.fas.org/nuke/control/seanwfz/text/seasiapr.htm> (Art. 2).
7. "Seminar on N on-proliferation", in *The ASEAN Regional Forum Documents*

Series 1994–2006, pp . 79–81. Also in <http://www .aseanregionalforum.org/
LinkClick.aspx?fileticket=RY4qiLjwQXo%3d&tabid= 66&mid=414>.

8. <http://www.fas.org/news/india/1998/05/98051501_npo.html> and <http://
www.fas.org/news/pakistan/1998/05/98052906_tpo.html>.

9. <http://www.undemocracy.com/S-1998-473.pdf>.

10. <http://daccessdds.un.org/doc/UNDOC/GEN/N98/158/60/PDF/
N9815860.pdf?OpenElement>.

11 "Chairman 's S tatement: The F ifth ASEAN R egional F orum, M anila, the
Philippines, 27 J uly 1998", in *The ASEAN Regional Forum Documents Series
1994–2006*, p. 89, para. 21. Also in <http://www   .aseanregionalforum.org/
PublicLibrary/ARFChairmansStatementsandReports/ChairmansStatement
ofthe5thMeetingoftheASE/tabid/180/Default.aspx>.

12. "Chairman's Statement: The Sixth ASEAN Regional Forum, Singapore, 26 July
1999", in *The ASEAN Regional Forum Documents Series 1994–2006*, p . 128,
para. 13. Also in <http://www   .aseanregionalforum.org/PublicLibrary/ARF
ChairmansStatementsandReports/ChairmansStatementofthe6thMeeting
oftheASE/tabid/177/Default.aspx>.

13. Alex Wagner: "B ush Waives N uclear-Related Sanctions on I ndia, Pakistan", in
Arms Control Today (Washington, D.C.: Arms Control Association, O ctober
2001). See <http://www.armscontrol.org/act/2001_10/sanctionsoct01>.

14. <http://www.america.gov/st/washfile-english/2005/July/20050718191301
cpataruK0.5283625.html>.

15. <http://www.whitehouse.gov/news/releases/2006/03/20060302-5.html>.

16. <http://www.armscontrol.org/projects/India/20060306_Singh_Statement.asp>.

17. <http://www.america.gov/st/washfile-english/2005/July/20050718191301
cpataruK0.5283625.html>.

18. <http://www.iaea.org/NewsCenter/News/2008/board010808.html>.

19. Reuters, "India Nuclear Trade Waiver Approved", in <http://www.nytimes.com/
reuters/world/international-nuclear-india-suppliers.html?hp>.

20. "ARF Statement on Non-proliferation", in *The ASEAN Regional Forum Documents
Series 1994–2006*, pp . 345–47. Also in <http://www   .aseanregional
forum.org/PublicLibrary/ARFChairmansStatementsandReports/
TheEleventhASEANRegionalForum20032004/tabid/68/Default.aspx>.

21. <http://daccessdds.un.org/doc/UNDOC/GEN/N04/328/43/PDF/
N0432843.pdf?OpenElement>.

22. "Chairman's Statement: The Twelfth ASEAN R egional Forum, Vientiane, Lao
PDR, 29 J uly 2005", in *The ASEAN Regional Forum Documents Series 1994–
2006*, pp . 357–58, and in <http://www .aseansec.org/17642.htm>, para. 26,
"Chairman's Statement: The Thirteenth ASEAN Regional Forum, Kuala Lumpur,
Malaysia, 28 July 2006", in *The ASEAN Regional Forum Documents Series 1994–
2006*, p . 434, and in <http://www .aseansec.org/18599.htm>, para. 32, and
"Chairman's Statement: 14th ASEAN Regional Forum, Manila, 2 August 2007"
in <http://www.aseansec.org/20807.htm>, para. 31.

23. "Chairman's Statement of the 15th ASEAN Regional Forum, Singapore, 24 July 2008", in <http://www.aseansec.org/21816.htm>, para. 29.

24. <http://www.aseanregionalforum.org/LinkClick.aspx?fileticket=RbahNhjo2E8%3d&tabid=66&mid=940>, para. 31.

25. Mely Caballero-Anthony, head of the Centre for Non-traditional Security Studies at the S. Rajaratnam School of International Studies, Nanyang Technological University, Singapore, in an interview with the author in Singapore on 10 July 2008, pointed out that peacekeeping operations no wadays almost invariably deal with "human security", noting that food, water, the environment, health and migration have become potential or actual sources of conflict.

26. "Co-chairmen's Summary Report of the ARF CBM Workshop on Peace Arrangements Ensuring Stability and Security in the Region, Including Civil-Military Cooperation, Tokyo, Japan, 22–23 March 2005", in *The ASEAN Regional Forum Documents Series 1994–2006*, pp. 375–79.

27. <http://www.aseanregionalforum.org/LinkClick.aspx?fileticket=T%2b0XBqj4oz0%3d&tabid=66&mid=401>.

28. "Chairman's Statement of the 15th ASEAN Regional Forum Singapore, 24 July 2008", in <http://www.aseansec.org/21816.htm>, para. 8.

29. Ibid., para. 8a.

30. The 1982 UN Convention on the Law of the Sea defines piracy as being carried out "for private ends ... in a place outside the jurisdiction of any State" (Art. 101). The International Maritime Bureau's broader definition, although not recognized under international law, embraces attacks on ships wherever they are.

31. <http://www.iccwbo.org/iccbghna/index.html>.

32. "ASEAN Regional Forum Statement of Cooperation Against Piracy and Other Threats to Maritime Security", 17 June 2003, in *The ASEAN Regional Forum Documents Series 1994–2006*, pp. 269–72. Also in <http://www.aseanregionalforum.org/PublicLibrary/ARFChairmansStatementsandReports/ARFStatementonCooperationAgainstPiracyandOt/tabid/78/Default.aspx>.

33. Amitav Acharya, *A New Regional Order in South-East Asia: ASEAN in the Post-Cold War Era* (London: Brassey's for the International Institute for Strategic Studies, Adelphi Paper 279, 1993), p. 37.

34. <http://www.icc-ccs.org/prc/piracy_maps_2006.php>.

35. Adam J. Young and Mark J. Valencia, "Conflation of Piracy and Terrorism in Southeast Asia: Rectitude and Utility", *Contemporary Southeast Asia* 25, no. 2 (2003): 271.

36. <http://www.icc-ccs.org/index.php?option=com_content&view=article&id=332:imb-reports-unprecedented-rise-in-maritime-hijackings&catid=60:news&Itemid=51>.

37. Joshua Ho, "The Importance and Security of Regional Sea Lanes", in *Maritime Security in Southeast Asia*, edited by Kwa Chong Guan and John K. Skogan (London and New York: Routledge, 2007), p. 22.

38. Barry Desker, "Re-thinking the Safety of Navigation in the Malacca Strait", in *Maritime Security in Southeast Asia*, edited by Kwa Chong Guan and John K. Skogan (London and New York: Routledge, 2007), p. 14.

39. Joshua Ho, "The Security of Regional Sea Lanes", IDSS Working Paper No. 81 (Singapore: Institute of Defence and Strategic Studies, Nanyang Technological University, June 2005), p. 10.

40. Martin N. Murphy, *Contemporary Piracy and Maritime Terrorism*, Adelphi Paper No. 388 (London: International Institute for Strategic Studies, 2007), p. 45.

41. "Regional Cooperation in Maritime Security", in *Navy News* (Singapore: Republic of Singapore Navy, February 2005), p. 3.

42. Young and Valencia, op. cit., pp. 274–77.

43. "Piracy Surge Raises Terrorism Concerns", in *International Herald Tribune*, 26 November 2008.

44. "ASEAN Regional Forum Maritime Security Shore Exercise, 22–23 January 2007, Singapore: Chairman's Report".

45. "Chairman's Statement: The Fourteenth ASEAN Regional Forum, Manila, the Philippines", in <http://www.aseanregionalforum.org/LinkClick.aspx?fileticket=RbahNhjo2E8%3d&tabid=66&mid=940>, para. 30.

46. Interview by the author, Beijing, 19 September 2007.

47. Australia, Bangladesh, Brunei Darussalam, Cambodia, Canada, China, European Union, India, Indonesia, Japan, the Republic of Korea, Malaysia, New Zealand, Pakistan, the Philippines, Singapore, Thailand and Vietnam were represented.

48. "Co-chairs' Summary Record of the ASEAN Regional Forum (ARF) Seminar on Anti-personnel Mines, 8–10 April 2008, Penang, Malaysia" (unpublished document).

49. "Chairman's Statement: The Eighth ASEAN Regional Forum, Ha Noi, Viet Nam, 25 July 2001", in *The ASEAN Regional Forum Documents Series 1994–2006*, p. 193. Also in <http://www.aseanregionalforum.org/LinkClick.aspx?fileticket=w%2fMjx3xLGRU%3d&tabid=66&mid=410>, para. 34.

50. "Chairman's Statement: The Ninth ASEAN Regional Forum, Bandar Seri Begawan, Brunei Darussalam, 31 July 2001", in *The ASEAN Regional Forum Documents Series 1994–2006*, p. 227. Also in <http://www.aseanregionalforum.org/PublicLibrary/ARFChairmansStatementsandReports/ChairmansStatementofthe9thMeetingoftheASE/tabid/88/Default.aspx>, para. 14.

51. "Statement by the Chairman of the ARF on the Terrorist Acts of the 11th September 2001, Bandar Seri Begawan, Brunei Darussalam, 4 October 2001", in *The ASEAN Regional Forum Documents Series 1994–2006*, p. 253. Also in <http://www.aseanregionalforum.org/PublicLibrary/ARFChairmansStatementsandReports/StatementbytheChairmanoftheASEANRegionalFo/tabid/108/Default.aspx>.

52. <http://www.aseansec.org/589.htm>.

53. <http://www.aseanregionalforum.org/LinkClick.aspx?fileticket=Hn4UnDG3WVY%3d&tabid=66&mid=1009>, para. 37.

54. "Chairman's Summary of the First ARF Security Policy Conference, Beijing, China, 4–6 November 2004", in *The ASEAN Regional Forum Documents Series 1994–2006*, pp. 397–99.
55. The chairman's statements of the three seminars are reproduced in Desmond Ball and Amitav Acharya, eds., *The Next Stage: Preventive Diplomacy and Security Cooperation in the Asia-Pacific Region* (Canberra: Australian National University, 1999), pp. 279–91.
56. See Appendix A.
57. Mely Caballero-Anthony, *Regional Security in Southeast Asia: Beyond the ASEAN Way* (Singapore: Institute of Southeast Asian Studies, 2005), p. 135.
58. "Co-chairs' Summary of ARF Workshop on Preventive Diplomacy, Tokyo, Japan, 16–17 March 2004", in *The ASEAN Regional Forum Documents Series 1994–2006*, pp. 330–32. Also in <http://www.aseanregionalforum.org/Public Library/ARFChairmansStatementsandReports/CoChairsSummaryofARF WorkshoponPreventiveD/tabid/74/Default.aspx>.

6

DOES THE ARF NEED CENTRAL INSTITUTIONS?

The ASEAN R egional F orum has been, since 1994, a useful for um for foreign ministers and for senior officials, both fom the foreign ministries and the defence and other security agencies, to get together periodically for discussions on regional security in the Asia-P acific. In these gatherings, national positions on security issues, broad or specific, long-term or short-term, traditional or non-traditional, ar e pr esented and clarified, if not reconciled. There, valuable networ ks ar e formed. Kno wledge is shar ed. Common problems are identified. International cooperation on those problems is promoted. Participants and observers express the hope that these processes help build mutual confidence and diminish mutual suspicions and thus reduce the risk of miscalculation and ultimately of conflict.

However, some in the academic world and a few in government press the ARF to go beyond its curr ent minimalist r ole and do something directly to prevent conflict and even resolve disputes between states or between warring factions within countries. Failing in this, the ARF is derided as a "talk shop", as if an oppor tunity for rival po wers to hold r egular discussions and consultations had no value. Some profess to want to see results rather than be content with mere "process", which is what they consider the ARF to be.

For example, B ryan J. Couchman, a Visiting F ellow at Cambridge University, asserted:

> If China continues to incr ease the pressur e in the S outh China S ea by, for example, taking control of more territory claimed by one or more of the ASEAN states, the ARF is unlikely to present a coher ent stance, let

alone negotiate a solution to the problem. Likewise, a sudden deterioration in the situation on the Korean Peninsula could not be managed by the Forum. In either scenario, the ARF would most likely be shown to be a paper tiger and so lose credibility, especially if other smaller bilateral discussions and security alliance structures proved more useful in dealing with these disputes. [1]

On the other hand, one could argue that participation in the ARF could serve as a deterrent to a unilateral act of aggression. An ARF participant would think twice before upsetting a security environment from which it presumably benefited unless it felt that its core interests were threatened.

In any case, it is difficult to see how the ARF can undertake preventive diplomacy, whether with respect to traditional or non-traditional threats, or contribute directly to the resolution of conflicts without effective regional institutions to carry out the task. After the ARF has reached consensus on what needs to be done about this or that security threat — a difficult and rare enough achievement — who is to take action? Ong Keng Yong, former ASEAN Secretary-General, deplores the absence of what he calls "follow through" of ARF decisions. [2] His successor, Surin Pitsuwan, former Thai foreign minister, has noted that ARF decisions will have to be "followed through". [3]

The Institute of Defence and Strategic Studies at Nanyang Technological University in Singapore has categorically called for the establishment of an ARF secretariat. [4] Urging that the ARF Unit in the ASEAN Secretariat be strengthened, Nopadol Gunavibool, then ASEAN Director-General at Thailand's Ministry of Foreign Affairs and later Thai ambassador to Singapore, has argued that a regional outlook can come only from regional institutions. [5]

The report of the first meeting of the ARF Experts and Eminent Persons in June 2006 delicately pointed out:

> Despite its progress, the ARF lacks some of the institutional structure and cohesion among members to respond effectively to regional security concerns and challenges. Many participants agreed that it is time for the ARF to shift from a forum for discussion to more of an institution of implementation. Participants discussed two categories of changes: institutional and substantive. Institutional issues include enhancing the role of the ARF Chair, reexamining the leadership structure, creating a Secretariat, and strengthening relations with other multilateral and regional organizations, specifically the United Nations. [6]

It is clear in this account, with its reference to "many participants", that not all participants agree that the ARF should become " an institution of implementation". With little b y way of common strategic inter ests to bind the disparate participants together, they have scant incentive to build effectie central institutions and mechanisms to achiee common purposes in peventive diplomacy, much less in conflict resolution. There is always the fear that the regional institution will act too independently or , worse, ser ve as a tool of rival powers. Confidence-building still has a long way to go .

Nevertheless, the ARF has sought to establish certain minimal central institutions. It has resolved to "enhance" the role of the chair. It has tried to organize the "friends of the chair" to help the chair in its "enhanced" role. It has designated Experts and Eminent Persons to offer advice to the forum and its chair. An ARF U nit is in place and at wor k in the ASEAN S ecretariat, serving as a small secretariat for the forum. The ARF now has its own website, closely linked to that of the ASEAN Secretariat and accessible through it. The ARF Unit operates the site, which is open to the public but also has a page accessible only to authorized officials. The ARF no w has a fund to finance specific projects. Are these regional constructs, actual or proposed, adequate to move the forum from discussion, consultation, dialogue and confidence-building — valuable though these ar e — to pr eventive action and even conflict resolution? Are they enough to enable the ARF itself as distinct from its individual participants, to get involved in operational action on traditional or non-traditional security threats? Or do they merely conjure the illusion of movement but are actually without substance?

Perhaps, the way for ward lies in organizing institutions pragmatically , incrementally, informally, and sector-specific, provided they are acceptable to all as useful for meeting common needs. This is illustrated by the operation of a " shepherds" system for disaster r elief, in which A ustralia, China, the European Union, Indonesia, Malaysia and the United States have volunteered to ser ve as " shepherds" and lead the wor k of drawing up guidelines and standard operating procedures for ARF coordination in disaster relief and of conducting a desktop ex ercise for that purpose. The work plan that the United States proposed to the ISM on Counter-terrorism and Transnational Crime in F ebruary 2008 envisaged a system of shepher ds.[7]

THE CHAIR AND ITS FRIENDS

In the absence of permanent, effective r egional institutions with a certain degree of independence of action, the ARF has looked to its chairman to act as its agent between meetings. The ARF chair is also that of ASEAN, which rotates annually among the ASEAN foreign ministers in the usual alphabetical order. The chairmanship of the for um, as w ell as of ASEAN, used to be turned over immediately after the mid-year series of foreign ministers' meetings that include those of ASEAN and the ARF. On the basis of the new ASEAN Charter, the chairmanships are to coincide with the calendar year, so that, in the transition, Thailand chairs the ARF, as well as ASEAN, from July 2008 to December 2009.

The 1998 ARF ministerial meeting asked the I ntersessional Group on Confidence Building Measures (ISG-CBM) to consider " an enhanced r ole for the ARF Chairman, particularly the idea of a good offices role", as one of the proposed measur es straddling the confidence-building and pr eventive-diplomacy stages of the ARF' s evolution. The 1998–99 ISG-CBM defined the elements making up such a r ole as extending the chair 's good offices, "particularly in helping to promote tr ust and confidence among ARF participants", "liaising" with external parties, conducting "informal dialogue" with Track Two, and coor dinating activities between ministerial meetings, including the calling of special sessions and the issuance of statements. As Chapter 4 of this book discussed, the ISG-CBM hemmed in the chair with restricting conditions, holding him on a short leash. Chapter 4 also r ecalled how thr ee ARF chairmen sought to carr y out their " enhanced" r ole, with little effect.

As directed by the 1999 ARF S enior Officials Meeting, the ISG-CBM, meeting in N ovember 2000 and A pril 2001, discussed a paper on the "principles, procedures and mechanisms for the E nhanced Role of the ARF Chair". D rafted by Japan and subsequently r evised according to comments submitted by other participants, the paper was adopted by the ARF ministers at their 2001 meeting. Although it speaks of " enhancing" the ARF chair 's role, the document seeks to ensur e that that r ole is to be carried out within narrow, defined limits and always with the consent of all ARF participants. I t makes clear that the chair's role is to be confined to pr omoting the building of mutual confidence, easing information exchange and dialogue, facilitating discussion on " potential ar eas of cooperation " and on " norms building ", serving as a focal point for consultations, and "promoting the continuity and efficiency of the ARF process". The paper does envision the chair carrying out "good offices" and coor dination between ministerial meetings. I t sees the chair as "liaising with external parties ", but only informally, and after *prior consultation* with *all* ARF members and with their consent. S imilarly, the chair may convene "*ad hoc*" meetings (which it has never done) and "draw on the expertise and resources of external parties and Track II organisations", but with the *prior consent* of *all* ARF participants. The exchange of information that the chair is to encourage is to be pur ely voluntary. I n ever y case, the principles of international law and inter-state r elations ar e to be obser ved, including those enshrined in the UN Charter, the Five Principles of Peaceful Co-existence, and the Treaty of Amity and Cooperation in S outheast Asia, specifically "sovereign equality, territorial integrity, and non-inter ference in the internal affairs of a state ".[8]

Clearly, the paper on the Enhanced Role of the ARF Chair is the ppduct of a series of compromises betw een those who wish to see an activist ARF chair exercising diplomacy in potential conflict situations, as the EU pasidency sometimes does in its o wn continent, and those who pr efer to hav e such situations dealt with by the powers directly concerned. And then there is the ambiguity as to whether the chair is acting on behalf of ASEAN or on behalf of the ARF.

As part of the effort to "enhance" the role of the chair the ARF ministers, at their 2003 meeting, agreed to support the chair with " friends" assisting him "in dealing with international situations. In 2005, they formally decided to "establish 'Friends of the Chair' in the ARF". The ministers approved, at their 2007 meeting, the body 's terms of r eference, which had been initially drafted by the Philippines. The document specified the body's composition as the previous and next ARF chairs and the foreign minister of one of the non-ASEAN par ticipants, while giving the chair the pr erogative of deciding on "the specific composition of the FOC, depending on the issue at hand." However, the terms of reference made it clear that the " friends of the chair" would focus on confidence-building and "shall not be intervention-oriented" and that they wer e to be "an ad hoc group" and "advisory body" and "not a decision-making body". Evidently, some par ticipants had sought to pr event the emergence of a combination of 'friends of the chair" capable of colluding against those par ticipants' inter ests. I n any case, the " friends of the chair " have never been activated since the adoption of the terms of r eference.

The 2008 ARF ministerial meeting cr eated the position of ARF vice-chair. The vice-chair would be the foreign minister who was next in line to be in the ARF chair according to the ASEAN alphabetical order. Thus, the 2008 chairman's statement specified that Vietnam would be the vice-chair during Thailand's chairmanship. How the new position would serve the purposes of ARF institutionalization remains to be seen. [9]

EXPERTS AND EMINENT PERSONS

Another institution that the ARF has cr eated is the r egister of E xperts and Eminent Persons. The co-chairmen's report on the 1998–99 meetings of the ISG-CBM said, " The par ticipants agr eed in principle on the pr oposal to develop a register of experts/eminent persons to ser ve as a pool of r esources in CBMs and preventive diplomacy whose services would be made available to par ticipants in pr oviding non-binding pr ofessional advice and recommendations as well as to under take in-depth studies. I n addition, the ARF Chair at ministerial and SOM lev els and ISG/ISM Co-Chairs, upon concurrence from all par ticipants, might also r equest the experts/eminent persons to serve as resource persons at their respective meetings. Furthermore, some participants felt that the exper ts/eminent persons could play a useful advisory role in dev eloping preventive diplomacy ...." [10]

The May 2000 ARF senior officials' meeting gave the go-ahead for ARF participants to nominate experts and eminent persons pending the adoption of their terms of reference. The July 2000 ministerial meeting "welcomed the establishment" of the EEP register. At their July 2001 meeting, the ministers adopted the EEP s' terms of refer ence, which had been drawn up by the 2000–01 ISG-CBM co-chaired by M alaysia and S outh Korea. [11]

According to the terms of r eference, each ARF par ticipant-state may nominate up to five of its o wn nationals as EEP s. The terms of r eference specify the items to be r eflected in the r egister, mainly the personal circumstances, expertise and contact details of each EEP. The ARF chair is to manage the r egister. As for funding, the ARF participant that engages the services of the EEP s is to bear the costs involv ed. If the ARF chair r equests those services, he can "mobilize voluntary contributions" for the purpose.

The portion of the terms of references on "scope and procedures" places rather restrictiv e conditions on the EEP s' wor k, ensuring contr ol b y each ARF state over any EEP activity. The EEPs' views and recommendations are expressly to be " non-binding" and only on "issues of relev ance to their expertise". The EEPs can be "activated" only if none of the "concerned ARF participants" objects. The ARF chair is to share the findings of the EEPs with all ARF par ticipants.

The "guidelines" for the EEP that the July 2004 ARF ministerial meeting adopted further circumscribe the role and functions of the EEP s by limiting them to ARF interests and concerns that are "not being adequately addressed elsewhere and to which their exper tise is dir ectly applicable " and to the process of the ARF's evolution. The guidelines prohibit the publication of the EEPs' findings outside of the ARF . [12]

Going beyond being items on a r egister, the EEPs met as a body for the first time in J une 2006 on J eju Island in K orea. This was pursuant to the ministers' agreement at their July 2005 meeting to convene the EEPs. Among their eight recommendations, the EEPs sought operational roles for themselves — their use in fact-finding missions or as special envoys and their engagement in planning ex ercises r elated to international terr orism, maritime security , disaster management, pandemics and peacekeeping operations. A second meeting, in F ebruary 2007 in M anila, focused on r egional cooperation in Northeast Asia in non-traditional security matters and on v arious aspects of the management of the tensions in that ar   ea. The 2007 and 2008 ARF ministerial meetings adopted the " assessments" of the " practicability" of the EEP recommendations that the ARF SOM had undertaken upon the ministers instructions. The assessments have not been made public, and it may be too early to tell whether the EEP r ecommendations — and which ones — will actually be carried out.

In any case, as their terms of r eference and the " guidelines" go verning their functions make clear, the EEPs' role, as a body or as individuals, is of an advisory, rather than operational, natur e. Accordingly, the EEP s are, at the moment, no differ ent in r eality from CSCAP or ASEAN-ISIS, although at their first meeting they explicitly urged that their "   role and functions " be distinguished from those of the two advisor   y bodies dealing with ARF matters on Track Two. Nevertheless, it remains conceivable that, sometime in the future, the ARF will ask one or more of the EEPs to undertake operational duties on its behalf, but this would certainly be done on the basis of individual cases or issues and with all par   ticipants' consent, something difficult to imagine at this time. Like other ARF matters, it would depend on the dynamics of the relationships among the ARF's major participants, including ASEAN. I n the meantime, having a r   egister of EEP s on hand is useful, although the EEPs have limited functions so far .

THE ARF UNIT, ARFNET AND THE ARF FUND

In the early years of the ARF , no office in the ASEAN S ecretariat formally attended to ARF affairs, or to any other subject dealing with security . From the beginning, the ASEAN Secretariat had been enjoined, at least implicitly, not to be involved in anything having to do with political or security matters; those were the domains and prerogatives of the member-states. Yet, someone had to pr ocess ARF matters that went thr ough the S ecretariat. M ore and more such matters did so . M oreover, the S ecretary-General attended ARF ministerial meetings. The stopgap solution that the Secretary-General arrived at was to designate his S pecial Assistant to deal with ARF affairs.

At their J une 2003 meeting, the ARF ministers called for " the ASEAN Secretariat's assistance for the ARF Chair in carr   ying out the mandates outlined in the paper on the 'E nhanced Role of the ARF Chair ' ".[13] Soon thereafter, after having earlier floated the idea of an ARF secr   etariat, the United States circulated a concept paper pr oposing the establishment of an

ARF Unit in the ASEAN S ecretariat. However, the ASEAN senior officials decided to ensure that ASEAN retained control of the ARF Unit, agreeing on the unit's terms of r eference, which I ndonesia had drafted, without fur ther consultation with the non-ASEAN participants in the ARF . The ASEAN senior officials, at their meeting in May 2004, also decided to launch the unit into operation right away. The unit's main task would be to support the ARF chair. I t would be funded entir ely b y ASEAN. ASEAN countries could second officials to the unit, but not the non-ASEAN participants. The ASEAN senior officials formally adopted the terms of eference in June 2004.

Both ARF SOM and the ARF ministers explicitly defined the main function of the ARF Unit as supporting the ARF chair in its "enhanced" role. The unit would also be the r epository of ARF documents and manage databases and r egistries. H owever, it would not r eceive additional funding but would be supported by the Secretariat's regular budget. The result is that only three persons manned the unit at the beginning, with that complement subsequently increasing to four — a head at assistant director level, who was simply mo ved fr om another assignment, two locally r ecruited " technical officers" and one secr etary, also locally r ecruited. The terms of refer ence do allow for the secondment of additional personnel fom other ASEAN countries, but so far such a step has not been taken. Sme non-ASEAN ARF participants have pr essed for the secondment of their o wn people to the ARF U nit. However, ASEAN has resisted these suggestions.

The principal functions of the unit so far have been the management of ARFNet, the publication of the ARF Documents Series, acting as the repository of ARF documents, custody of the r egister of Experts and E minent Persons, the maintenance of a matrix of ARF decisions and their status, the conduct of activities that the ARF dir ects it to under take (e.g. the 2007–08 study of practices by other international and r egional organizations in pr eventive diplomacy), and otherwise serving as the ARF's *de facto* secretariat. These are useful functions, and the creation of an ARF Unit in the ASEAN Secretariat is a step for ward, but the unit is clearly not meant to enable the U nit or the Secretariat to ser ve as a r egional institution for pr eventive diplomacy or conflict resolution.

A number of ARF officials have expr essed their desir e to see the ARF Unit strengthened. Bounkeut Sangsomsak, Laos' Deputy Minister for Foreign Affairs, for example, thinks that the ARF U nit should be " empowered for research".[14] However, the lack of independent funding pr ecludes the unit 's growth and any expansion of its mandate. F or ten y ears, the ASEAN Secretariat's par ticipation in ARF activities was limited to the S ecretary-General's attendance at ministerial meetings. The establishment of the ARF

Unit in the Secretariat in 2004 paved the way for the Secretariat's presence in most ARF meetings and activities, including the ISG-CBM/PD, from which it had previously been ex cluded.

In the late 1990s, the U nited S tates openly recommended the establishment of what several participants thought the ARF ought to have — an ARF website, or ARFNet. The United States presented an "interim report" of a group pr eviously formed to study the ARFN et pr oposal. The U nited States suggested that the site be located in and run by the U   niversity of Washington in Washington State. ASEAN countries balked at this, contending that it would be more appropriate — and less expensive — were the website to be located in Southeast Asia, preferably at the ASEAN Secretariat. ARFNet was finally launched at the ARF ministerial meeting in J   uly 2005, to be operated by the ARF U nit and accessible dir ectly or thr ough the ASEAN Secretariat's website.

ARFNet (http://www.aseanregionalforum.org) has the usual page "about us". Its Public Library has the texts of chairman's statements, reports, terms of reference, concept papers, and defence " white papers". The P ublic Librar y contains lists of Track One and Track Two activities b y year and b y subject and a matrix of ARF cooperation in disaster management. It also reproduces the contents of *The ARF Document Series 1994–2006* and of all volumes of the *Annual Security Outlook*. " ARF in the N ews" featur es ARF-r elated dispatches, supplied by Agence France-Presse (AFP), from a number of news agencies, including AFP itself There is a calendar of forthcoming ARF events and a " photo gallery". The site carries contact data for persons inv olved in areas of ARF cooperation, including disaster relief, export licensing, maritime security, and illicit trade in small arms and light weapons. I t is linked to the websites of several international and regional organizations, including CSCAP members, defence univ ersities and colleges, and ARF for   eign ministries. ARFNet has a page accessible only to selected officials. All in all, ARFN et is an extremely useful w ebsite for getting at published documents and data.

Institutions cannot function as regional bodies unless they are adequately funded. The ARF took a step forward in this respect by establishing an ARF Fund in July 2005, when the ministers adopted the fund's terms of reference. The fund is to be devoted to "implementing projects, activities, and decisions of the ARF...."[15] However, the terms of r eference and subsequent practice seem to pr eclude the fund 's use for institutional support. Thus, the ARF Unit is financed out of the ASEAN Secretariat's regular budget and not out of the ARF F und.

As the terms of reference make clear, the fund is to be used according to an annual work plan approved by ARF SOM on the basis of recommendations by the ISG-CBM/PD and ARF inter-sessional meetings. I t is to be in the custody of the ARF Unit and disbursed in accordance with ASEAN Secretariat rules and procedures. With a contribution from the United States, the fund supported the development of the ARF's website. However, the ARF Unit has been managing the site's daily operation at the ASEAN Secretariat's expense. The ARF Fund also financed the study on pr eventive diplomacy referred to above to the amount of US$129,034.50. Contributions are entirely voluntary. The chairman's statement of the 2007 ministerial meeting " welcomed the voluntary contributions" of Indonesia, Pakistan, the Philippines, New Zealand, Singapore and the United States.

COOPERATING WITH THE UN

A concept paper drawn up b y Thailand, appr oved by ARF SOM and "welcomed" by the ministers at their meeting in July 2006 stated, "ARF may, at the initial stage, wish to dev elop contacts with the UN, SCO, CICA, NAM, OAS and OSCE on issues r elevant to its wor k. For the UN, such bodies as UN Office for D rugs and Crime and the Counter Terrorism Executive Dir ectorate may be giv en special consideration in view of the significance given by ARF to related issues."[16] This was a fairly recent reiteration of previous calls for closer ARF cooperation with the UN.

In fact, the participation of UN bodies in ARF activities has been quite extensive, at least since 1996. The UN Department of Humanitarian Affairs, the UN Office for the Coor dination of Humanitarian Affairs (OCHA), the UN High Commissioner for R efugees (UNHCR), the UN D evelopment Programme (UNDP), and the World Health Organization (WHO) have all taken par t in ARF inter-sessional meetings and other activities on disaster relief. The International Maritime Organization (IMO) and the International Civil Aviation Organization (ICAO) have shared their expertise and experience at ARF meetings on search and rescue, with the IMO being involved also in maritime-security wor kshops and confidence-building efforts. The UN Department of P eacekeeping Operations has par ticipated in ARF meetings and seminars on peacekeeping, as hav e the UNHCR and the UNDP . UNOCHA and UNHCR have taken part in the ARF seminar on the law on armed conflict, while OCHA has done so also in an ARF wor kshop on the consequences of a major terrorist attack. The UN S ecurity Council's 1540 Committee was present at the 2007 ARF workshop on UN Security Council Resolution No. 1540 regarding the proliferation of weapons of mass destruction to non-state actors, a matter discussed in Chapter 5 of this book. The UN Educational, Scientific and C ul:ural Organization (UNESCO) has taken part in an I ntersessional Meeting on Counter Terrorism and Trans-national Crime. The UN D epartment of P olitical Affairs and the UN I nstitute for Training and R esearch (UNIT AR) have par ticipated in ARF Track Two activities on pr eventive diplomacy.

Romualdo Ong, retired Philippine ambassador to China and to Malaysia and former ASEAN S enior O fficial for the P hilippines, has pr oposed the further expansion of the involvement of UN and other international agencies in ARF discussions and activities. He cited as examples the participation of the International Atomic Energy Agency (IAEA) in matters of nuclear non-proliferation and of the World H ealth O rganization (WHO) and the World Organisation for Animal H ealth (OIE) in activities per taining to avian influenza. [17]

IDSS at Nanyang Technological University, Singapore, has recommended, "The ARF should build closer r elationships with the U nited N ations." However, the areas of such relationships that IDSS had in mind were conflict prevention and early-warning capabilities. [18] Similarly, CSCAP has suggested that "the ARF should consider developing closer ties and more collaboration with the UN and its various agencies, drawing upon their experience and expertise". Just as similarly, it specified conflict pr evention and resolution as areas for such collaboration. [19]

SUBSIDIARY BODIES?

There hav e been suggestions for setting up ARF subsidiar y offices. O ne proposes three such offices, each to attend to humanitarian activities, including search and rescue and natural disasters, to the environment and public health, and to terrorism, transnational crime and maritime security . The ARF Unit in the ASEAN Secretariat would coordinate them. This proposal was evidently inspired by the example of the Organization for Security and Cooperation in Europe (OSCE), which has offices for media freedom in Vienna, democratic institutions and human rights in Warsaw, and national minorities in The Hague, in addition to a branch office of the Secretariat in Prague. The OSCE also has six missions in Southeastern Europe and three in South Caucasus and four centres in Central Asia. S everal officials of ARF countries with whom I tested this proposal professed to welcome the idea. Some ARF supporters wax wistful about the perceived efficacy and activism of the OSCE. H owever, aside from the matter of funding — the fifty-six-member OSCE' s 2007 "unified budget" was €168.2 million — the ARF is clearly not going the way of the OSCE, which has about 450 people in its central institutions and some 3,000 in its field operations, at least not anytime soon. The more fundamental obstacle, of course, is the divergence in strategic inter ests among the major powers of the Asia-Pacific, an obstacle in the way of other forms of ARF institutionalization.

CONCLUSION

The ARF does not have the permanent regional institutions that are necessary for it to carry out preventive diplomacy or conflict resolution. The position of ARF chair, although "enhanced" to act for the forum between ministerial meetings and supported by "friends" and Experts and Eminent Persons, is severely circumscribed in its functions and held by the participant-states on a short leash — upon the insistence of some of those participants. The EEPs could conceivably be used in the future for fact-finding or as special envoys on specific issues, but their role is explicitly laid down as advisory rather than operational. The creation of an ARF Unit in the ASEAN Secretariat is a step forward in the ARF's institutionalization, but it remains small and receives no funding separate from that which the ASEAN member-states contribute to the Secretariat. The ARF Fund is devoted strictly to projects and not to institutions. Although it is now allowed greater participation in ARF meetings and activities, the Secretariat's role in ARF matters remains tightly restricted.

The ARF Concept Paper observed, "Without a high degree of confidence among ARF participants, it is unlikely that they will agree to the establishment of mechanisms which are perceived to be intrusive and/or autonomous. This is a political reality the ARF should recognize."[20] That was in 1995, but the "political reality" that the Concept Paper referred to is still very much with us.

As everything else about the ARF, the existence and effectiveness of ARF institutions depend on the dynamics in the relationships among the great powers, all of which are participants in the forum. Today, the nature of those relationships precludes the emergence of viable regional institutions that can take the ARF beyond what it currently is — a useful forum for consultation, dialogue, networking and confidence-building.

Regional institutions are necessary for the ARF to go beyond confidence-building, but a sufficient convergence of national interests is required for such institutions to be established. Clearly, that condition is not present in the ARF. However, the ARF is needed precisely because the national interests of the Asia-Pacific powers are at odds.

Notes

1. Bryan J. Couchman, *The ASEAN Regional Forum: Does the Reality Match the Rhetoric?* (Johannesburg: East Asia Project, University of Witwatersrand, October 1996), p. 11.

2. Interview by the author, Jakarta, 13 July 2007.

3. Interview by the author, Singapore, 15 October 2007.

4. *A New Agenda for the ASEAN Regional Forum*, IDSS Monograph No. 4 (Singapore: Institute of Defence and Strategic Studies, Nanyang Technological University, 2002), p. 63.

5. Interview by the author, Bangkok, 1 October 2007.

6. "Co-chairs' Summary Report of the Inaugural Meeting of the Experts and Eminent Persons, the ASEAN Regional Forum, Jeju Island, 29–30 June 2006", in *The ASEAN Regional Forum Documents Series 1994–2006*, p. 440, para. 6.

7. "Co-chairs' Summary Report: The Sixth ASEAN Regional Forum Inter-sessional Meeting on Counter-terrorism and Transnational Crime, Semarang, Indonesia, 21–22 February 2008", para. 9.

8. "Enhanced Role of the ARF Chair (Shared perspectives among the ARF members)", in *The ASEAN Regional Forum Documents Series 1994–2006*, pp. 217–19. Also in <http://www .aseanregionalforum.org/PublicLibrary/ARFChairmansStatementsandReports/EnhancedRoleoftheARFChairEEPs/tabid/112/Default.aspx>.

9. "Chairman's Statement: The Fifteenth ASEAN Regional Forum, 24 July 2008, Singapore" in <http://www .aseanregionalforum.org/LinkClick.aspx?fileticket=Hn4UnDG3WVY%3d&tabid=66&mid=1009>, para. 32.

10. "Co-Chairmen's Summary Report of the Meetings of the ARF Intersessional Support Group on Confidence Building Measures, Honolulu, 4–6 November 1998, and Bangkok, 3–5 March 1999", in *The ASEAN Regional Forum Documents Series 1994–2006*, pp. 143–44. Also in <http://www .aseanregional forum.org/PublicLibrary/ARFChairmansStatementsandReports/CoChairmensSummary ReportoftheMeetingsofth/tabid/178/Default.aspx>, para. 41(B).

11. "Co-Chairs' Paper on the Terms of Reference for the ARF Experts/Eminent Persons (EEPs)", in *The ASEAN Regional Forum Documents Series 1994–2006*, pp. 220–21. Also in <http://www .aseanregionalforum.org/PublicLibrary/ARFChairmansStatementsandReports/CoChairsPaperontheTermsofReference forthe/tabid/114/Default.aspx>.

12. "Guidelines for the Operation of the ARF EEP", in *The ASEAN Regional Forum Documents Series 1994–2006*, pp. 348–49. Also in <http://www . aseanregionalforum.org/LinkClick.aspx?fileticket=7CZjUqEWIsA%3d&tabid=89&mid=453>.

13. "Chairman's Statement of the Tenth ASEAN Regional Forum, Phnom Penh, Cambodia, 18 June 2003", in *The ASEAN Regional Forum Documents Series 1994–2006*, p. 267. Also in <http://wwwaseanregionalforum.org/PublicLibrary/ARFChairmansStatementsandReports/ChairmansStatementofthe10thMeeting oftheAS/tabid/76/Default.aspx>, para. 38.

14. Interview by the author, Singapore, 27 August 2007.

15. "Chairman's Statement of the Thirteenth ASEAN Regional Forum, Kuala Lumpur, Malaysia, 28 July 2006", in *The ASEAN Regional Forum Documents*

Series 1994–2006, p. 438. Also in <http://www .aseanregionalforum.org/Link Click.aspx?fileticket=0v9rLDy0uvQ%3d&tabid=66&mid=401>, para. 51.

16. "A Concept Paper on Enhancing Ties between Track I and Track II in the ARF, and between the ARF and O ther R egional and I nternational S ecurity Organizations, Kuala Lumpur, Malaysia, 28 July 2006", in *The ASEAN Regional Forum Documents Series 1994–2006*, p. 532, para. 9.

17. Interview by the author, Manila, 7 June 2007.

18. *A New Agenda for the ASEAN Regional Forum*, IDSS M onograph N o. 4, pp. 65–66.

19. "The ARF into the 21st Century" (Paper presented to the 9th ASEAN Regional Forum Ministerial meeting, Bandar Seri Begawan, 31 July 2002), p. 3.

20. Appendix A, para. 13.

7

ASSESSING THE ARF

The ASEAN R egional Forum was founded as a v enue and mechanism for ministerial-level consultation and dialogue among states in East Asia and others with interests in it on political and security issues in the Asia-P acific. The only r egion-wide security forum for the Asia-P acific, the ARF was established in the early 1990s in the light of and in r esponse to the ne w regional security envir onment that had dev eloped at the time. This new environment had emerged from the end of the Cold War, the break-up of the Soviet Union, the r emoval of U nited S tates forces from their bases in the Philippines, the withdrawal of Soviet forces from Cam Ranh Bay, the opening up of China and the accompanying surge in China's economy, military power and political influence, and J apan's policy foray into r egional security multilateralism from an almost total dependence on the Japan-United States security treaty. Vietnamese forces had pulled out of Cambodia, the Cambodian conflict had been politically settled, and the Southeast Asian divide had been narrowed. A t the same time, cer tain "flashpoints" r emained in the r egion. This was an environment in which stability r equired not only traditional alliance-building and balance-of-po wer manœuvers but also r egional multilateral processes to supplement, if not supplant or transcend, them.

The ARF is neither a militar y alliance nor a defence pact. I t has no adversary, actual or potential, against which to devise military plans, conduct military exercises, or direct weapon systems. Indeed, all possible adversaries in the Asia-Pacific are inside the ARF fold; that is the whole point of the forum. However, the principal reality and consideration from which the ARF proceeds

is the fact that the strategic inter   ests of the major par   ticipants differ and
diverge, differences that produce misunderstandings and mutual suspicions,
if not political, diplomatic or military collisions. The ARF's main objectives
are to reduce the chances of these differences, misunderstandings and suspicions
leading to conflict and to ensure that inter-state relations all around, especially
among the major participants, progr ess towards a cer tain degree of stability.
A r elated goal is to expand the ar   ea where their inter   ests conv erge and
cooperation becomes possible.

For this purpose, ASEAN, J   apan and the so-called "   middle po wers",
Australia, Canada and N ew Zealand, succeeded in r oping both China and
the United States into the forum — to engage China in the regional security
process and keep the U nited States engaged in it. After an initial r eluctance
on the part of both, China and the United States have come to use the forum
on behalf of their r   espective inter ests, having seen par   ticipation in it as
serving those interests.

The ARF's inclusiveness is both its vir tue and its w eakness. As the only
Asia-Pacific forum on regional security, it includes China, the U nited States
and states leaning to one or the other or standing betw een them. It is meant
to promote mutual confidence and cooperation among such disparate powers
and thus, presumably, diminish the chances of conflict. O n the other hand,
the divergent, if not clashing, interests of rival major powers within the ARF
prevent the forum from moving forward in terms of "concrete results" as fast
as some may want or expect. Yet, the conclusion is inevitable: it is better to
have the ARF, slow and ineffectual though it may often seem to be, than not
to have it at all.

The national interest also plays a critical role in the ARF' s expansion.
Despite repeated moratoriums on additional membership and attempts at
establishing objective cr.teria for admission, participation in the ARF swelled
from the original eighteen to twenty-seven in 2008. Cambodia, Myanmar,
India, Mongolia, North Korea, Pakistan, Timor-Leste, Bangladesh and S ri
Lanka were admitted since the ARF's inaugural meeting in 1994. Although
the merit of the par ticipation of Cambodia, M yanmar, I ndia and N orth
Korea is generally ackno wledged, that of the others is mor   e debatable.
Decisions on the admission of additional par ticipants have been driven in
most cases not b y regional considerations in terms of the forum 's efficacy
but by the curr ent ARF participants' relations with the states aspiring for
admission.

The Concept Paper that ASEAN produced and the ARF ministers adopted
at their second meeting in 1995 projected three stages in the forum's evolution

— promotion of confidence-building measures, development of preventive-diplomacy mechanisms, and development of conflict-resolution mechanisms.[1] The ministers changed the last stage to "elaboration of approaches to conflict". This was done upon the insistence of China, which apparently wanted to ensure that the ARF would not get involved in the Taiwan issue, the South China Sea disputes, or the other territorial questions to which Bijing is party. This change is discussed in Chapter 1 of this book. The Concept Paper and subsequent ARF documents have stressed that the forum's progress should take place "at a pace comfortable to all participants", that, is, slowly and by consensus, so as to assure all that the ARF would not be used to "gang up" on any participant.

The ARF at this point seeks primarily to build mutual confidence and dispel mutual suspicions among the participants. The reality of divergent, even clashing, interests — and strategic perceptions — among the participants, principally those of China and the United States, makes even the first stage of the ARF's projected evolution extremely difficult, not to mention its transition to the next stage of preventive diplomacy.

At this stage, does the ARF, in fact, promote mutual confidence? The ARF seeks to do this in three ways. The first is through meetings, dialogues and consultations at the ministerial, officials and "working" levels in many sectors, including among defence and national-security officials.This would include similar processes in CSCAP. It is also done through the exchange of defence white papers, contributions to the *Annual Security Outlook* and other transparency measures. In this way, positions on political and security issues are clarified and, presumably, understood. Common stances are negotiated on certain questions. Networks are formed. The second mode is through the adoption of the " ASEAN way ", which, contrary to the assumption of many, is hardly unique to ASEAN. The "ASEAN way" seeks to give reassurance to participants through its manner of decision-making by consensus and through incremental and evolutionary progress. It also means the centrality of ASEAN, a presumably neutral, objective and harmless party. Not least, it entails adherence to ASEAN's norms for inter-state relations: the rejection of the use or threat of force, the peaceful settlement of disputes, and non-interference in internal affairs. The third way of confidence-building is through the increasing number and frequency of inter-sessional activities in an increasing number of areas. These lead to familiarity, networking and, in some cases, operational coordination.

These are modalities for building confidence, but have they succeeded, and to what extent? It is difficult to say . Confidence is subjective, and government officials, if one asks them, will insist that mutual confidence is improving. The acceptance of non-traditional, non-militar y ar eas of cooperation as appropriate objects of preventive diplomacy is an indication of progress in confidence-building. However, the continuing absence of regional institutions that make region-wide cooperation possible, an absence arising largely fr om mutual suspicions and div ergent interests, demonstrates that confidence-building in the ARF has a long way to go .

Early in the ARF's existence, the question ar ose as to ho w quickly the forum was to mo ve to the pr eventive-diplomacy phase. O n this question, two div ergent tendencies hav e emerged. O ne tendency fav ours the enhancement and use of an activist chair, which raises the related question of ASEAN's monopoly of the ARF chair, and the establishment and use of regional institutions, like risk-reduction centres, to help prevent both inter-state and intra-state conflict.   This tendency would apply pr   eventive diplomacy to conflicts within states in the name of human security and the "responsibility to protect". The other tendency, exemplified by China but also by some ASEAN countries, resists these propositions, apparently out of wariness that pr eventive diplomacy applied to inter-state or intra-state conflict may be used to inter vene in countries' internal affairs, destabiliz e ruling regimes, or otherwise harm those countries or those regimes interests. Thus, adherents of this position have severely circumscribed the role of the chair and the functions of other central ARF institutions, no matter ho w innocuous they appear initially to be.   The ARF U nit in the ASEAN Secretariat, whose establishment was undeniably a step forward, is deliberately kept limited in siz e and function. ARFNet is merely a tool, albeit a useful one. The ARF F und is used only for specific pr   ojects rather than for institutional purposes. Even some Western ARF participants have accepted the realism behind this tendency, although efforts persist in Track Two to promote the establishment of central ARF institutions.

Both tendencies have apparently come to agree on the acceptability and desirability of applying preventive diplomacy to non-traditional, non-military security thr eats, like environmental degradation, natural disasters, communicable diseases, international terrorism and transnational crime, anti-personnel mines left behind b y armed conflict, trafficking in illicit drugs, persons and small arms and light w eapons, and piracy and r obbery at sea. ARF participants seem increasingly to recognize that such problems represent threats to all, without any state having an inter   est in any of them.   The foreseeable future of ARF cooperation seems to lie her e.

Indeed, the number of confer ences, seminars, workshops, joint exercises and other activities between ministerial meetings inv olving such thr eats has been steadily incr easing. Chapter 5 of this book categorizes such activities into the civilian use of militar y assets, civilian-militar y cooperation, pur ely civilian undertakings and non-traditional security issues, and the ARF process, as well as the exchange of security perceptions, arms control and management, and military cooperation.

The absence of central regional institutions has prevented the ARF itself, at the operational level, fr om countering the non-traditional, non-militar y threats or follo wing thr ough on the activities that the ARF carries out between ministerial sessions. Nevertheless, through its declarations and other statements and the increasing number of inter-sessional activities in different ARF countries, the ARF legitimiz es and giv es sanction to operational cooperation between two or mor e ARF par ticipants. I t also promotes the adoption of common positions on international issues, mutual understanding and networking, which not only help build mutual confidence but may also make operational coor dination possible.

Moreover, as Rizal Sukma, Deputy Executive at the Centre for Strategic and International Studies in I ndonesia, has noted, participation in the ARF cultivates the "habit of consultation ".[2] Vietnam's Nguy en Trung Thanh, former assistant for eign minister and later ambassador to S ingapore, has pointed out that the ARF "inculcates the notion of cooperativ e security".[3]

A lack of appreciation of the natur e and r ole of the ARF and of the mutual suspicions born of divergent inter ests among the major par ticipants has led to heckling by some media and academic commentators of the ARF as a mere "talk shop". M. Jawhar Hassan, chairman of Malaysia's Institute of Strategic and International Studies, urges that the ARF be judged on its own terms and not b y the standar ds of other regional institutions and pr ocesses, like the OSCE. H e says:

> The OSCE is cer tainly useful as a comparison and as a pointer to what kind of regional security cooperation may be developed, but it cannot be the standard against which the ARF should be judged. I t cannot be the standard because the strategic envir onments of the two organizations are markedly different. To put it more bluntly, the OSCE would be a non-starter in the Asia P acific r egion, and hence a failur e. S imilarly, the European states would hav e abandoned the ARF model if all the organization has to sho w after 7 years is what the ARF has no w. An understanding of the strategic envir onment is therefor e critically important. It helps to clarify not only the setting of the ARF , but also how this setting is shaping the natur e and evolution of the ARF.[4]

Thoughtful scholars and serious bodies have pr oduced balanced assessments of the ARF, although some observations, expectations and recommendations may be considered, in hindsight, as a bit unrealistic. In February 1997, for example, less than three years after the ARF's inception, Gary J. Smith, a former fellow at the Weatherhead Center for International Affairs at Harvard University and Canadian diplomat, wrote about the forum,

> It is succeeding in its aim of building a multilateral security dialogue that engages the relevant players and helps to forestall the possibility of conflict .... Concrete transparency and Confidence Building Measures are being adopted .... A spirit of cooperation is developing, helping to alleviate past tensions ..., and the ARF has provided a vehicle for dialogue between countries where formal diplomatic relations had not been achieved .... Potentially contentious issues between China and the US ... can be raised and dealt with by other countries rather than having every issue become a bilateral irritant. [5]

In April 1998, S. R. Nathan, then director of the Institute of Strategic and Defence Studies and later President of Singapore, gave this assessment of the forum's value:

> *Firstly*, it is the only regional security forum to bring together all major powers of the world. No other forum (apart from UN bodies) brings together the US, Russia, China, Japan, the EU, India to discuss security issues. *Secondly*, the "geographic footprint" of the ARF covers the region of the world, which has recently seen and will continue to see, in the next decade or so, the most significant shift of power seen in recent times. If the ARF did not exist, we would have had to invent it quickly to help manage these changes. *Thirdly*, the ARF is unique in having been launched by diplomatic initiatives emanating not from major powers but by the developing countries of Southeast Asia. If it succeeds, it will bring hope to many other developing countries. In short, for a Forum that is barely five years old, it has already made a difference.[6]

A month later, Alan Dupont, then a fellow at the Strategic and Defence Studies Centre, Australian National University, listed what he considered as the ARF's "accomplishments". The first one was the very fact that the forum was still alive, four years after its inaugural meeting, despite the immense diversity of the Asia-Pacific and the lack of precedents for such an arrangement in the region. The ARF had helped ASEAN to manage the new strategic environment arising from Russia's eclipse, China's rise, and the reduction of the United States' military capabilities in the area. Through the ARF, Dupont noted, ASEAN had been able to extend its influence in the wider region and achieve at least nominal parity with the world's great powers. The ARF had sown the seeds of a security community in the Asia-P acific, fostering within Southeast and Northeast Asia a better understanding of each other's security concerns, leading, D upont claimed, to a r eduction in tensions in the ar ea. Dupont declared, "East Asia's track record in confidence building and conflict management in the 1990s is cer tainly no worse, and arguably much better , than that of Europe." On the other hand, Dupont asserted, ASEAN's control of the ARF process and of its pace and dir ection was a source of the forum's weakness and of unhappiness among the U nited S tates, J apan and S outh Korea.[7] (Since then, however, these and other non-ASEAN participants seem to have resigned themselves to ASEAN leadership of the ARF process.)

In May 2002, B runei D arussalam, ARF chair at the time, cir culated a paper at the ARF SOM meeting " taking stock " of the ARF . The paper pointed out that the ARF had engaged its par ticipants in a r egional process of dialogue and confidence-building, despite their div erse and sometimes conflicting strategic inter ests and concerns. I t had inculcated a habit of dialogue and discussion, which had become increasingly frank and progressively extended into sensitive subjects like the K orean peninsula, the S outh China Sea, and nuclear pr oliferation. The ARF had laid do wn the foundations of security cooperation in such ar eas as confidence-building, disaster r elief, peacekeeping operations, search and rescue, and de-mining. Transparency in defence and militar y matters had been enhanced. F inally, the forum had elevated ASEAN's influence and pr estige in the r egion and in the world.

However, the Brunei paper also deplor ed the fact that the ARF did not have the institutional capacity to r espond to security developments in a timely manner. I t thus had not been able to deal effectiv ely with security issues, traditional or non-traditional. ASEAN' s monopoly of the ARF' s leadership and the adoption of the ASEAN model for the ARF had been questioned by Western par ticipants and had led to a lack of attention to Northeast Asia's security problems. Defence, military and police officials did not sufficiently participate in the ARF .

A CSCAP paper submitted in its co-chairs' name to the ARF ministerial meeting at the end of J uly 2002 enumerated the forum 's "utility":

> First, the ARF is the only r egional forum that discusses some sensitive regional issues and pro vides an oppor tunity for ex changes of views on potential flash points such as on the K orean peninsula.

> Second, the ARF has helped to build comfor t lev els and cr eate an atmosphere conducive to multilateral cooperative security in the r egion where previously there had been none. F or the ASEAN states, the ARF served as an insurance against uncertainty at a time when the strategic environment was changing in the Asia-P acific.

Third, the ARF has facilitated the r   eduction of tension and the management of r egional relationships. It has not r esolved disputes or prevented the outbr eak of conflicts but it has helped to minimiz e the impact of differing perceptions and interests.

Fourth, the ARF has helped begin the pocess of creating predictable and stable relations among the regional states. It has engendered an increasing awareness of r egional norms among the major po   wers .... M ost importantly, the ARF has engaged both China and the United States in shaping the new Asia-Pacific security agenda ....

The paper follo wed this with some suggestions for the ARF'   s " future agenda", which indicated CSCAP' s views on the forum 's deficiencies. I t urged a higher level of frankness in its discussions and the focus of each ISG-CBM meeting on a specific theme or issue. It called for the improvement of the *Annual Security Outlook,* particularly with respect to transparency in arms procurement. Institutionally, it recommended the establishment of an ARF secretariat, if only a "virtual" one, and a regional peacekeeping centre, although it was silent on ho w they would be funded. I t suggested that the ARF chair be "de-linked" from the ASEAN chair on the ground that some ASEAN countries might not be up to leading the ARF (although ASEAN and some other countries would surely resist this). The paper called for the involvement of senior legal and law-enforcement officials in ARF activities, the better to enable the for um to deal with what it called " transnational security issues". It recommended the convening of an ARF defence minister's forum in addition to the networking being carried out among senior defence and national-security officials.

Addressing a 26 May 2003 regional conference on the ARF and Europe's contribution to it, H or Namhong, Cambodia's Minister of F oreign Affairs and I nternational Cooperation, obser ved that the ARF had embar ked on building confidence, committed its participants to the discussion of political and security issues, and provided a venue for the management of bilateral and sub-regional problems. This had pr omoted a cultur e of dialogue and consultation. The ARF had also enabled and encouraged defence and national-security officials to form networ ks among themselves.

Scot Marciel, Deputy Assistant S ecretary for East Asian and P acific Affairs at the Department of State of the United States and the first person appointed as ambassador to ASEAN, told me in O ctober 2007 that he considered the ARF as " a key r egional-security for um", bringing together "key players ", " filling a v oid" and developing a " sense of community " among policy-makers. H owever, he also expressed the wish that the ARF were "more operational" and had stronger institutions.[8] Ralf Emmers of the

S. Rajaratnam School has obser ved that the ARF is the only forum that "brings everybody together".[9]

ASEAN-ISIS M emorandum N o. 4, circulated to the ASEAN senior officials in N ovember 2007, declared:

> Since its inception in 1994, the ASEAN Regional forum (ARF) has been and remains the foremost inter-governmental security forum in the Asia Pacific. It has successfully engaged a growing number of countries in the Asia Pacific region and beyond. The ARF Ministerial, SOM and Working Group pr ocesses have become firmly institutionaliz ed. Confidence building measur es continue to be intensely explor ed. A number of important initiativ es have also been launched, among them r egional cooperation to counter and eliminate terrorism.
>
> Despite this, however, the ARF has yet to emerge as an effectiv e forum for addressing emerging security issues in the region. The ARF has not been able to embar k upon concrete confidence building or pr eventive diplomacy measur es since inception. There has been a r esurgence of rivalry among the major powers, all of whom are also key participants of the ARF process. The ARF has also not given sufficient attention to non-military security issues.

An anonymous draft "discussion paper" drawn up either towards the end of 2007 or in J anuary 2008 cited the fact that the ARF had v astly expanded the scope and number of its activities, including its r esponses to non-traditional security threats, such as natural disasters, thr eats to maritime security and avian influenza. I t had str engthened its internal mechanisms, adopting the terms of reference of the Friends of the Chair and establishing the ARF F und. I t had star ted engaging other r egional organizations and Track Two in its discussions. The par ticipant-countries had appointed Experts and Eminent Persons. However, it pointed to a number of problems — the proliferation of meetings, the lack of concr ete and practical cooperation, the diffused focus of discussions, slo w decision-making, and the expansion in the number of par ticipants.

In November 2008, Amitav A charya, a long-time obser ver of security developments in Asia, contrasted the failed per formance of the EU and the OSCE in the case of Russia s actions in Georgia the month before with Asia's successful management of r egional or der. H e pointed out that Asia 's "talk shops", often derided as weak and ineffectual, had discouraged the adoption of a strategy based on the containment of China, had made multilateralism "palatable" to B eijing, and had used the r esulting r estraint between China and the United States to "soften" the region's balance-of-power geopolitics.[10] Made fr om a strategic standpoint, A charya's r emarks wer e about Asia in general but could ver y well apply specifically to the ARF .

Pointing out that confidence-building helps to r educe the likelihood of conflict through dialogue and consultation, M alaysia's Tan Sri Abdul Kadir Mohamad, former Secretary-General of the Ministry of Foreign Affairs and later for eign-affairs adviser to the P rime M inister, stressed that the ARF prevented the region fr om being dominated b y one or two po wers or by "Cold War-type antagonisms".[11]

On the other hand, José T. Almonte, national security adviser of President Fidel V. Ramos of the Philippines, wr ote, "ARF has been useful to the gr eat powers primarily as a club wher e their for eign ministers and other senior diplomats can meet each other informally. ARF has provided a discreet venue for bilateral talks — such as those betw een the U nited S tates and N orth Korea in Jakarta in July 2004."[12] Rizal Sukma has noted that the ARF serves as a "venue for consultation" among the N ortheast Asians.[13] Dewi F ortuna Anwar, vice chairman of the Indonesian Institute of Science, has made much the same point, only in mor e general terms.[14]

To some, these may indicate a minimalist view and rather modest expectations of the ARF , and they do . However, in assessing the ARF , it is important to r emember that it is a forum made up of so vereign states, the most powerful of which have divergent strategic outlooks and interests. This fact has prevented the forum from setting up regional institutions that could enable it to be more active and effective in preventing and resolving conflicts or in dealing with threats of a non-traditional nature that are common to all. Daljit Singh, a r egional-security exper t at the I nstitute of S outheast Asian Studies in Singapore, pithily advised, "Do not dismiss the ARF, but do not be seduced by it."[15]

Writing with remar kable prescience in 1996, the late M ichael Leifer put the potential and limitations of the ARF in the context of the r egional power balance:

> On the positive side, the embr yonic multilateral str ucture is unique to
> the Asia-Pacific and is also remarkable in how much it has accomplished
> in such a shor t space of time. M oreover, it is a conv enient point of
> diplomatic contact for the major Asia-P acific powers. For example, the
> US has sought to use the ARF' s inter-sessional activities to pr omote
> dialogue between its senior military and their Chinese counterparts. I t
> also values the opportunity for bilateral dialogue at foreign-minister level
> which might otherwise not be politically oppor tune ....

> Indeed, the prer equisite for a successful ARF may well be the prior
> existence of a stable balance of power. The central issue in the case of the
> ARF is whether, in addition to diplomatic encouragement for a futue of
> cooperation driv en par tly b y economic inter dependence, the r egion
> shows the makings of a stable, suppor ting balance or distribution of
> power that would allo w the multilateral v enture to pr oceed in
> circumstances of some pr edictability. The ARF's structural problem is
> that its viability seems to depend on the prior existence of a stable
> balance, but it is not r eally in a position to cr eate it.[16]

One might add that a mor e idealistic vie w of the ARF would harbour the
hope that the for um's gradual adoption of a cultur e of cooperativ e security
will in the futur e r educe, if not r emove, the need for balance-of-po wer
considerations in the relations among nations of the Asia-P acific. Indeed, as
Amitav Acharya implied, it has alr eady begun to do so .

M. Jawhar Hassan forecast in 2001, "The ARF is still in its embryonic
or early development stage. I f the ARF par ticipants ar e patient and
pragmatic but determined in their pursuit of regional cooperation for the
benefit of all and to the serious detriment of none, the Forum can have a
promising future."[17]

Considering its inclusion of all the world 's gr eat po wers, a significant
enough achievement, the ARF can proceed only at a pace comfortable to all,
that is, slowly. At the same time, this very inclusiveness has enabled the ARF
to proceed in its contribution to peace and stability in the Asia-P acific.

Some have expr essed the concern that the N ortheast Asian po wers,
including R ussia and the U nited S tates, would set up their o wn security
forum, perhaps on the foundations of the S ix-Party Talks on N orth Korea.
Such a development would, according to this view, render the ARF "irrelevant".
I do not share this concern. I f a Northeast Asian for um could contribute to
the reduction of tensions, the prevention of conflict or even the resolution of
disputes in that part of Asia, that would be good for all of East Asia, including
Southeast Asia. It would not necessarily reduce the ARF to irrelevance, since
China, the United States, Japan, Australia and all the others would not want
to be left out of the affairs of the Asia-Pacific, except in the unlikely event that
all decided to opt out.

The Prime Minister of Japan, the Premier of China's State Council and
the President of the R epublic of K orea have finally met for the first time
outside the ASEAN Hus Three context.[18] Originally scheduled for September,
the one-day meeting took place on 13 December 2008. I t is too early to
judge the significance of that event. If it leads to better relations among the

three Northeast Asian nations, so much the better for all, including the ARF's purposes.

Nor am I bother ed by the pr ospect of the ARF' s disappearance. That would likely happen only if disputes and tensions in the Asia-Pacific were to dissipate to such an extent that r egional stability was perceived as being guaranteed and confidence-building no longer necessar y. In that case, ther e would no longer be any need for the ARFThat ideal situation would be good for all. Unfortunately, that time is not y et upon us.

Notes

1. Appendix A.
2. Interview by the author, Jakarta, 13 July 2007.
3. Interview by the author, Singapore, 7 April 2008.
4. M. Jawhar Hassan, "The ASEAN R egional F orum: A Critical A ppraisal", in <http://www.ndu.edu/inss/symposia/pacific2001/jawharpaper.htm>.
5. Gary J. S mith, "Mu_tilateralism and R egional S ecurity in Asia: The ASEAN Regional F orum (ARF) and AP EC's Geopolitical Value", WCFIA Working Paper 97-02 (Cambridge, M assachusetts: The Weatherhead Center for International Affairs, Harvard University, February 1997), pp. 15–16.
6. S.R. Nathan: "Opening Address", in *The Future of the ARF*, edited by Khoo How San (Singapore: Institute of Defence and S trategic Studies, 1999), p. 9.
7. Alan Dupont, *The Future of the ASEAN Regional Forum: An Australian View* (Canberra: Strategic and Defence Studies Centre, Australian National University, May 1998), pp. 2–5.
8. Interview by the author, Washington, D.C., 22 October 2007.
9. Interview by the author, Singapore, 12 November 2007.
10. Amitav A charya, "R egionalism and I ntegration: EU and S outheast Asian Experiences" (unpubl_shed notes prepared for the conference on *Regional Economic Integration and Cultural Change* organized by the Bertelsmann Foundation and the Diplomatic Academy of Vietnam, Hanoi, 12–13 N ovember 2008).
11. Interview by the author, Putrajaya, Malaysia, 15 August 2007.
12. José T. Almonte, "H ow ar e We to Keep ARF R elevant to the R egion?" (unpublished notes c_r culated at the wor kshop of ASEAN ARF Exper ts and Eminent Persons, Kuala Lump ur, 9–10 October 2005), pp. 1–2.
13. Interview by the author, Jakarta, 13 July 2007.
14. Interview by the author, Jakarta, 8 May 2008.
15. Interview by the author, Singapore, 16 January 2008.
16. Michael Leifer, "The ASEAN R egional Forum: Extending ASEAN's Model of Regional Security", Adelphi Paper 302 (Oxford and New York: Oxford University Press for the I nternational Ins_tute for S trategic Studies, 1996), pp. 57–58.
17. M. Jawhar Hassan, op. cit.

18. ASEAN Plus Three refers to the linkage and pr ocess involving ASEAN, China, Japan and S outh K orea. It was formally initiated at the leaders ' lev el on the occasion of the ASEAN Summit in December 1997. ASEAN's leaders meet with the three par tners collectively and individually at the annual ASEAN S ummit meetings. As of the end of 2008, it pursues cooperation at various levels and with varying degrees of substance in twenty areas, driven by forty mechanisms.

APPENDICES

APPENDIX A

The ASEAN Regional Forum: A Concept Paper

Introduction

1.   The Asia-Pacific region is experiencing an unprecedented period of peace and prosperity. For the first time in a century or more, the guns are virtually silent. There is a growing trend among, the states in the region to enhance dialogue on political and security cooperation.The Asia-Pacific is also the most dynamic region of the world in terms of economic growth. The centre of the world's economic gravity is shifting into the region. The main challenge of the ASEAN Regional Forum (ARF) is to sustain and enhance this peace and prosperity.

2.   This is not an easy challenge. The region has experienced some of the most disastrous wars of the twentieth century. It is also a remarkably diverse region where big and small countries co-exist. They differ significantly in levels of development. There are cultural, ethnic, religious and historical differences to overcome. Habits of cooperation are not deep-seated in some parts of the region.

3.   ASEAN has a pivotal role to play in the ARF. It has a demonstrable record of enhancing regional cooperation in the most diverse sub-region of the Asia-Pacific. It has also fostered habits of cooperation and provided the catalyst for encouraging regional cooperation in the wider Asia-Pacific region. The annual ASEAN Ministerial Meetings have contributed significantly to the positive regional environment today. There would be great hope for the Asia-Pacific if the whole region could emulate ASEAN's record of enhancing the peace and prosperity of its participants.

4.   Although ASEAN has undertaken the obligation to be the primary driving force of the ARF, a successful ARF requires the active participation and cooperation of all participants. ASEAN must always be sensitive to and take into account the interests and concerns of all ARF participants.

The Challenges

5.   To successfully preserve and enhance the peace and prosperity of the region, the ARF must dispassionately analyse the key challenges facing the region. Firstly, it should acknowledge that periods of rapid economic growth are often accompanied by significant shifts in power relations. This can lead to conflict. The ARF will have to carefully manage these transitions to preserve the peace. Secondly, the region is remarkably diverse. The ARF should recognise and

accept the differ ent appr oaches to peace and security and tr   y to forge a consensual approach to security issues.   Thirdly, the r egion has a r esidue unresolved territorial and other differ ences. Any one of these could spark conflagration that could undermine the peace and prosperity of the r egion. Over time, the ARF will have to gradually defuse these potential pr oblems.

6.   It would be unwise for a y oung and fragile pr ocess like the ARF to tackle all these challenges simultaneous y. A gradual ev olutionary approach is required. This evolution can take place in thr ee stages:

Stage I: Promotion of Confidence-Building Measures

Stage II: Development of Preventive Diplomacy Mechanisms

Stage III: Development of Conflict-Resolution Mechanisms

7.   The participants of the first ARF Ministerial Meeting in Bangkok in July 1994 agreed on "the need to develop a more predictable and constructive pattern of relations for the Asia-P acific r egion". I n its initial phase, the ARF should therefore concentrate on enhancing, the tr   ust and confidence amongst participants and thereby foster a regional environment conducive to maintaining the peace and pr osperity of the r egion.

Stage I: Promotion of Confidence-Building Measures

8.   In promoting confidence-building measur es, the ARF may adopt two complementary approaches. The first appr oach derives fr om ASEAN' s experience, which provides a valuable and pr oven guide for the ARF. ASEAN has succeeded in r educing, tensions among, its member states, pr   omoting region cooperation and cr eating a r egional climate conduciv e to peace and prosperity without the implementation of explicit confidence-building measues, achieving conditions appro ximating those envisaged in the D   eclaration of Zone of Peace, Freedom and Neutrality (ZOPFAN). The concepts of ZOPFAN and its essential component, the S outheast Asia N uclear Weapons-Free Zone (SEANWFZ), ar e significantly contributing to r egional peace and stability . ASEAN's well established practices of consultation and consensus (musyawarah and mufakat) hav e been significantly enhanced b y the r egular ex changes of high-level visits among ASEAN countries.   This pattern of r egular visits has effectively developed into a preventive diplomacy channel. In the Asian context, there is some merit to the ASEAN approach. It emphasises the need to develop trust and confidence among neighbouring states.

9.   The principles of good neighbourliness, which are elaborated in the concept of ZOPFAN, ar e enshrined in the 1976   Treaty of Amity and Cooperation in

Southeast Asia (TAC). One simple concr ete way of expanding the ASEAN experience is to encourage the ARF par ticipants to associate themselv es with the TAC. I t is significant that the first ARF meeting in B angkok agr eed to "endorse the purposes and principles of ASEAN   Treaty of Amity and Cooperation in Southeast Asia as a code of conduct governing relations between states and a unique diplomatic instrument for r egional confidence-building, preventive diplomacy, and political and security cooperation."

10.   The second approach is the implementation of concrete confidence-building measures. The first ARF meeting, in B angkok entrusted the next Chairman of the ARF , B runei Darussalam, to study all the ideas pr esented by ARF participants and to also study other relevant internationally recognised norms, principles and practices. After extensive consultations, the ASEAN countries have prepared two lists of confidence-building measures. The first list (Annex A) spells out measur es which can be explor ed and implemented b y ARF participants in the immediate future. The second list (Annex B) is an indicative list of other proposals which can be explored over the medium and long-term by ARF par ticipants and also consider ed in the immediate futur e b y the Track Two process. These lists include possible pr eventive diplomacy and other measures.

11.   Given the delicate nature of many of the subjects being considered by the ARF, there is merit in mo ving, the ARF process along two tracks.   Track One activities will be carried out b y go vernments. Track Two activities will be carried out by strategic institutes and non-go vernment organisations in the region, such as ASEAN-ISIS and CSCAP. To be meaningful and relevant, the Track Two activities may focus, as much as possible, on the current concerns of the ARF. The synergy between the two tracks would contribute gr eatly to confidence-building measur es in the region. Ov er time, these   Track Two activities should r esult in the cr eation of a sense of community among participants of those activities.

Moving Beyond Stage 1

12.   There remains a residue of unresolved territorial and other disputes that could be sources of tension or conflict. I   f the ARF is to become, o   ver time, a meaningful vehicle to enhance the peace and pr osperity of the r egion, it will have to demonstrate that it is a relevant instrument to be used in the event that a crisis or problem emerges. The ARF meeting in B angkok demonstrated this by taking a stand on the Korean issue at the very first meeting. This was a signal that the ARF is ready to address any challenge to the peace and security of the region.

13.   Over time, the ARF must develop its o   wn mechanisms to carr y preventive
       diplomacy and conflict-resolution. In doing so, the ARF will unique challenges.
       There are no established r oads or procedures for it to follo w. Without a high
       degree of confidence among ARF participants, it is unlikely that they will agre
       to the establishment of mechanisms which are perceived to be intrusive and/or
       autonomous. This is a politica. reality the ARF should r ecognise. However, it
       would be useful in the initial ℈hase for the Track Two process to consider and
       investigate a variety cf preventive diplomacy and conflict-resolution mechanisms.
       A good star t was made with the thr ee workshops organised b y International
       Studies Centre (Thailand) and I   nstitute of P olicy S tudies (S ingapore) on
       ASEAN-UN Cooperation for P   eace and P reventive D iplomacy, and the
       Indonesia-sponsored series of workshops on the S outh China S ea.

Stage II: Development of Preventive Diplomacy

14. P reventive diplomacy would be a natural follo   w-up to confidence building
       measures. Some suggestions for preventive diplomacy measures are spelled out
       in Annexes A and B .

Stage III: Conflict Resolution

15.   It is not envisaged that the ARF would establish mechanisms conflictresolution
       in the immediate future. The establishment of such mechanisms is an eventual
       goal that ARF participants shculd pursue as they proceed to develop the ARF
       as a vehicle for pr omoting regional peace and stability.

Organisation of ARF activities

16.   There shall be an annual ARF M inisterial Meeting, in an ASEAN capital just
       after the ASEAN Ministerial Meeting. The host country will chair the meeting.
       The incoming Chairman of the ASEAN S tanding Committee will chair all
       inter-sessional Track One activities of the ARF .

17.   The ARF shall be apprised of all   Track Two activities thr ough the curr ent
       Chairman of the Track One activities, who will be the main link between Track
       One and Track Two activities.

18.   In the initial phase cf the ARF no institutionalisation is expected. N or should
       a Secretariat be established in ℈he near futur e. ASEAN shall be the r epository
       of all ARF documents and information and pr ovide the necessary support to
       sustain ARF activities.

19.   The participants of the ARF comprise the ASEAN member states, the observers,
       and consultative anc dialogue partners of ASEAN. Applications to participate
       in the ARF shall be submitted to the Chairman of the ARF who will then
       consult the other ARF participants.

20.   The rules of procedure of ARF meetings shall be based on prevailing, ASEAN norms and practices. Decisions should be made by consensus after careful and extensive consultations. No voting will take place. h accordance with prevailing ASEAN practices, the Chairman of the ASEAN S tanding Committee shall provide the secretarial support and coordinate ARF activities.

21.   The ARF should also pr ogress at a pace comfor table to all par ticipants. The ARF should not move "too fast for those who want to go slow and not too slow for those who want to go fast ".

Conclusion

22.   ARF participants should not assume that the success of the ARF can be taken for granted. ASEAN' s experience sho ws that success is a r esult of har d work and careful adherence to the rule of consensus. ARF par ticipants will have to work equally hard and be equally sensitive to ensure that the ARF process stays on track.

23.   The ARF must be accepted as a "sui generis" Organisation. It has no established precedents to follow. A great deal of innovation and ingenuity will be required to keep the ARF moving forward while at the same time ensur e that it enjoys the support of its diverse participants. This is a major challenge both for the ASEAN countries and other ARF par ticipants. The UN S ecretary-General's "Agenda for Peace" has recognised that "just as no two regions or situations are the same, so the design of cooperative wor k and its division of labour must adjust to the r ealities of each case with flexibility and cr eativity".

Note

Appendix A is r eproduced with the kind permission of the ASEAN S ecretariat at <http://www.asean.org>.

APPENDIX B

Chairman's Statement
The Second Meeting of the ASEAN Regional Forum
Brunei Darussalam, 1 August 1995

1.   The Second ASEAN Regional Forum (ARF) was held on 1 August 1995 in
     Bandar Seri Begawan. The Meeting was chaired by His Royal Highness Prince
     Mohamed Bolkiah, Minister of Foreign Affairs of Brunei Darussalam.

2.   The Forum was attended by all ARF participants. The Secretary-General of
     ASEAN was also present.

3.   The Ministers welcomed Cambodia to the ARF.

4.   The Ministers expressed their satisfaction at the level of stability in the Asia
     Pacific Region. They noted the ways in which cooperative relationships were
     developing constructively. In this regard, the Ministers noted the many positive
     steps taken since the first ARF in Bangkok in July 1994, particularly those
     which built confidence and created greater transparency. In this respect, they
     noted the participants' willingness to address substantive security issues in a
     spirit of mutual respect, equality and cooperation.

5.   The Ministers expressed their appreciation for the consultations conducted by
     the Chairman of ARF, Brunei Darussalam, with ARF participants to obtain
     their views in preparation for the ARF. Based on the inputs and proposals,
     ASEAN has produced "The ASEAN Regional Forum — A Concept Paper", as
     annexed.

6.   The Ministers considered and endorsed the Report of the Chairman of the
     ARF-SOM. In particular, they adopted the following proposals in the context
     of the Concept Paper:

A.   GOALS AND EXPECTATIONS

*   The ARF participants shall continue to work closely to ensure and
    preserve the current environment of peace, prosperity and stability in the
    Asia Pacific;
*   The ARF shall continue to be a forum for open dialogue and consultation
    on regional political and security issues, to discuss and reconcile the
    differing views between ARF participants in order to reduce the risk to
    security; and

- The ARF recognises that the concept of comprehensive security includes not only military aspects but also political, economic, social and other issues.

B. METHOD AND APPROACH

- A successful-ARF requires the active, full and equal participation and cooperation of all participants. However, ASEAN undertakes the obligation to be the primary driving force;
- The ARF process shall move at a pace comfortable to all participants;
- The approach shall be evolutionary, taking place in three broad stages, namely the promotion of confidence building, development of preventive diplomacy and elaboration of approaches to conflicts. The ARF process is now at Stage I, and shall continue to discuss means of implementing confidence building. Stage II, particularly where the subject matter overlap, can proceed in tandem with Stage I. Discussions will continue regarding the incorporation of elaboration of approaches to conflicts, as an eventual goal, into the ARF process.
- Decisions of the ARF shall be made through consensus after careful and extensive consultations among all participants.

C. PARTICIPATION

- The participants of the ARF comprise ASEAN Member States, Observers, Consultative and Dialogue Partners of ASEAN. Any new application should be submitted to the Chairman of the ARF who will then consult the other ARF participants; and
- To request the next Chairman, to study the question of future participation and develop the criteria for the consideration of the Third ARF through the ARF-SOM.

D. ORGANISATION OF THE ARF

- There shall be an annual ARF in the context of the ASEAN Ministerial Meeting and Post Ministerial Conferences to be preceded by ARF-SOM;
- The ARF process would move along two tracks. Track one activities will be carried out by ARF governments. Track Two activities shall be carried out by strategic institutes and relevant non-governmental organisations to which all ARF participants should be eligible. To be meaningful and relevant, the ARF Chairman shall ensure that Track Two activities as indicated in ANNEX B result from full consultations with all ARF participants; and

- The ARF shall be apprised of all Track One and Track Two activities through the current Chairman of the ARF , who will be the main link between Track One and Track Two.

E. IMPLEMENTATION OF IDEAS AND PROPOSALS

- In order to assist the Chairman of the ARF-SOM to consider and make recommendations to the ARF on the implementation of the proposals agreed by the ARF participants as indicated in ANNEX A of the Concept Paper, the following shall be convened at the inter-go vernmental level:
  - Inter-sessional Support Group (ISG) on Confidence Building, in particular, dialogue on security per ceptions and defence policy papers; and
  - Inter-sessional Meetings (ISMs) on Cooperative Activities including inter-alia, Peacekeeping.
- ISG and ISMs shall be go verned by the following guidelines:
  - ISG and ISMs shall be co-chair ed by ASEAN and non-ASEAN participants;
  - ISG and ISMs shall be held in between ARF-SOMs; and
  - Findings of the ISG and ISMs shall be pr esented to the ARF-SOM in I ndonesia in 1996. The possible continuation of the mandate of the ISG and ISMs shall be r eviewed at that time.

7. In this regard the Ministers agreed that Indonesia would co-chair the ISGs on CBMs with J apan; Malaysia would co-chair the ISMs on P   eacekeeping Operations with Canada; and Singapore would co-chair the ISMs Seminar on Search and Rescue Coordination and Cooperation with the U nited States.

8. The Ministers also agr eed on the follo wing:
  - to encourage all ARF countries to enhance their dialogues and consultations on political and security cooperation including ex changes on security perceptions on a bilateral, sub-r egional and r egional basis;
  - for the ARF countries to submit to the ARF or ARF-SOM, on a voluntary basis, an annual statement of their defence policy;
  - on the benefits of increased high lev el contacts and ex changes between military academies, staff colleges and training; and
  - to take note of the increased participation in the UN conventional Arms Register since the first ARF and encourage those not yet participating to soon do so.

9. The Ministers expressed the view that their endorsement of such specific ideas and proposals pr ovided sufficient direction for the ARF pr ocess at this stage. They also reaffirmed their belief that the Asia Pacific Region currently had an

historically unprecedented opportunity to establish and consolidate long term conditions for peace and stability.

10.   The Ministers also received the reports of the following seminars on Building of Confidence and   Trust in the Asia P   acific, held in N   ovember 1994 in Canberra, Australia; Seminar on Peacekeeping: Challenges and opportunities for the ASEAN Regional Forum, held in March 1995 in Bandar Seri Begawan, Brunei D arussalam; S eminar on P reventive D iplomacy, held in M ay 1995, Seoul, Republic of K orea. They commended the hosts and sponsors of those seminars for their efforts and agreed that the arrangements under the   Track Two process should continue. They also noted the Russian offer to host a Track Two seminar in S pring of 1996 on the proposed P   rinciples of S ecurity an Stability in the Asia-P   acific R egion. They also commended bilateral and multilateral, governmental and non-governmental consultations and seminars in the Asia P acific region including the I ndonesian Workshop (co-sponsored by Canada) series on Managing Potential Conflicts in the S outh China Sea as a useful means of enhancing dialogue and cooperation.

11.   Noting the o verall stable envir onment and many ar eas of ongoing r egional cooperation, the M inisters ex changed vie ws on r egional security issues, and highlighted the follo wing:
   *   expressed concern on overlapping sovereignty claims in the region. They encouraged all claimants to reaffirm their commitment to the principles contained in relevant international laws and convention, and the ASEAN's 1992 D eclaration on the S outh China S ea;
   *   recognized that the Korean Peninsula issue has a direct bearing on peace and security in the Asia-P acific. They welcomed the r ecent US-DPRK talks held in Kuala Lumpur and expressed the hope that this would lead to the full implementation of the Agr   eed F ramework of 21 October 1994. The M inisters urged the r esumption of dialogue betw een the Republic of K orea and the D emocratic People's Republic of K orea and believed that it would assist in the successful implementation of the Agreed F ramework and the maintenance of peace and stability on the Korean Peninsula. The Ministers also recognised the impor tance which international suppor t for the K orean P eninsula E nergy O rganisation (KEDO) has for the implementation of the Agr eed Framework;
   *   expressed their suppor t for the efforts of the R   oyal G overnment of Cambodia to achieve security, promote national stability and economic recovery; and
   *   emphasised the impor tance of non-pr oliferation of nuclear w eapons in promoting regional peace and stability. They welcomed the commitment by all parties to the Non-Proliferation Treaty to conclude a Comprehensive

Test Ban Treaty by 1996. Those countries who plan to conduct fur ther nuclear tests were called upon by all other ARF member states to bring immediate end to such testing. They also endorsed the nuclear-weapon free zones, such as the South Pacific Nuclear Free Zone, in strengthening the international non-proliferation regime and expr essed the hope that all nuclear w eapon states would in the v ery near futur e adher e to the relevant Protocols. They noted with satisfaction the progress made towards the establishment of the South East Asia Nuclear Weapon Free Zone and encouraged fur ther consultations on this issue with those states that would be significantly affected b y the establishment of the zone.

Note

Appendix B is repr oduced with the kind permission of the ASEAN S   ecretariat at <http://www.asean.org>.

APPENDIX C

Treaty of Amity and Cooperation in Southeast Asia Indonesia, 24 February 1976

The High Contracting Parties:

CONSCIOUS of the existing ties of histor y, geography and cultur e, which have bound their peoples together;

ANXIOUS to pr omote r egional peace and stability thr ough abiding r espect for justice and the r ule of law and enhancing r egional resilience in their r elations;

DESIRING to enhance peace, friendship and mutual cooperation on matters affecting Southeast Asia consistent with the spirit and principles of the Charter of the U nited Nations, the Ten Principles adopted by the Asian-African Conference in Bandung on 25 April 1955, the Declaration of the Association of Southeast Asian Nations signed in B angkok on 8 A ugust 1967, and the Declaration signed in K uala L umpur on 27 November 1971;

CONVINCED that the settlement of differences or disputes between their countries should be regulated by rational, effective and sufficiently flexible procedures, avoiding negative attitudes which might endanger or hinder cooperation;

BELIEVING in the need for cooperation with all peace-loving nations, both within and outside Southeast Asia, in the furtherance of world peace, stability and harmony;

SOLEMNLY AGREE to enter into a Treaty of Amity and Cooperation as follo ws:

CHAPTER I: PURPOSE AND PRINCIPLES

Article 1

The purpose of this Treaty is to pr omote perpetual peace, everlasting amity and cooperation among their peoples which would contribute to their strength, solidarity and closer r elationship.

Article 2

In their relations with one another, the High Contracting Parties shall be guided by the following fundamental principles:

a.   Mutual respect for the independence, sovereignty, equality, territorial integrity and national identity of all nations;

b.   The right of ever y S tate to lead its national existence fr   ee fr om external interference, subversion or coer cion;

c.   Non-interference in the internal affairs of one another;

d.   Settlement of differ ences or disputes b y peaceful means;

e.   Renunciation of the thr eat or use of force;

f.   Effective cooperation among themselves.

CHAPTER II: AMITY

Article 3

In pursuance of the purpose of this   Treaty the H igh Contracting P arties shall endeavour to dev elop and str ength en the traditional, cultural and historical ties of friendship, good neighbourliness and cooperation which bind them together and shall fulfill in good faith the obligations assumed under this   Treaty. In or der to promote closer understanding among them, the H   igh Contracting P arties shall encourage and facilitate contact and inter course among their peoples.

CHAPTER III: COOPERATION

Article 4

The H igh Contracting P arties shall promote activ e cooperation in the economic, social, technical, scientific and administrative fields as well as in matters of common ideals and aspirations of international peace and stability in the r egion and all other matters of common inter est.

Article 5

Pursuant to Article 4 the High Contracting Parties shall exert their maximum efforts multilaterally as w ell as bilaterally on the basis of equality , non-discrimination and mutual benefit.

Article 6

The High Contracting Parties shall collaborate for the acceleration of the economic growth in the r egion in or der to str engthen the foundation for a prosper ous and peaceful community of nations in Southeast Asia. To this end, they shall promote the greater utilization of their agriculture and industries, the expansion of their trade and the impro vement of their economic infrastructur e for the mutual benefit of their peoples. I n this r egard, they shall continue to explor e all av enues for close and beneficial cooperation with other S tates as w ell as international and r egional organisations outside the r egion.

Article 7

The H igh Contracting P arties, in or der to achieve social justice and to raise the standards of living of the peoples of the region, shall intensify economic cooperation. For this purpose, they shall adopt appr opriate r egional strategies for economic development and mutual assistance.

Article 8

The High Contracting Parties shall strive to achieve the closest cooperation on the widest scale and shall seek to pro vide assistance to one another in the form of training and r esearch facilities in the social, cultural, technical, scientific and administrative fields.

Article 9

The High Contracting Parties shall endeavour to foster cooperation in the furtherance of the cause of peace, harmony , and stability in the r egion. To this end, the H igh Contracting P arties shall maintain r egular contacts and consultations with one another on international and regional matters with a view to coordinating their views actions and policies.

Article 10

Each High Contracting P arty shall not in any manner or form par ticipate in any activity which shall constitute a thr eat to the political and economic stability , sovereignty, or territorial integrity of another H igh Contracting Party.

Article 11

The H igh Contracting P arties shall endeav our to str engthen their r espective national resilience in their political, economic, socio-cultural as w ell as security fields in conformity with their respective ideals and aspirations, free from external interference as w ell as internal sub versive activities in or der to pr eserve their respective national ident.ties.

Article 12

The H igh Contracting P arties in their efforts to achieve regional pr osperity and security, shall endeavour to cooperate in all fields for the pr omotion of regional resilience, based on the principles of self-confidence, self-r eliance, mutual r espect, cooperation and solidarity which will constitute the foundation for a str ong and viable community of nations in S outheast Asia.

CHAPTER IV: PACIFIC SETTLEMENT OF DISPUTES

Article 13

The High Contracting Parties shall have the determination and good faith to prevent disputes from arising. In case disputes on matters directly affecting them should arise, especially disputes likely to disturb r egional peace and harmony , they shall r efrain from the thr eat or use of force and shall at all times settle such disputes among themselves through friendly negotiations.

Article 14

To settle disputes through r egional pr ocesses, the H igh Contracting P arties shall constitute, as a continuing body , a H igh Council comprising a R epresentative at ministerial level from each of the High Contracting Parties to take cognizance of the existence of disputes or situations likely to disturb r egional peace and harmony.

Article 15

In the event no solution is r eached through dir ect negotiations, the H igh Council shall take cognizance of the dispute or the situation and shall r ecommend to the parties in dispute appropriate means of settlement such as good offices, mediation, inquiry or conciliation. The H igh Council may ho wever offer its good offices, or upon agr eement of the par ties in dispute, constitute itself into a committee of mediation, inquiry or conciliation. When deemed necessary, the High Council shall recommend appropriate measures for the prevention of a deterioration of the dispute or the situation.

Article 16

The foregoing provision of this Chapter shall not apply to a dispute unless all the parties to the dispute agree to their application to that dispute. H owever, this shall not preclude the other H igh Contracting P arties not par ty to the dispute fr om offering all possible assistance to settle the said dispute. Parties to the dispute should be well disposed towards such offers of assistance.

Article 17

Nothing in this Treaty shall pr eclude recourse to the modes of peaceful settlement contained in Article 33(l) of the Charter of the United Nations. The High Contracting Parties which are parties to a dispute should be encouraged to take initiatives to solve it by friendly negotiations before resorting to the other procedures provided for in the Charter of the United Nations.

CHAPTER V: General Provision

Article 18

This Treaty shall be signed by the Republic of Indonesia, Malaysia, the Republic of the Philippines, the Republic of Singapore and the Kingdom of Thailand. It shall be ratified in accordance with the constitutional pr ocedures of each signatory State. It shall be open for accession by other States in Southeast Asia.

Article 19

This Treaty shall enter into force on the date of the deposit of the fifth instrument of ratification with the Go vernments of the signator y S tates which ar e designated Depositories of this Treaty and the instr uments of ratification or accession.

Article 20

This Treaty is drawn up in the official languages of the High Contracting Parties, all of which are equally authoritative. There shall be an agr eed common translation of the texts in the English language. Any div ergent interpretation of the common text shall be settled by negotiation.

IN FAITH THEREOF the H igh Contracting P arties have signed the Treaty and have hereto affixed their S eals.

DONE at Denpasar , Bali, this tw enty-fourth day of F ebruary in the y ear one thousand nine hundr ed ar d seventy-six.

For the Republic
of Indonesia:

SOEHARTO
President

For the Republic
of Singapore:

LEE KUAN YEW
Prime Minister

For Malaysia:

DATUK HUSEIN ONN
Prime Minister

For the Kingdom
of Thailand:

KUKRIT PRAMOJ
Prime Minister

For the Republic
of the Philippines:

FERDINAND E. MARCOS

Protocol Amending the Treaty of Amity and Cooperation in Southeast Asia
Philippines, 15 December 1987

The Government of Brunei Darussalam
The Government of the Republic of Indonesia
The Government of Malaysia
The Government of the Republic of the Philippines
The Government of the Republic of Singapore
The Government of the Kingdom of Thailand

DESIRING to further enhance cooperation With all peace-lo ving nations, both within and outside S outheast Asia and, in par ticular, neighbouring S tates of the Southeast Asia region

CONSIDERING Paragraph 5 of the preamble of the Treaty of Amity and Cooperation in Southeast Asia, done at Denpasar, Bali, on 24 February 1976 (hereinafter referred to as the Treaty of Amity) which r efers to the need for cooperation with all peace-loving nations, both within and outside S outheast Asia, in the fur therance of world peace, stability and harmony.

HEREBY AGREE TO THE FOLLOWING:

Article 1

Article 18 of the Treaty of Amity shall be amended to r ead as follows:

"This Treaty shall be signed by the Republic of Indonesia, Malaysia, the Republic of the Philippines, the Republic of Singapore and the Kingdom of Thailand. It shall be ratified in accordance with the constitutional pr ocedures of each signatory State.

It shall be open for accession by other S tates in S outheast Asia.

States outside Southeast Asia may also accede to this Treaty by the consent of all the States in Southeast Asia which are signatories to this Treaty and Brunei Darussalam."

Article 2

Article 14 of the Treaty of Amity shall be amended to r ead as follows:

"To settle disputes thr ough r egional processes, the H igh Contracting P arties shall constitute, as a continuing body , a H igh Council comprising a R epresentative at ministerial level from each of the High Contracting Parties to take cognizance of the existence of disputes or situations likely to disturb r egional peace and harmony.

However, this ar ticle shall apply to any of the S tates outside S outheast Asia which have acceded to the Treaty only in cases wher e that state is dir ectly involved in the dispute to be settled through the r egional processes."

Article 3

This Protocol shall be subject to ratification and shall come into foce on the date the last instrument of ratification of the H igh Contracting Parties is deposited.

DONE at M anila, the fifteenth day of December in the y ear one thousand nine hundred and eighty-seven.

For Brunei Darussalam :

PRINCE HAJI MOHAMED BOLKIAH
Minister of Foreign Affairs

For the Republic of Indonesia :

PROF. DR. MOCHTAR KUSUMAATMADJA
Minister of Foreign Affairs

For Malaysia :

DATO HAJI ABU HASAN HAJI OMAR
Minister of Foreign Affairs

For the Republic of the Philippines :

RAUL S. MANGLAPUS
Secretary for Foreign Affairs

For the Republic of Singapore :

S. DHANABALAN
Minister of Foreign Affairs

For the Kingdom of Thailand :

AIR CHIEF MARSHALL SIDDHI SAVETSILA
Minister of Foreign Affairs

Second Protocol Amending the Treaty of Amity and Cooperation in Southeast Asia
Manila, Philippines, 25 July 1998

The Government of Brunei Darussalam
The Government of the Kingdom of Cambodia
The Government of the Republic of Indonesia
The Government of the Lao People's Democratic Republic
The Government of Malaysia
The Government of the Union of Myanmar
The Government of the Republic of the Philippines
The Government of the Republic of Singapore
The Government of the Kingdom of Thailand
The Government of the Socialist Republic of Vietnam
The Government of Papua New Guinea

Hereinafter referred to as the High Contracting Parties:

DESIRING to ensure that there is appropriate enhancement of cooperation with all peace-loving nations, both within and outside Southeast Asia and, in particular, neighboring States of the Southeast Asia region;

CONSIDERING Paragraph 5 of the preamble of the Treaty of Amity and Cooperation in Southeast Asia, done at Denpasar, Bali, on 24 February 1976 (hereinafter referred to as the Treaty of Amity) which refers to the need for cooperation with all peace-loving nations, both within and outside Southeast Asia, in the furtherance of world peace, stability and harmony.

HEREBY AGREE TO THE FOLLOWING:

Article 1

Article 18, Paragraph 3, of the Treaty of Amity shall be amended to read as follows:

> "States outside Southeast Asia may also accede to this Treaty with the consent of all the States in Southeast Asia, namely, Brunei Darussalam, the Kingdom of Cambodia, the Republic of Indonesia, the Lao People's Democratic Republic, Malaysia, the Union of Myanmar, the Republic of the Philippines, the Republic of Singapore, the Kingdom of Thailand and the Socialist Republic of Vietnam."

Article 2

This Protocol shall be subject to ratification and shall come into force on the date the last instrument of ratification of the High Contracting Parties is deposited.

DONE at M anila, the twenty-fifth day of J   uly in the year one thousand nine hundred and ninety-eight.

For Brunei Darussalam :

PRINCE MOHAMED BOLKIAH
Minister of Foreign Affairs

For the Kingdom of Cambodia :

CHEM WIDHYA
Special Envoy of the
Royal Government of Cambodia

For the Republic of Indonesia :

ALI ALATAS
Minister for Foreign Affairs

For the Lao People's Democratic Republic :

SOMSAVAT LENGSAVAD
Deputy Prime Minister and
Minister of Foreign Affairs

For Malaysia :

DATUK SERI ABDULLAH
HAJI AHMAD BADAWI
Minister of Foreign Affairs

For the Union of Myanmar :

U OHN GYAW
Minister for Foreign Affairs

For the Republic of the Philippines :

DOMINGGO L SIAZON, JR.
Secretary of Foreign Affairs

For the Republic of Singapore :

S JAYAKUMAR
Minister for Foreign Affairs

For the Kingdom of Thailand :

SURIN PITSUWAN
Minister of Foreign Affairs

For the Socialist Republic of
Vietnam

NGUYEN MANH CAM
Deputy Prime Minister and
Minister of Foreign Affairs

For Papua New Guinea :

ROY YAKI
Minister of Foreign Affairs

Note

Appendix C is r eproduced with the kind permission of the ASEAN S   ecretariat at <http://www.asean.org>.

APPENDIX D

Treaty on the Southeast Asia Nuclear Weapon-Free Zone Bangkok, Thailand 15 December 1995

The States Parties to this Treaty:

DESIRING to contribute to the r ealization of the purposes and principles of the Charter of the United Nations;

DETERMINED to take concr ete action which will contribute to the pr ogress towards general and complete disarmament of nuclear weapons, and to the promotion of international peace and security;

REAFFIRMING the desire of the S outheast Asian S tates to maintain peace and stability in the region in the spirit of peaceful coexistence and mutual understanding and cooperation as enunciated in various communiques, declarations and other legal instruments;

RECALLING the Declaration on the Z one of P eace, F reedom and N eutrality (ZOPFAN) signed in Kuala Lumpur on 27 November 1971 and the Programme of Action on ZOPFAN adopted at the 26th ASEAN Ministerial Meeting in Singapore in July 1993;

CONVINCED that the establishment of a S outheast Asia N uclear Weapon-Free Zone, as an essential component of the Z OPPAN, will contribute to wards strengthening the security of S tates within the Z one and to wards enhancing international peace and security as a whole;

REAFFIRMING the importance of the Treaty on the Non-Proliferation of Nuclear Weapons (NPT) in preventing the proliferation of nuclear weapons and in contributing towards international peace and security;

RECALLING Article VII of the NPT which r ecognizes the right of any gr oup of States to conclude r egional treaties in or der to assume the total absence of nuclear weapons in their r espective territories;

RECALLING the F inal D ocument of the Tenth S pecial S ession of the U nited Nations General Assembly which encourages the establishment of nuclear w eapon-free zones;

RECALLING the P rinciples and O bjectives for N uclear N on-Proliferation and Disarmament, adopted at the 1995 Review and Extension Conference of the Parties to the NPT, that the cooperation of all the nuclear-w eapon States and their r espect and support for the relevant protocols is important for the maximum effectiveness of this nuclear w eapon-free zone tr eaty and its r elevant protocols.

DETERMINED to protect the region from environmental pollution and the hazards posed by radioactive wastes and other radioactive material;

HAVE AGREED as follows:

Article I
USE OF TERM

For the purposes of this Treaty and its P rotocol:

(a)   "Southeast Asia N uclear Weapon-Free Z one", her einafter r eferred to as the "Zone", means the ar ea comprising the territories of all S tates in S outheast Asia, namely, Brunei Dar ussalam, Cambodia, I ndonesia, Laos, M alaysia, Myanmar, Philippines, Singapore, Thailand and Vietnam, and their respective continental shelves and Ex clusive Economic Z ones (EEZ);

(b)   "territory" means the land ter ritory, internal waters, territorial sea, archipelagic waters, the seabed and the sub-soil ther eof and the airspace abo ve them;

(c)   "nuclear w eapon" means any explosiv e device capable of r eleasing nuclear energy in an uncontrolled manner but does not include the means of transport or delivery of such device if separable from and not an indivisible part thereof;

(d)   "station" means to deploy, emplace, implant, install, stockpile or stor e;

(e)   "radioactive material" means material that contains radionuclides above clearance or exemption levels recommended by the International Atomic Energy Agency (IAEA);

(f)   "radioactive wastes" means material that contains or is contaminated with radionuclides at concentrations or activities gr eater than clearance levels recommended by the IAEA and for which no use is for eseen; and

(g)   "dumping" means

    (i)   any deliberate disposal at sea, including seabed and subsoil insertion, of radioactive wastes or other matter from vessels, air craft, platforms or other man-made str uctures at sea, and

(ii)   any deliberate disposal at sea, including seabed and subsoil insertion, of
         vessels, aircraft, platforms or other man-made structures at sea, containing
         radioactive material,but does not include the disposal of wastes or other
         matter incidental to, or deriv ed from the normal operations of v essels,
         aircraft, platforms or other man-made str   uctures at sea and their
         equipment, other than wastes or other matter transpor   ted b y or to
         vessels, aircraft, platforms or other man-made structures at sea, operating
         for the purpose of disposal of such matter or derived from the treatment
         of such wastes or other matter on such vessels, air   craft, platforms or
         structures.

Article 2
APPLICATION OF THE TREATY

1.   This Treaty and its P rotocol shall apply to the territories, continental selv es,
       and EEZ of the States Parties within the Zone in which the Treaty is in force.

2.   Nothing in this Treaty shall prejudice the rights or the ex ercise of these rights
       by any State under the pr ovisions of the U nited Nations Convention on the
       Law of the Sea of 1982, in particular with regard to freedom of the high seas,
       rights of innocent passage, ar chipelagic sea lanes passage or transit passage of
       ships and aircraft, and consistent with the Char ter of the U nited Nations.

Article 3
BASIC UNDERTAKINGS

1.   Each State Party undertakes not to, anywher e inside or outside the Z one:

       (a)   develop, manufacture or otherwise acquire, possess or have control over
               nuclear weapons;
       (b)   station or transpor t nuclear weapons b y any means; or
       (c)   test or use nuclear weapons.

2.   Each State Party also undertakes not to allow, in its territory, any other State to:

       (a)   develop, manufacture or otherwise acquire, possess or have control over
               nuclear weapons;
       (b)   station nuclear w eapons; or
       (c)   test or use nuclear weapons.

3.   Each State Party also under takes not to:

       (a)   dump at sea or discharge into the atmospher e anywhere within the Zone
               any radioactive material or wastes;

(b)   dispose radioactive material or wastes on land in the territory of or under the jurisdiction of other States except as stipulated in Paragraph 2 (e) of Article 4; or

(c)   allow, within its territory, any other State to dump at sea or discharge into the atmosphere any radioactive material or wastes.

4.   Each State Party undertakes not to:

(a)   seek or receive any assistance in the Commission of any act in violation of the provisions of Paragraphs 1, 2 and 3 of this Article; or

(b)   take any action to assist or encourage the Commission of any act in violation of the provisions of Paragraphs 1, 2 and 3 of this Article.

Article 4
USE OF NUCLEAR ENERGY FOR PEACEFUL PURPOSES

1.   Nothing in this Treaty shall prejudice the right of the States Parties to use nuclear energy, in particular for their economic development and social progress.

2.   Each State Party therefore undertakes:

(a)   to use exclusively for peaceful purposes nuclear material and facilities which are within its territory and areas under its jurisdiction and control;

(b)   prior to embarking on its peaceful nuclear energy programme, to subject its programme to rigorous nuclear safety assessment conforming to guidelines and standards recommended by the IAEA for the protection of health and minimization of danger to life and property in accordance with Paragraph 6 of Article III of the Statute of the IAEA;

(c)   upon request, to make available to another State Party the assessment except information relating to personal data, information protected by intellectual property rights or by industrial or commercial confidentiality, and information relating to national security;

(d)   to support the continued effectiveness of the international non-proliferation system based on the Treaty on the Non-Proliferation of Nuclear Weapons (NPT) and the IAEA safeguard system; and

(e)   to dispose radioactive wastes and other radioactive material in accordance with IAEA standards and procedures on land within its territory or on land within the territory of another State which has consented to such disposal.

3.   Each State Party further undertakes not to provide source or special fissionable material, or equipment or material especially designed or prepared for the processing, use or production of special fissionable material to:

(a)   any non-nuclear-weapon State except under conditions subject to the safeguards required by Paragraph 1 of Article III of the NPT; or

(b)   any nuclear-weapon State except in conformity with applicable safeguards agreements with the IAEA.

Article 5
IAEA SAFEGUARDS

Each State Party which has not done so shall conclude an agreement with the IAEA for the application of full scope safeguards to its peaceful nuclear activities not later than eighteen months after the entry into force for that State Party of the Treaty.

Article 6
EARLY NOTIFICATION OF A NUCLEAR ACCIDENT

Each State Party which has not acceded to the Convention on Early Notification of a Nuclear Accident shall endeavour to do so.

Article 7
FOREIGN SHIPS AND AIRCRAFT

Each State Party, on being notified, may decide for itself whether to allow visits by foreign ships and aircraft to its ports and airfields, transit of its airspace by foreign aircraft, and navigation by foreign ships through its territorial sea or archipelagic waters and overflight of foreign aircraft above those waters in a manner not governed by the rights of innocent passage, archipelagic sea lanes passage or transit passage.

Article 8
ESTABLISHMENT OF THE COMMISSION FOR THE SOUTHEAST ASIA NUCLEAR WEAPON-FREE ZONE

1.   There is hereby established a Commission for the Southeast Asia Nuclear Weapon-Free Zone, hereinafter referred to as the "Commission".

2.   All States Parties are ipso facto members or the Commission. Each State Party shall be represented by its Foreign Minister or his representative accompanied by alternates and advisers.

3.   The function of the Commission shall be to oversee the implementation of this Treaty and ensure compliance with its provisions.

4.   The Commission shall meet as and when necessary in accordance with the provisions of this Treaty including upon the request of any State Party. As far

as possible, the Commission shall meet in conjunction with the ASEAN Ministerial Meeting.

5.   At the beginning of each meeting, the Commission shall elect its Chairman and such other officers as may be r equired. They shall hold office until a new Chairman and other officers ar e elected at the next meeting.

6.   Unless otherwise provided for in this Treaty, two-thirds of the members of the Commission shall be pr esent to constitute a quor um.

7.   Each member of the Commission shall have one v ote.

8.   Except as pr ovided for in this Treaty, decisions of the Commission shall be taken by consensus or , failing consensus, by a two-thir ds majority of the members present ar d v oting

9.   The Commission shall, by consensus, agree upon and adopt rules of procedure for itself as well as financial rules governing its funding and that of its subsidiary organs.

Article 9
THE EXECUTIVE COMMITTEE

1.   There is her eby established, as a subsidiar y organ of the Commission, the Executive Committee.

2.   The Executive Committee shall be composed of all States Parties to this Treaty. Each State Party shall be represented by one senior official as its representative, who may be accompanied b y alternates and advisers.

3.   The functions of the E xecutive Committee shall be to:

(a)   ensure the proper operation of verification measures in accordance with the provisions on the contr ol system as stipulated in Ar ticle 10;

(b)   consider and decide or r equests for clarification and for a fact-finding mission;

(c)   set up a fact-finding mission in accor dance with the Annex of this Treaty;

(d)   consider and decide or the findings of a fact-finding mission and report to the Commission;

(e)   request the Commission to conv ene a meeting when appr opriate and necessary;

(f)   conclude such agr eements with the IAEA or other international organizations as referred to in Article 18 on behalf of the Commission after being duly authorized to do so b y the Commission; and

(g)   carry out such other tasks as may, from time to time, be assigned by the Commission.

4.   The Executive Committee shall meet as and when necessar y for the efficient exercise of its functions. As far as possible, the Executive Committee shall meet in conjunction with the ASEAN S enior Officials Meeting.

5.   The Chairman of the Ex ecutive Committee shall be the r epresentative of the Chairman of the Commission. Any submission or communication made b y a State Party to the Chairman of the Executive Committee shall be disseminated to the other members of the E xecutive Committee.

6.   Two-thirds of the members of the Ex ecutive Committee shall be pr esent to constitute a quor um.

7.   Each member of the E xecutive Committee shall hav e one v ote.

8.   Decisions of the E xecutive Committee shall be taken b y consensus or, failing consensus, by a two-thir ds majority of the members pr esent and v oting.

Article 10
CONTROL SYSTEM

1.   There is her eby established a contr ol system for the purpose of verifying compliance with the obligations of the S tates Parties under this Treaty.

2.   The Control System shall comprise:

(a)   the IAEA safeguar ds system as pro vided for in Ar ticle 5;

(b)   report and ex change of information as pro vided for in Ar ticle 11;

(c)   request for clarification as pr ovided for in Ar ticle 12; and

(d)   request and procedur es for a fact-finding mission as pr ovided for in Article 13.

Article 11
REPORT AND EXCHANGE OF INFORMATION

1. Each State Party shall submit reports to the Executive Committee on any significant event within its territory and areas under its jurisdiction and control affecting the implementation of this Treaty.

2. The States Parties may exchange information on matters arising under or in relation to this Treaty.

Article 12
REQUEST FOR CLARIFICATION

1. Each State Party shall have the right to request another State Party for clarification concerning any situation which may be considered ambiguous or which may give rise to doubts about the compliance of that State Party with this Treaty. It shall inform the Executive Committee of such a request. The requested State Party shall duly respond by providing without delay the necessary information and inform the Executive Committee of its reply to the requesting State Party.

2. Each State Party shall have the right to request the Executive Committee to seek clarification for another State Party concerning any situation which may be considered ambiguous or which may give rise to doubts about compliance of that State Party with this Treaty. Upon receipt of such a request, the Executive Committee shall consult the State Party from which clarification is sought for the purpose of obtaining the clarification requested.

Article 13
REQUEST FOR A FACT-FINDING MISSION

A State Party shall have the right to request the Executive Committee to send a fact-finding mission to another State Party in order to clarify and resolve a situation which may be considered ambiguous or which may give rise to doubts about compliance with the provisions of this Treaty, in accordance with the procedure contained in the Annex to this Treaty.

Article 14
REMEDIAL MEASURES

1. In case the Executive Committee decide in accordance with the Annex that there is a breach of this Treaty by a State Party, that State Party shall, within a reasonable time, take all steps necessary to bring itself in full compliance with this Treaty and shall promptly inform the Executive Committee of the action taken or proposed to be taken by it.

2.   Where a State Party fails or refuses to comply with the provisions of Paragraph 1 of this Ar ticle, the Ex ecutive Committee shall request the Commission to convene a meeting in accor dance with the pro visions of P aragraph 3(e) of Article 9.

3.   At the meeting conv ened pursuant to P aragraph 2 of this Ar ticle, the Commission shall consider the emergent situation and shall decide on any measure it deems appropriate to cope with the situation, including the submission of the matter to the IAEA and, when the situation might endanger international peace and security the Security Council and the General Assembly of the United Nations.

4.   In the event of br each of the P rotocol attached to this Treaty by a S tate Party to the P rotocol, the E xecutive Committee shall convene a special meeting of the Commission to decide on appr opriate measures to be taken.

Article 15
SIGNATURE, RATIFICATION, ACCESSION, DEPOSIT AND REGISTRATION

1.   This Treaty shall be open for signature by all States in Southeast Asia, namely, Brunei Darussalam, Cambodia, I ndonesia, Laos, M alaysia, M yanmar, Philippines, Singapore, Thailand and Vietnam.

2.   This Treaty shall be subject to ratification in accordance with the constitutional procedure of the signator y states. The instr uments of ratification shall be deposited with the Government of the Kingdom of Thailand which is hereby designated as the D epositary State.

3.   This Treaty shall be open for accession. The instruments of accession shall be deposited with the Depositar y State.

4.   The Depositary State shall inform the other States Parties to this Treaty on the deposit of instr uments of ratification or accession.

5.   The Depositar y S tate shall r egister this Treaty and its P rotocol pursuant to Article 102 of the Char ter of the U nited Nations.

Article 16
ENTRY INTO FORCE

1.   This Treaty shall enter into for ce on the date of the deposit of the sev enth instrument of ratification and/or accession.

2. For States which ratify or accede to this Treaty after the date of the sev enth instrument of ratification or accession, the Treaty shall enter into force on the date of deposit of its instr ument of ratification or accession.

Article 17
RESERVATIONS

This Treaty shall not be subject to r eservations.

Article 18
RELATIONS WITH OTHER INTERNATIONAL ORGANIZATIONS

The Commission may conclude such agreements with the IAEA or other international organizations as it considers likely to facilitate the efficient operation of the contr ol system established by this Treaty.

Article 19
AMENDMENTS

1. Any State Party may propose amendments to this Treaty and its Protocol and shall submit its proposals to the E xecutive Committee, which shall transmit them to all the other States Parties. The Executive Committee shall immediately request the Commission to conv ene a meeting to examine the pr oposed amendments. The quorum required for such a meeting shall be all the members of the Commission. Any amendment shall be adopted by a consensus decision of the Commission.

2. Amendments adopted shall enter into force 30 days after the r eceipt by the Depositary S tate of the sev enth instrument of acceptance fr om the S tates Parties.

Article 20
REVIEW

Ten years after this Treaty enters into for ce, a meeting of the Commission shall be convened for the purpose of reviewing the operation of the Treaty. A meeting of the Commission for the same purpose may also be conv ened at anytime ther eafter if there is consensus among all its members.

Article 21
SETTLEMENT OF DISPUTES

Any dispute arising from the interpr etation of the pro visions of this Treaty shall be settled by peaceful means as may be agreed upon by the States Parties to the dispute.

If within one month, the par ties to the dispute ar e unable to achiev e a peaceful settlement of the dispute by negotiation, mediation, enquir y or conciliation, any of the par ties concerned shall, with the prior consent of the other parties concerned, refer the dispute to arbitration or to the I nternational Court of J ustice.

Article 22
DURATION AND WITHDRAWAL

1.   This Treaty shall r emain in for ce indefinitely.

2.   In the event of a br each b y any S tate P arty of this Treaty essential to the achievement of the objectiv es of the Treaty, every other S tate Party shall have the right to withdraw fr om the Treaty.

3.   Withdrawal under Paragraph 2 of Article 22, shall be effected by giving notice twelve months in adv ance to the members of the Commission.

IN WITNESS WHEREOF, the undersigned have signed this Treaty.

DONE at **Bangkok,** this fifteenth day of December one thousand nine hundred and ninety-five, in one original in the E nglish language.

FOR BRUNEI DARUSSALAM

HAJI HASSANAL BOLKIAH
Sultan of Brunei Darussalam

FOR THE KINGDOM OF CAMBODIA

Samdech Krom Preah NORODOM RANARIDH
First Prime Minister

FOR THE LAO PEOPLE'S DEMOCRATIC REPUBLIK

KHAMTAY SIPHANDONE
Prime Minister

FOR THE UNION OF MYANMAR

SENIOR GENERAL THAN SHWE
Chairman of the State Law and Order Restoration Council
and Prime Minister

FOR THE REPUBLIC OF SINGAPORE

GOH CHOK TONG
Prime Minister

FOR THE SOCIALIST REPUBLIC OF VIETNAM

VO VAN KIET
Prime Minister

FOR THE REPUBLIC OF INDONESIA

SOEHARTO
President

Samdech HUN SEN
Second Prime Minister

FOR MALAYSIA

DR MAHATHIR BIN MOHAMAD
Prime Minister

FOR THE REPUBLIC OF THE PHILIPPINES

FIDEL V. RAMOS
President

FOR THE KINGDOM OF THAILAND

BANHARN SILPA-ARCHA
Prime Minister

Note

Appendix D is reproduced with the kind permission of the ASEAN Secretariat at
<http://www.asean.org>.

APPENDIX E

Declaration on the Conduct of Parties
in the South China Sea

The G overnments of the M ember S tates of ASEAN and the G overnment of the People's Republic of China,

REAFFIRMING their determination to consolidate and develop the friendship and cooperation existing between their people and governments with the view to promoting a 21st centur y-oriented par tnership of good neighbourliness and mutual trust;

COGNIZANT of the need to pr omote a peaceful, friendly and harmonious environment in the South China Sea between ASEAN and China for the enhancement of peace, stability, economic growth and prosperity in the r egion;

COMMITTED to enhancing the principles and objectives of the 1997 Joint Statement of the Meeting of the Heads of State/Government of the Member States of ASEAN and President of the P eople's Republic of China;

DESIRING to enhance favourable conditions for a peaceful and durable solution of differences and disputes among countries concerned;

HEREBY DECLARE the follo wing:

1.   The Parties reaffirm their commitment to the purposes and principles of the Charter of the U nited Nations, the 1982 UN Conv ention on the Law of the Sea, the Treaty of Amity and Cooperation in Southeast Asia, the Five Principles of P eaceful Coexistence, and other univ   ersally r ecognized principles of international law which shall ser ve as the basic norms go verning state-to-state relations;

2.   The Parties are committed to exploring ways for building trust and confidence in accordance with the above-mentioned principles and on the basis of equality and mutual r espect;

3.   The P arties r eaffirm their respect for and commitment to the fr   eedom of navigation in and overflight above the South China Sea as provided for by the universally recognized principles of international law, including the 1982 UN Convention on the Law of the S ea;

4.   The Parties concerned undertake to r esolve their territorial and jurisdictional disputes by peaceful means, without r esorting to the thr eat or use of force, through friendly consultations and negotiations b y so vereign states dir ectly concerned, in accordance with universally recognized principles of international law, including the 1982 UN Convention on the Law of the S ea;

5.   The Parties undertake to exer cise self-restraint in the conduct of activities that would complicate or escalate disputes and affect peace and stability including, among others, refraining from action of inhabiting on the presently uninhabited islands, reefs, shoals, cays, and other features and to handle their differences in a constructive manner.

Pending the peaceful settlement of territorial and jurisdictional disputes, the P arties concerned undertake to intensify efforts to seek ways, in the spirit of cooperation and understanding, to build tr ust and confidence between and among them, including:

a.   holding dialogues and exchange of views as appropriate between their defense and military officials;

b.   ensuring just and humane treatment of all persons who are either in danger or in distress;

c.   notifying, on a v oluntary basis, other P arties concerned of any impending joint/combined military exercise; and

d.   exchanging, on a voluntar y basis, relevant information.

6.   Pending a compr ehensive and durable settlement of the disputes, the P arties concerned may explore or undertake cooperative activities. These may include the following:

a.   marine environmental protection;

b.   marine scientific resear ch;

c.   safety of navigation and communication at sea;

d.   search and rescue operation; and

e.   combating transnational crime, including but not limited to trafficking in illicit dr ugs, piracy and armed r obbery at sea, and illegal traffic in arms.

The modalities, scope and locations, in respect of bilateral and multilateral cooperation should be agreed upon by the Parties concerned prior to their actual implementation.

7.   The Parties concerned stand ready to continue their consultations and dialogues concerning relevant issues, through modalities to be agreed by them, including regular consultations on the observance of this Declaration, for the purpose of promoting good neighbourliness and transparency, establishing harmony, mutual understanding and cooperation, and facilitating peaceful resolution of disputes among them;

8.   The Parties undertake to respect the provisions of this Declaration and take actions consistent therewith;

9.   The Parties encourage other countries to respect the principles contained in this Declaration;

10. The Parties concerned reaffirm that the adoption of a code of conduct in the South China Sea would further promote peace and stability in the region and agree to work, on the basis of consensus, towards the eventual attainment of this objective.

Done on the Fourth Day of November in the Year Two Thousand and Two in Phnom Penh, the Kingdom of Cambodia.

For Brunei Darussalam

Mohamed Bolkiah
Minister of Foreign Affairs

For the People's Republic of China

Wang Yi
Special Envoy and
Vice Minister of Foreign Affairs

For the Kingdom of Cambodia

HOR Namhong
Senior Minister and Minister of
Foreign Affairs and International Cooperation

For the Republic of Indonesia

Dr. Hassan Wirayuda
Minister for Foreign Affairs

For the Lao People's Democratic Republic

Somsavat Lengsavad
Deputy Prime Minister and
Minister for Foreign Affairs

For Malaysia

Datuk Seri Syed Hamid Albar
Minister of Foreign Affairs

For the Union of Myanmar

Win Aung
Minister for Foreign Affairs

For the Republic of the Philippines

Blas F. Ople
Secretary of Foreign Affairs

For the Republic of Singapore

Prof. S. Jayakumar
Minister for Foreign Affairs

For the Kingdom of Thailand

Dr. Surakiart Sathirathai
Minister of Foreign Affairs

For the Socialist Republic of Viet Nam

Nguyen Dy Nien
Minister of Foreign Affairs

Note
Appendix E is r eproduced with the kind permission of the ASEAN S ecretariat at
<http://www.asean.org>.

APPENDIX F
ARF Ministerial Meetings: 1994–2008

Meeting	Place	Date
First	Bangkok	25 July 1994
Second	Bandar Seri Begawan	1 August 1995
Third	Jakarta	23 July 1996
Fourth	Subang Jaya, Malaysia	27 July 1997
Fifth	Manila	27 July 1998
Sixth	Singapore	27 July 1999
Seventh	Bangkck	27 July 2000
Eighth	Hanoi	25 July 2001
Ninth	Bandar Seri Begawan	31 July 2002
Tenth	Phnom Penh	18 June 2003
Eleventh	Jakarta	2 July 2004
Twelfth	Vientiane	29 July 2005
Thirteenth	Kuala Lumpur	28 July 2006
Fourteenth	Manila	2 August 2007
Fifteenth	Singapore	24 July 2008
Sixteenth	Phuket, Thailand	23 July 2009

Note
The data in A ppendix F is compiled fr om the ASEAN S ecretariat website <http://www.asean.org>.

INDEX

www.ingramcontent.com/pod-product-compliance
Lightning Source LLC
Chambersburg PA
CBHW021541260326
41914CB00001B/103